The Secret Life
of Bletchley Park

Sinclair McKay writes for the *Daily Telegraph* and the *Mail on Sunday* and has written books about James Bond and Hammer horror for Aurum. His next book, *Secret Listeners*, is about the Overseas Listening Service during World War II, to be published by Aurum in 2012. He lives in London.

1 Reporting for Duty

Sarah Baring – and her good friend Osla Henniker-Major – received the summons by means of a terse telegram. She remembers that it read: 'You are to report to Station X at Bletchley Park, Buckinghamshire, in four days time. Your postal address is Box 111, c/o The Foreign Office. That is all you need to know.'

These two aristocratic young women arrived one evening in the spring of 1941, having travelled by rail from Euston. Their journey had been rendered a little fraught by a male fellow passenger sitting opposite in their compartment, apparently manipulating himself obscenely through his trouser pockets. After some whispered conference, the two outraged young women decided that Osla should deal with the grubby man by reaching up to the luggage rack and then 'accidentally dropping their case of gramophone records' on his lap. The man got the message and 'fled up the corridor'.

Just over an hour later, they were there. 'We decanted ourselves from the train at Bletchley station,' recalls the Honourable Sarah Baring, 'and then, weighed down by our luggage, we staggered up a rutted narrow path. On the side of the tracks, there was an eight foot high chained fence. It was topped by a roll of barbed wire.'

The boundary of the Bletchley Park estate is adjacent to the railway station. The two women struggled with their suitcases through the twilight along this long, quiet path, up a gentle slope running along the fenced side of the wooded grounds, until they reached the short driveway and the concrete RAF sentry post that stood on the road towards the house. The sentry on duty swiftly established that these incongruously elegant ladies were expected.

Then they caught their first view of the big house itself, with the lake before it, the thick branches of a Wellingtonia tree obscuring some of the windows. One or other of them raised an eyebrow at the prospect. For these two young women – both of whom would have been familiar with grander properties – initial impressions were not remotely favourable. 'It was a bit of a shock,' says Sarah Baring lightly now. 'We thought the house was perfectly monstrous.'

Scattered around outside the mansion, on its lawns, were spartan-looking single-storey wooden huts, with little chimneys coughing out thick, inky smoke, and windows covered for the blackout. Round to the side of the house were what had been the old stables, and a sturdy red-brick outbuilding referred to as 'the Cottage'. The paving around the house, and on the concrete driveway, was in a state of disrepair, with potholes.

It was difficult to see beyond this, but the grounds went on further, much further; there were meadows filled with more huts, and concrete blocks. 'And there were,' Sarah Baring says, 'men and women emerging from all these huts, giving the impression of a labyrinth from which there was no exit.' She also immediately noted a disconcerting 'absence of people in uniform'.

The front of the house, looking across the pretty ornamental lake and beyond into the gloaming, down the hill, faced towards the town; but any glimpse of Bletchley was obscured by trees. The only reminder of the outside world was the distant shrieks of train whistles echoing in the spring air.

Once through the door of the big house – which bustled with more intense-looking young men and women in civilian clothes –

the two young women were pointed up the stairs, and presented themselves on the first floor to the man who had sent them the telegram: Commander Travis, Deputy Director of Bletchley Park.

Travis immediately asked the two bemused young women to sign the Official Secrets Act. He then told them of a temporary billet in town – a hotel – in which they would be staying, and added that their duties would begin the following morning. 'He said to me, "I hear you've got the German,"' says Sarah Baring, 'which at that moment I thought was rather funny because I thought he meant a man.' At that point, Commander Travis told the two women very little of what their duties would entail; only that the need for secrecy was absolutely paramount.

And after this faintly dreamlike introduction, Sarah and Osla's years at Bletchley Park began.

Other recruits to the Park often arrived late at night. During the blackout, there would have been no lights visible from the dowdy Buckinghamshire town; these people would not have been able to make out through the murk a single detail of the small red-brick houses, or the long terraced streets, or the pubs. 'In the early hours of the morning, I alighted on the station platform, and was met by an army captain,' said one veteran. 'I might as well have found myself in Outer Mongolia.'

'I got to Bletchley around midnight,' recalled another veteran. 'Everything was in darkness. There were some iron steps going over the bridge. There wasn't a soul about.'

There is, perhaps, a touch of the Graham Greene thriller about this image: the steam train drawing away, its red rear lights disappearing into the black distance; then a thick silence, broken only by the click of solitary footsteps pacing in the deep shadows of an unlit platform, waiting for the mysterious contact to arrive. 'A system of passwords has been instituted to enable authorised persons to circulate in the grounds after dark,' stated an early Bletchley Park memo in October 1939. '[It will] enable them to identify themselves to the military police when challenged.'[1]

Many of those who reported for duty at Bletchley Park recall that suspense; the anticipation and excitement of not knowing what kind of work they were about to step into. For those who arrived on a winter evening, or even in the small hours, the total darkness around the station acquired a chillingly metaphorical depth.

And even for the others who reported for duty in more conventional, brighter daylight, the introduction to Bletchley Park was no less disorientating. The experience of another veteran, Sheila Lawn (née MacKenzie), just nineteen years old at the time, was not untypical.

Sheila was a young nineteen, too; she had never previously left her native Scotland. She had received the summons in some bewilderment, uncertain how anyone would have known about her, or who might have recommended her. She embarked upon a deeply uncomfortable eleven-hour train journey from Inverness to Bletchley (trains during the war were often jammed, and people would often have to sit on their suitcases in the corridors, and try to do without the lavatories, which were gothically horrible); eleven hours with the tension – and the thrill – of having no idea what was coming next.

She now recalls: 'When I arrived at Bletchley station, I had been instructed to find a phone, which I did. The voice at the other end said: "Ah, yes, Miss MacKenzie, we are expecting you." And a car came down to take me up there. How could I really speculate about what I was getting into? This was a very secretive business, you see.'

The most secretive business there could be. Years before the outbreak of the Second World War, one branch of the Foreign Office was acutely aware of the immense challenge it was facing; a challenge that would require not merely diamond-sharp minds, but also young people with the energy and the character to face exhausting trials of patience. Recruits with the strength to focus every single day upon tasks of stunning complexity, without letting the pressure undermine their mental well-being.

Upon arrival, most of the young recruits to this establishment immediately gathered that they were to be engaged upon intelligence work of the most crucial nature. There were sharp, serious warnings about total secrecy; glimpses of former university tutors, in civilian clothing; then the swift, giddying realisation that they were now close to the nerve centre of the British war effort.

Here, in these grounds fifty miles to the north of London, they would be introduced to the gravest secret of the war. Every intercepted enemy message, every signal from every captain, commander, military division, battleship, U-boat; all these encrypted communications, jumbled up into seemingly random letters in groups of four and five, and transmitted by radio, were gathered in by the many listening posts around the British coastline. And they were all assiduously sent on to Bletchley Park. It was here, in these nondescript huts, that the most powerful intellects of a generation struggled with a proposition that German High Command considered completely insoluble: that of outwitting – and mastering – its ingenious Enigma encoding technology.

The Enigma machines – compact, beautifully designed devices, looking a little like typewriters with lights – were used by all the German military forces; these portable machines generated the countless millions of different letter combinations in which most coded German communications were sent.

In the early stages of the war, when the Nazis had conquered much of western Europe, Britain looked alarmingly vulnerable – relatively ill-prepared and underarmed. From the beginning, the desperate need to break the Enigma codes was about much more than simple tactical intelligence. It was about survival.

To unlock the secrets of Enigma would mean penetrating to the heart of the enemy's campaign; it would allow the British to read the encoded messages from U-boats, from Panzer divisions, from the Gestapo. It would allow them to read Luftwaffe messages, with their clues about bombing targets, and even to read messages from High Command itself. The codebreakers of Bletchley Park aimed at reading the enemy's every message, and in so doing potentially trying to anticipate his every move.

And in the initial push to find some incredibly abstruse mathematical way into these constantly changing codes – all the settings were changed every night, at midnight – it was immediately apparent to the few who knew the secret that this intelligence was much more than getting a head start on the enemy. This was intelligence that could help decide the course of the war.

Most people these days are vaguely aware that the work of Bletchley and its supply of intelligence – codenamed Ultra – helped, in the words of President Eisenhower, to shorten the war by two years. Indeed, according to the eminent historian – and Bletchley Park veteran – Professor Sir Harry Hinsley, the figure should be three years. Prominent critic and essayist George Steiner went further: he stated that the work done at Bletchley was one of 'the greatest achievements of the twentieth century'.

From the Battle of Britain to the Blitz; from Cape Matapan to El-Alamein; from Kursk to the V-1 rockets, to D-Day and Japan, the work of Bletchley Park was completely invisible, yet right at the heart of the conflict. It was a key player whose presence, at all times, had to be kept utterly hidden from the enemy. For if even a suggestion of what was happening at Bletchley were to reach German High Command, all the cryptography efforts could have been ruined. The effect on the war could have been catastrophic.

'When you think that about nine or ten thousand people worked in all the various sections of Bletchley Park,' says Park veteran Mavis Batey, 'it is really quite incredible that the secret never got out. Imagine so many people keeping such a secret now.' More than this, though. The austere wooden huts on the lawns and in the meadows played host to some of the most gifted – and quirky – individuals of their generation. Not only were there long-standing cryptographers of great genius; there were also fresh, brilliant young minds, such as Alan Turing, whose work was destined to shape the coming computer age, and the future of technology.

Also at Bletchley Park were thousands of dedicated people, mostly young, many drawn straight from university. Some came straight from sixth form.

As the war progressed, numbers grew. Alongside the academics, there were platoons of female translators and hundreds of eager Wrens, there to operate the fearsomely complicated prototype computing machines; there was also a substantial number of well-bred debutantes, sought out upon the social grapevine, and equally determined to do their bit.

A surprising number of people at Bletchley Park were either already famous, or would become famous not long after their time there. These ranged from glamorous film actress Dorothy Hyson (with occasional appearances from her paramour, actor Anthony Quayle) and novelist-to-be Angus Wilson (who was to become renowned at the Park for his stretched-out nerves, extravagantly camp mannerisms, wild temper tantrums, and richly coloured bow ties) to future Home Secretary Roy Jenkins (a 'terrible code-breaker'). James Bond's creator Ian Fleming, then working in London on naval intelligence, would drop by on a regular basis.

The comparative youth of most of the recruits was to colour the atmosphere of the establishment quite deeply. They worked with tremendous vigour and intensity, but they also brought a sharp, lively creativity to their off-duty hours. These young people – many of whom were part of an emerging, strengthening middle class – found that rather than being a 'pause' in their educations, Bletchley Park was to form its own peculiar kind of university experience.

There was also to be a great deal of romance, perhaps unsurprisingly in what one veteran described as 'the hothouse atmosphere' of Bletchley Park. Many who fell in love at Bletchley stayed happily married for many years afterwards. Some are still married today.

Yet this 'hothouse' also imposed an extraordinary burden. The oaths of secrecy that the recruits were made to swear lasted for many decades beyond the end of the war. Husbands and wives were forbidden to discuss the work they had done there; they could not tell their parents what they had achieved, even if their parents were dying. They were not allowed to tell their children.

Which is why, since the silence lifted in the late 1970s, the recollections of Bletchley Park veterans seem to have a special vividness and clarity; they have not been smoothed out or transformed or muddled by endless retelling. Added to this, there was a focus and intensity about life at the Park that would burn itself on to the memory.

Architectural historian Jane Fawcett MBE, who was recruited to the Park as a young woman in 1940, recalls the almost unfathomable sense of pressure that they were under. 'We knew that what we were doing was making all the difference,' she says. 'We knew that it really did depend on us.'

'It would get too much for some,' says one veteran. 'The strain really did tell.' Another veteran, S. Gorley Putt, commented: 'One after another – in one way or another – we would all go off our rockers.'[2]

Gorley Putt was exaggerating a little. Not everyone went off their rockers. Indeed, many Bletchley Park veterans now look back at their experiences – the frustrations, the exhausting night shifts, the flashing moments of insight and genius, even the outbreaks of youthful, high-spirited laughter – as a formative experience that they were uniquely privileged to enjoy.

2 1938–39: The School of Codes

Until the outbreak of war (and indeed for many years afterwards), the town of Bletchley – in the north of Buckinghamshire, and sited roughly halfway between London and Birmingham – was notable chiefly for being completely unworthy of note.

Even the well-respected architectural chronicler Nikolaus Pevsner counselled his readers against visiting the place. He felt it had nothing to offer either in terms of interesting buildings or beguiling landscape. It was a railway town, sitting on a busy junction. Bletchley's other chief industry was the manufacture of bricks. The smell of the works had a distinct tang that hung over the town on warm summer days.

And the idiosyncratic nineteenth-century house, with its fifty-five acres of grounds, located on the other side of the railway tracks from the main streets of Bletchley, was selected as the wartime base for the Government Code and Cypher School largely for reasons of security, as opposed to aesthetic considerations.

Ever since 1919, all foreign encrypted messages – largely those from the fledgling Soviet Union – had been dealt with by the Government Code and Cypher School (GC&CS), a small, esoteric government department which was in essence the codebreaking arm of the Foreign Office. Since the 1930s, the department had been based just around the corner from Whitehall, in Broadway Buildings, St James's Park; a smart London address that it shared with MI6.

It was actually a good eighteen months before 1939 that the decision was made to move GC&CS out to the countryside. The reason was that its central London location would put it at very high risk from potential German bomber raids. The horrifying Blitzkrieg campaign in Spain had demonstrated just how lethally effective such attacks could be.

Previously, the Bletchley Park estate had belonged to the wealthy Leon family. But in 1937, the heir, Sir George, lost interest in maintaining the trappings of country life. And thus the place went on the market. A relative of the family, Ruth Sebag-Montefiore – who quite by chance was recruited to become a codebreaker at Bletchley Park herself – said of the house: 'Only by stretching my imagination to the utmost could I picture the place . . . in its heyday, when there were hunters in the stables, house-parties most weekends and children in the top floor nurseries.'[1]

By 1937, the grand house-parties were over. In 1938, a small team of property developers, led by a Captain Faulkner, made the highest bid for the estate. It is reported that the head of MI6, or the Secret Intelligence Service (SIS), Admiral Sir Hugh Sinclair, was so adamant that the move was necessary, and so frustrated by lumbering Whitehall interdepartmental bureaucracy, that he paid for the house out of his own pocket.

Work began at once. Violent events in Europe were casting shadows. Admiral Sinclair was sharply aware – perhaps more so than many in the government – that the house and its grounds would be needed urgently.

In May of that year, engineers from the Post Office began laying cables from the house that would connect it up to the nerve endings of Whitehall. Over the summer of 1938 – which was dominated by the excruciating tension of the Munich summit and

Chamberlain's calculated but misguided appeasement of Hitler over mounting German aggression towards Czechoslovakia – 'Captain Ridley's Shooting Party', as the codename went, came to stay at the Bletchley Park estate by way of a rehearsal.

In fact, Captain Ridley was a naval officer with MI6. His job was to organise the logistics of the move of GC&CS (known by some jokingly as the 'Golf Club and Chess Society') from London to Bletchley. 'We were told that this was a "rehearsal",' wrote senior codebreaker Josh Cooper in a contemporary diary. 'But we all realised that the "rehearsal" might well end in a real war.'

This 1938 rehearsal also gave an idea of the difficulties involved. The presence of so many visitors to Bletchley Park milling around the grounds was explained to the curious local people by that very 'Captain Ridley's Shooting Party' catch-all phrase. The Wodehousian flavour of the term – faintly anachronistic, even back then – was to find echoes in the years to come.

There was a lot of work to be done. It was immediately clear that the house itself would not be large enough to accommodate the anticipated code-cracking activity. As such, wooden huts, insulated with asbestos, were to be built in the grounds 'To begin with, when there were only a handful of us, we worked in the house,' recalled Ruth Sebag-Montefiore. 'Subsequently we moved into one of the wooden huts that sprang up like mushrooms.'

Although records are not completely clear, it seems that the first of the huts – those brilliantly makeshift, weather-exposed synecdoches of British improvisational spirit, and the eventual beehives of the Bletchley operation – was built not too long after the time of the Munich crisis. Hut 1 was originally intended to house the Park's wireless station. The huts that were built soon afterwards – some of which still survive today – strike the modern eye as puzzlingly temporary structures; they put one in mind of prefab houses.

Bletchley was both far enough away yet convenient enough to reach to make it an ideal location. And the town and surrounding villages were reckoned to have sufficient space for billeting all the codebreakers and translators. Bletchley Park itself was (and is) next to what is now referred to as the West Coast railway line. And in the days before Dr Beeching axed so much of the network, Bletchley station teemed with activity. To the west, the railways reached Oxford; to the east Cambridge. Meanwhile, anyone travelling from London, Birmingham, Lancashire or Glasgow could get to the town with ease. 'Or relative ease,' says Sheila Lawn, who became used to these long-distance hauls. 'The trains were always absolutely packed with soldiers.' Nevertheless, the location was a great boon to the many young people scattered across the country who would find themselves receiving the summons.

Throughout 1938, work on further customising the estate progressed at speed. One wing of the house was demolished; the outbuildings were converted into office space.

At the very top of the house, in a small, dingy attic room near a large water tank, lay 'Station X'. In essence, it was an SIS radio listening post. Outside the tiny little window was a huge Wellingtonia tree, around which was arranged the necessary rhombic array aerial. 'Station X', a wonderfully Ian Fleming-esque designation, was in fact so named because it was simply the tenth station of its sort. The station didn't last long there – later, it was moved six miles away to Whaddon Hall.

There was a temporary decrease in diplomatic tension in the aftermath of Munich. Prime Minister Neville Chamberlain famously had in his hand a piece of paper, which promised peace in our time. According to some contemporaneous Mass Observation reports, not many ordinary people were wholly convinced by this. And on the intelligence side, the quiet, furtive preparations for the coming, inevitable conflict became ever more intense.

Bletchley Park was placed under the control of Commander Alistair Denniston. Originally the establishment was supposed to have been run by Admiral Sir Hugh Sinclair, but he was becoming very ill by this point and Denniston rapidly assumed day-to-day responsibility for the operation. This delegation of responsibility –

with the head of MI6 being in ultimate, rather than everyday, control – was one of the elements that in the years to come was to give Bletchley Park its unusual and sometimes unpredictable flavour. It had a degree of quirky autonomy. Certainly quirky enough not to be appreciated by some senior figures in Whitehall.

Back in 1919, just after the end of the First World War, Alistair Denniston had been made head of the Government Code and Cypher School, and he presided over the department in the interwar years. When Denniston came to Bletchley Park in 1939, he saw to it that some fellow codebreakers from the early days of the department came too – including the mercurial but brilliant Alfred Dillwyn Knox and Frank Birch.

Birch had a rather unusual hinterland; as well as being incredibly sharp with codes, he was a theatre actor and director with an amusingly exaggerated manner. In fact, in 1930 he had essayed a highly memorable Widow Twankey in a sumptuous West End production of *Aladdin*. Birch and Knox had been at Cambridge together.

On arrival at Bletchley, 'Dilly' Knox, as senior cryptographer, was allocated working space in 'the Cottage' – in reality, a row of chunky converted interlinked houses – just across the courtyard from the main house, near the stables. Fifty-five-year-old Knox was, in the words of a colleague, 'the mastermind behind the Enigma affair', a gangling figure with a prominent forehead, 'unruly black hair and his eyes, behind glasses, some miles away in thought'.

Knox had been interested in ciphers since boyhood, noted the novelist (and his niece) Penelope Fitzgerald. Also as a boy, Dilly had precociously 'detected a number of inaccuracies, even downright contradictions in the Sherlock Holmes stories,' wrote Fitzgerald, 'and sent a list of them to Conan Doyle in an envelope with four dried orange pips, in allusion to the threatening letter in "The Sign of Four"'.[2]

He was also a man prone to terrific bursts of temper, and quickly became noted by his colleagues for the fact that he seemed to get on much better with women than he did with men. He certainly had a most enlightened approach to the employment of women at that period – one might even be tempted to call it positive discrimination. Although that was not how many more lascivious-minded colleagues saw it at the time.

Indeed, it was not long before the female recruits to 'the Cottage' became known widely around the Park as 'Dilly's Fillies'. These days, the expression causes one of Knox's more illustrious female recruits – Mavis Batey, née Lever – to tut-tut and roll her eyes with good-humoured exasperation. 'A myth has grown up that Dilly went around in 1939 looking at the girls arriving at Bletchley and picking the most attractive for the Cottage,' Mrs Batey says, perhaps protesting a little too much. 'That is completely untrue. Dilly took us on our qualifications.'

Other experienced codebreakers who had served alongside Denniston in that interwar period, and who were to make such a difference at Bletchley Park, were Josh Cooper, John Jeffreys, Frank Lucas, Nigel de Grey, Oliver Strachey and Colonel John Tiltman, an utterly brilliant veteran cryptographer.

Oliver Strachey, related to Lytton, was noted for his colourful good humour and his intense musicality. He was a friend of Benjamin Britten. When back in London, Strachey and Britten would enjoy playing duets. As the war intensified, Strachey would find himself taking a pivotal role in the Park's decoding of Gestapo signals, heading a special department which in the 1940s began to slowly decrypt the hideous bureaucracy of death – the railway timetables, the numbers of people being transported – that surrounded the Holocaust.

Also highly notable among the codebreakers was Josh Cooper, a physically imposing presence – known to some as 'the Bear' – in his middle years, and singular in his mannerisms, often given to exclaiming to himself. In the very early days of Bletchley, he was rather taken with this move from London to the country. 'We all sat down to lunch together at one long table in the House,' Cooper wrote. Elsewhere he recalled, 'a large room on the ground floor had been set aside for Air Section . . . I remember coming into a scene of chaos with a great mound of books and papers piled on the floor.'

Cooper also noted right from the start that 'service personnel wore civilian clothes in the office', but 'put on uniform to go on leave, or on duty trips to London etc., in order to be able to use Service travel warrants'. As a security precaution, all personal post had to be sent to Bletchley Park via a London PO box. This postal system broke down, according to Cooper, when a relative of one codebreaker 'attempted to send a grand piano'.[3]

Cooper's own recollections fail to include his own spectacular bouts of eccentricity, such as the later occasion, recalled by another veteran, when Cooper was present at the interrogation of a captured German pilot. When the pilot gave out a 'Heil Hitler!' Cooper inadvertently did the same, and in his haste to sit down after this embarrassment ended up missing the chair and falling under his desk. But what we do hear in these accounts of the very first days of Bletchley Park is the notion of a deliberate ethos, a studied atmosphere of genteel chaos that was perhaps fostered to encourage freethinking improvisation. Certainly, the way Bletchley Park was run was to become the source of future friction in the War Office.

The permanent staff of GC&CS – a platoon redolent of cardigans, tweed and pipes – around this time numbered around 180. Around thirty of these people were codebreakers. The rest were Intelligence and support staff. It was swiftly understood in 1938 that rather more were going to be needed.

And so the serious business of wider recruitment was beginning. One internal memo from February 1939 stated that 'three professors will be available as soon as required', as though such men were machine components. The looming conflict also brought a shift in attitude from GC&CS.

In previous years, according to one veteran, the department

didn't want to use mathematicians for codebreaking. The reason was that mathematicians, as a class, were not considered temperamentally appropriate. 'They were definitely persona non grata,' recalled John Herivel, himself a fine mathematician (and author of one of the Park's greatest breakthroughs). 'Supposedly because of their impractical and unreliable nature.'4

All this was about to change dramatically. Alistair Denniston had spent a few months visiting Oxford and Cambridge, assessing the likeliest young candidates. Among them was a deeply promising young mathematician called Peter Twinn; then there was a dazzlingly clever 33-year-old mathematics lecturer, Gordon Welchman, of Sidney Sussex College, Cambridge. Welchman – a handsome fellow with an extremely neat moustache – swiftly proved to be an assiduous, enthusiastic and fantastically ambitious recruiting officer.

The most talented young mathematician of them all, 27-year-old Alan Turing, from King's College, Cambridge, had been sounded out even earlier, as far back as 1937. Between them, Turing and Welchman would quickly prove to be crucial to the Bletchley operation. And it is of course Turing's name that lives on, inseparable from the Park and its work. In part, the success that this brilliant, tragically misunderstood figure was to enjoy at Bletchley subsequently led to the computerised world that we live in today. But it was also at the Park that Turing was to find a rare sort of freedom, before the narrow, repressive culture of the post-war years closed in on him and apparently led to his early death.

'Turing,' commented Stuart Milner-Barry, 'was a strange and ultimately a tragic figure.' That is one view. Certainly his life was short, and it ended extremely unhappily. But in a number of other senses, Alan Turing was an inspirational figure. 'Alan Turing was unique,' recalled Peter Hilton. 'What you realise when you get to know a genius well is that there is all the difference between a very intelligent person and a genius. With very intelligent people, you talk to them, they come out with an idea, and you say to yourself, if not to them, I could have had that idea. You never had that feeling with Turing at all. He constantly surprised you with the originality of his thinking. It was marvellous.'[5]

The popular misconception is that of a brooding, asocial homosexual, trapped in a hostile time, unable to find happiness. The story is not so simple as that. Thanks to biographies, an official apology from the government and the Prime Minister, and even a play by Hugh Whitemore, the name of Alan Turing has become, above all others, synonymous with the breaking of the Enigma codes.

Like Dilly Knox, Turing had attended Cambridge, though by the 1930s the university's former Edwardian atmosphere of homoerotic decadence was being gradually usurped by the apparent urgency of politics. Some accounts of Turing make mention of his high-pitched voice, his hesitating stammer, a laugh that would try the patience of even the closest of friends, and a habit of concluding any social interaction by sidling out of the room, eyes lowered, murmuring something about thanks.

In other words, the portrait we appear to be presented with is one of a classic borderline-Asperger's boffin. His eccentricities have been well rehearsed: among them was his bicycle, with a chain that was poised to fall off after so many rotations, which meant that Turing had to calculate exactly the moment at which to start moving the pedals backwards to avert this. And he had the habit of cycling around the countryside while wearing a full gas mask.

Yet perhaps there was a logical advantage in having a bicycle that no one else would know how to use without the thing falling to bits? And the simple fact was that Turing suffered badly from hay fever. The gas mask was a practical, if drastic, solution to the difficulty.

Moreover, unlike the usual shambling professor, Turing was remarkably physically fit. Though he had no time for organised field games, he was extremely keen on running, and took part in a great many races. Around the time he joined Bletchley Park, he had built up sufficient endurance to run marathons. It has been suggested that he channelled a great deal of sexual frustration into these distance runs; but the real satisfaction may have derived from a sport in which he had complete control, and which relied as much on concentration and mental focus as it did on physical power.

As Sarah Baring recalls: 'We just knew him as "The Prof". He seemed terribly shy.' Certainly, while at Bletchley, Turing certainly was not greatly interested in social interaction. Yet he was a more radical, open, honest soul than the accounts suggest.

Turing became a Fellow of King's College before, in the late 1930s, heading for the United States, to Princeton. Building bridges between the two disciplines of mathematics and applied physics, he threw himself into the construction of a 'Turing machine', a machine that could carry out logical binary calculations. Having seen a tide-predicting machine some years back in Liverpool, it occurred to him that the principle of this device could be applied to his own machine, greatly speeding its function.

By 1938, when it was increasingly clear that war was coming to the whole of Europe, Turing returned to England, and to King's, with his electric multiplier machine mounted on a bread-board. It was now that he decided to share his talent with the Government Code & Cypher School in the Broadway Buildings.

There he was given training sessions in the basics of code work and intelligence gathering. After one of these sessions, at Christmas 1938, he found himself working alongside Dilly Knox. Nine months before Britain went to war with Germany, Alistair Denniston had wisely started to speed up the process of cracking the problem of Enigma. At the beginning of 1939, Turing returned to Cambridge, now apprised of the intense secrecy of the matter, and began to apply himself to the intellectual challenge.

Throughout 1939, Turing and Gordon Welchman attended 'short courses' in cryptography organised by GC&CS. Their names are to be seen on contemporary memos, in pencil, with ticks beside them, as though they were part of a school register.

But it was not just mathematicians that were needed. Other

disciplines lent themselves to the work of codebreaking equally well. One could be a historian, or a classicist. Famously, one could be an expert at solving the *Daily Telegraph* cryptic crossword in under twelve minutes. One could also be a chess expert or grand master – as indeed were young Bletchley recruit Hugh Alexander and a number of the young recruits that he in turn bought along. 'Of course, we were also very good at Scrabble and anagrams,' says one veteran.

Secret service officer Captain Frederick Winterbotham, author of the pioneering book on Ultra, noted that many of the young people coming in had strong musical predilections; an inclination also recalled by Gordon Welchman, who summoned the rather beautiful image of youthful codebreakers 'singing madrigals on a summer's evening' by the waters of the Grand Union Canal.

But very quickly, Alistair Denniston detected that the gentle setting itself, the house and its spacious grounds, might be regarded as a nuisance by those who worked there, many of whom were coming from London. In a letter of September 1939, to Sir Stewart Menzies, the deputy (soon-to-be) head of the Secret Intelligence Service, Denniston wrote:

> The Government Code and Cypher School was moved out of London by the orders of the Admiral and not by order of the Foreign Office . . . the work [requires] a high degree of concentration in over-crowded rooms . . . billeting has forced the staff to live many miles from their work, We have tried to raise a force of volunteers and ask them to give their time and their cars to help their colleagues.[6]

In other words, the core of these teething problems was the fact that the codebreakers were finding it difficult to adjust to the change from fast metropolitan life to what many of them regarded as a provincial backwater.

It is broadly assumed nowadays that the work at Bletchley required its inmates to be near-autistic, socially inept geniuses. In fact, the more prized quality would have been a certain nimbleness and litheness of mind, the ability to approach and solve a problem from hitherto unconsidered angles.

This was certainly the case with Enigma. The breaking of the German codes would turn out to be the result of a combination of flashes of logical and mathematical insight plus a certain psychological brilliance. And this is even without mentioning the formidable technical skills of the men who built the 'bombe' machines, the vast, revolutionary proto-computer constructions that could sift through the dizzying millions of potential combinations of each code.

Nor was it just codebreakers who were needed. Bletchley Park also required the services of able, fast-witted linguists – young men and women fluent especially in German.

It also needed stalwart administrative backup; people who could attend to the grindingly tedious yet crucial roles of filing and archives. For not only were there enemy transmissions to be logged, translated, decoded – they also had to be filed in such a way that they could be cross-referenced with other messages in the future. At the beginning, this was a role that largely fell to the higher-class sort of 'gel'.

There was no embarrassment about this extension of the upper-class 'shooting party' idea. Debutantes and daughters of 'good families' were actively sought after, apparently to ensure the very highest levels of security and secrecy; Alistair Denniston felt that the smarter girls would have a more acutely refined sense of duty. Such wildly generalised social assumptions were not unusual at the time. But questions of class aside, that sense of duty led these well-bred girls to undertake with great good humour some of the most breathtakingly tedious work.

On top of all this, the Park needed secretaries, office managers and messengers, even waitresses for the canteen of the House. Quite a lot of people, all in all, to descend on a very small, un-note-worthy town.

3 1939: Rounding Up the Brightest and the Best

Almost instantly, Commander Denniston found himself sinking in a quagmire of difficulties. Indeed, he complained at the time that he was 'most anxious to take my share of the work on the increasing numbers of cryptographic problems confronting us'. Such a desire was simply not practical.

So, on 4 September 1939, further summonses to Bletchley started to go out discreetly. A surviving memo states: 'immediate personnel for Hut 3: I suggest 15 people be asked for at once. As you know I have already approached Pembroke College Oxford and they have promised to send me some names in a few weeks time.'

This need for discretion was paramount, which is why so many of the first codebreaking and translating recruits were known personally and socially to their recruitors. But there was much more than just plain nepotism and snobbery going on. For the linguists recruited to translate the German messages, there is a suggestion that the security services played a part in the approaches. Certainly, reasonably stringent background checks were made on these early young arrivals. Other than this, though, there seemed to be a pleasing breeziness about the way candidates were picked.

Mavis Batey is one of the few people to have worked closely

alongside the volcanic Dilly Knox, and she herself was to play a key role in the Park's story. She was by no means a debutante. Rather, she was a fiercely intelligent middle-class girl.

Today Mrs Batey, whose husband Keith is a fellow Bletchley Park veteran, is wryly amused by the reasoning that led to the Park's upper-class recruitment drive: 'The first two girls in the Cottage were the daughters of two chaps that Denniston played golf with at Ashtead. Denniston knew the family, he knew that they were nice people and . . . well, that their daughters wouldn't go around opening their mouths and saying what was going on. The background was so important if they were the sort of people who were not going to go around telling everyone what they were doing.'

For Keith Batey, a 20-year-old undergraduate reading mathematics at Cambridge – who was to participate in some of the greatest inspirational leaps made at the Park, and who was to meet his future wife Mavis there after a chance encounter in one of the huts – his own recruitment was reasonably straightforward. So much so, in fact, that unlike many of his fellow codebreakers-to-be, he realised instantly as soon as he received the summons. He recalls: 'They [the university authorities] were allowing mathematicians to stay on to finish degrees. I took my maths finals in Cambridge in May 1940 – it all seemed highly artificial, with the Germans charging across Europe – anyway, I took it and then one had to wait to be told what to do.

'I went home to Carlisle. A letter arrived, scruffily handwritten, from a chap called Gordon Welchman. He was writing to offer me a job. He couldn't tell me what it was, where it was, or anything of that kind, but he could say that it was very important, very interesting, and that the pay was lousy.

'Such was the security,' continues Mr Batey with a certain dryness, 'it was well known among the maths undergraduates in my year in Cambridge that in January 1940, one Welchman had taken a couple of his own graduates off to a certain "Room 40". And I knew Room 40 was cryptography.'

His wife-to-be, a linguist and student of German literature, also had the benefit of a certain amount of inside knowledge. Just as the war broke out, she had been seconded to the old GC&CS near St James's Park – a distinctly unusual position for a young woman at that time. 'I worked at Broadway Buildings first, in the Ministry of Economic Warfare,' Mrs Batey says. 'The job involved blacklisting all the people who were dealing with Germany – through commodities they were using. Then I got called for the interview at the Foreign Office – conducted by a formidable lady called Miss Moore – I don't know whether she knew what we were going to do. At the time of the interview, we didn't know whether we were going to be spies or what. But then I got sent to Bletchley.

'I didn't want to go on with academic studies,' Mrs Batey continues. 'University College London [where she had been studying] was just evacuating to the campus at Aberystwyth, in west Wales. But I thought I ought to do something better for the war effort than reading German poets in Wales. After all, German poets would soon be above us in bombers. I remarked to someone that I should train to be a nurse. But that person told me: "No you don't, you go and see someone at the Foreign Office. They can use your German." And so I did.'

Harry Hinsley, who was later to become the official historian of British wartime intelligence, recalled being interviewed in St John's College, Cambridge by Alistair Denniston and Colonel John Tiltman. Of this experience Hinsley said: 'The kind of questions they asked me were: "You've travelled a bit, we understand. You've done quite well in your Tripos. What do you think of government service? Would you rather have that than be conscripted? Does it appeal to you?"'[1]

This, at least, was rather more subtle than an approach made two years before to Professor E.R.P. Vincent, who was invited to dinner by Room 40 veteran Frank Adcock. Professor Vincent recalled: 'We dined very well, for he [Adcock] was something of an epicure, and the meal was very suitably concluded with a bottle of 1920 port. It was then that he did something which seemed to me most extraordinary: he went to the door, looked outside and came back to his seat. As a reader of spy fiction, I recognised the procedure but never expected to witness it.'[2]

However corny, the approach worked, and Professor Vincent was to join the team engaged with wrestling with the Japanese codes.

For Sheila Lawn there was a definite element of taking an active role in the conflict. 'I was in my second year in Aberdeen University studying for a Modern Languages honours degree. But I was very troubled because I was reserved as a future teacher. I felt I ought to be doing something – like so many of my friends – about fighting Hitler. So I took my name away from the Reserve list, didn't consult anyone, just took it away. I waited for developments, which came very quickly. A letter from the Foreign Office in London, asking me to go down for an interview.

'I had my interview,' Sheila continues. 'And shortly after that – it was the vacation – I got another letter, simply asking me to report to Bletchley.'

The man whom she met at Bletchley Park, and whom she was later to marry – Oliver Lawn – was similarly young and eager when he found himself being approached. Mr Lawn was later to find himself overseeing one of the most important technological breakthroughs of the entire war. But for this young man, only nineteen years old, not long out of a respectable minor public school, there was little hint at the beginning of the intellectual excitement that lay ahead.

Now he finds himself recalling the start of his Bletchley Park career with a certain amused seriousness. 'At the time, I was doing maths tripos at Cambridge. When I finished my tripos, my Part Three, in 1940, I expected to be called straight up into the army – Engineers or whatever. When I went up to Cambridge in July to take my degree, I was asked to go and see a chap called Gordon Welchman, who I knew by name, but not in person. He was a mathematics lecturer, who had not been one of my lecturers.

'So I didn't know, of course, that he had gone to Bletchley. I went to his rooms, and he said: "Would you like to work with me?" Without telling me, of course, what the work was. Obviously, since I was due for call-up, I had no choice, in that sense. And a fortnight later, I turned up at Bletchley Park, and sat at Welchman's feet, to learn about Enigma.'

For the Hon. Sarah Baring – a young debutante, goddaughter of Lord Mountbatten and a photographic model for Cecil Beaton – the route to Bletchley Park was a little less cloak-and-dagger and rather more patriotic gung-ho. As soon as the war broke out, she knew that she wanted to throw herself into the effort. The only problem was that the first job she found was less than ideal.

'When the war started, me and a great friend of mine, Osla Henniker-Major, decided we wanted to do something really important,' Sarah Baring says. 'And we thought: making aeroplanes. So we trooped off to the Slough Trading Estate – ghastly place – and said to the people there: "Here we are – we want to make aeroplanes." So we were shoved in to something like a school.

'We had to learn how to cut Durol,' she continues, 'which the planes were made of. We did that for a while, and then Osla and I felt we weren't really doing enough. Then suddenly, through the post, came a letter, God knows who from, asking us to report to the head of Bletchley – forthwith. That was all. So we thought: "Anything's better than making aeroplanes at the moment."

'We had to have a language test,' she continues. 'And it was a funny one. I knew German, luckily, because my mother had sent me to Germany when I was sixteen – I hated it, by the way – so I had the German. And French was easy. And I suddenly realised that the lady who was talking to me and finding out about my linguistic skills didn't have a clue what she was talking about.

'So I lost my head completely and said: "Oh! Would you like to hear my Spanish?" I couldn't really speak Spanish at all. She said: "Oh no, dear, I think that'll be . . ." I added: "I can do Portuguese."

The whole thing was going to my head. She said: "No, no, dear, that's fine, you've passed the thing." It was the German this lady was after, of course.'

Others too found that the language test didn't seem to be as rigorous as one would expect. One recruit was asked if she could speak Italian. 'Only opera Italian,' she replied. 'Yes, that will do,' she was told.

One young mathematician did have an idea of what was coming, and his approach was more cloak-and-dagger than almost anyone else's. But as the man who would provide one of the most brilliant intuitive leaps of the war, this is perhaps appropriate. John Herivel – whose 'Herivel Tip' was to prove vital in the struggle to crack Enigma – remembered his introduction to the institution as a young undergraduate in 1940: 'Gordon Welchman in the early days had done most of the recruiting. A lot of them inevitably were people that he knew. The men and also, I think, some of the women.'

Welchman also happened to be Herivel's old mathematics lecturer, so the link could not have been more direct. From the undergraduates' point of view, he was a figure who had disappeared from the university under a cloud of mystery; now, one cold midwinter's evening in Cambridge, 21-year-old Herivel got an unexpected visit in his rooms from the very man himself.

Welchman was brisk, though civil, wasting little time in telling Herivel that there was important war work going on at Bletchley Park and asking him if he would like to come and help.

The young man responded equally briskly; Mr Herivel recalls that at that time 'the university was a ghostly place', and that Part III of his Mathematics tripos could wait until after the war. And so a date was agreed. Welchman told Herivel where to go and whom to present himself to; and just a few moments later, the former Cambridge lecturer was gone, with a cheery 'Au revoir.'

Several days later, Herivel was on the train from Cambridge to Bletchley, speculating madly about what he was getting into. 'The very first thing I had to do on arrival there,' he recalls, 'was swear an oath. About not revealing a single detail to anyone. I remember there was a fearsome looking naval officer there – presumably to instil a measure of fear!'

Some veterans recalled their utter dismay upon arriving at Bletchley; the railway station itself was frowsy, and the small town that it served did not look much more promising. Architectural historian Jane Fawcett MBE recalls simply that Bletchley was 'a dump'. Even the first prospect of the Park itself – which from 1939 was surrounded with wire fencing, 'like Whipsnade Zoo', as veteran Diana Plowman put it – might not have seemed especially enticing. One or two of these young people, when being sized up for their new duties, had imagined that their top secret missions would involve them being parachuted in behind enemy lines. Drab, dreary, provincial Bletchley seemed a long way from such excitement.

Indeed, for a few, such as Scot Irene Young, the initial impressions of their new surroundings were downright depressing. Directly upon arriving, she recalled,

I fell on the gravel, severely grazing my knee and what was worse, ruining one of my two pairs of stockings ... The matron of Sick Bay, a formidable lady by the name of Mrs de Courcey-Meade, painted my wound (unwashed) with gentian violet, and I had to suffer the embarrassment of meeting my colleagues with a tattered and fluorescent leg. It duly went septic.

I found no great welcome. People seemed quite oblivious of my arrival, and no doubt it was unconscious arrogance to expect it to be otherwise.[3]

Not everyone recruited was an expert. The place, after all, needed a certain amount of mundane work doing, such as the role of messenger. And it was to 14-year-old Mimi Gallilee that one such role fell. Indeed, the very nature of the job that she did then – and the duties to which she was later promoted – gave her an almost uniquely broad view of the people, and of the Park. For everyone else, there was strict compartmentalisation; but a girl like Mimi could roam everywhere, and saw more than most.

As a schoolgirl, she had been evacuated from Islington, north London, the year before, and had eventually been joined by her mother and sister. School, for all these extra children imported into the Buckinghamshire countryside, consisted of cobbled-together lessons and improvised schoolrooms. Young Mimi couldn't stand it.

Her mother, a bookkeeper by profession, had been desperate for work of any sort and had been taken on as a canteen waitress at the Park. As such, she had a quiet word with one of the Park's directorate concerning her daughter.

'My mother knew Commander Bradshaw,' says Mrs Gallilee. 'She must have been talking to him about me and saying, "Mimi's fourteen now, she's learning nothing, she doesn't seem interested in what's going on" . . .

'Commander Bradshaw said to my mother, "Bring her up to see me." He talked to me and the result was that I was offered a job at Bletchley Park as a messenger. You could hardly call it an interview. He just talked to me. I started work there the following day.

'All of the messengers were girls and I was the youngest at the time. We had to deliver anything and everything to the Huts. In those days, there were only – I think – Huts 1 to 11a, no blocks yet. And that was my job, going around and delivering the mail, messages – everything of course was in big envelopes and we weren't even interested in knowing what was inside them.'

Gordon Welchman himself reflected a little on the need to enlist as many good women as men. 'Recruitment of young women went on even more rapidly than that of men,' he wrote. 'We needed more of them to staff the Registration Room, the Sheet-Stacking Room, and the Decoding Room. As with the men, I believe that the early recruiting was largely on a personal-acquaintance basis, but with the whole of Bletchley Park looking for qualified women, we got a great many recruits of high calibre.'[4]

Life was to acquire a terrific intensity, not all of it generated by the sometimes nightmarish pressure of breaking codes or the sheer feats of hard work required. There was a great deal more to life at Bletchley Park than that.

4 The House and the Surrounding Country

When talking to veterans of Bletchley Park now, one looming background visual feature of their lives seems to polarise opinion rather sharply, and that is the house itself.

A grand structure had stood on the site for a long time; there is apparently mention of some kind of property there in the Domesday Book. The Victorian house was acquired in 1883 by Sir Herbert Leon and his wife Fanny. With them came an extravagant building programme that saw the house expand, and also embrace a bewildering array of architectural styles.

The Leons were enthusiastic travellers and their journeys throughout Europe seemed to guide their aesthetic whims. As well as mock-Gothic twirls, there were Italian pillars by the entrance, rococo detailing on the ceiling of the ballroom, and a copper dome, inspired again by Italy, and jammed rather awkwardly on to the roof on the left of the house.

The building itself – all dark panelling, faux stained glass, little passageways and oaken stairs – stands as an interesting example of the general architectural confusion of the period, when heavy Victorian Gothic was starting to give way to the more natural contours that would be found in the Edwardian age. Some of the older landowners in the area, with their charmingly decayed honey-stone properties, might also have regarded Bletchley Park as having a nouveau feel to it – the modern house, with all the modern comforts, of a man who had finally arrived into wealth, and was keen for the world to know.

'It's a nightmare. It's hideous,' says Sarah Baring with some feeling. 'We called the house The Victorian Monstrosity.' The detailing of the house's interior was, she felt, equally off-putting. The ornate plasterwork on the ballroom ceiling, she says, 'looked like a cascade of drooping bosoms'. Others look more kindly upon the property as a form of brave architectural experiment. And for some, it was the sort of stately home that they never imagined that they would be working around.

Although from the beginning it had been clear that the house was not remotely big enough for the recruits either to live or work in it (though during the 1938 'rehearsal', those few who covered night shifts were permitted to sleep there), it would be a place in which, in the years to come, leisure hours could be spent, either in the library or at musical events held in the ballroom.

A suite of rooms on the first floor, initially the domain of the Secret Intelligence Service, were eventually used by Alistair Denniston, Edward Travis and Nigel de Grey for administrative purposes. Colonel John Tiltman, the veteran cryptographer and head of the military section, had an office right upstairs which had not long ago been the nursery to one of the Leon children. The walls of Tiltman's office were still decorated with Peter Rabbit wallpaper.

Having started working at Bletchley Park as a young messenger, Mimi Gallilee was within a couple of years promoted to secretarial work within the house itself. Mrs Gallilee recalls the high, decorative ceilings and the big, light windows which looked out over the lawn, and beyond that on to the pretty lake, fringed with trees. As the war went on, and as the activities of Bletchley multiplied, there was soon much more to the Park than that. 'I never realised the grounds were so extensive,' says Mrs Gallilee. 'Or that they had all those RAF camps there. It was all shaded off.'

For a very young person such as Mimi, the house had a somewhat overbearing air, which would be reflected in the personalities of those that she worked for – not merely the austere ways of her immediate superior Miss Reed, secretary to Nigel de Grey, but also what Mrs Gallilee calls the 'forbidding' manner of de Grey himself.

De Grey had previously been president of the Medici Society, Miss Reed his assistant. When he was called to Bletchley, de Grey ensured that the very strict Miss Reed came too. 'Not that Nigel de Grey was at all unpleasant,' Mrs Gallilee recalls. 'But you had to know your place. You'd never have joined in with a conversation. You would never butt in. People were very respectful.'

Directly outside the front door of the house was a path that led, both left and right, to various huts. Mrs Gallilee recalls often seeing Alan Turing 'walking along the path – intense – always looking worried. People thought he was a bit of a weirdo.'

The front lawn of the house was in the early days of 1939 used for sporting activities. The journalist and broadcaster Malcolm Muggeridge, who in his capacity as an intelligence operative passed through the Park a few times himself, recalled these contests in one of his volumes of memoirs:

> Every day after luncheon when the weather was propitious, the cipher crackers played rounders on the manor house lawn, assuming the quasi-serious manner dons affect when engaged in activities likely to be regarded as frivolous or insignificant in comparison with their weightier studies. Thus they would dispute some point about the game with the same fervour as they might the question of free will or determinism, or whether the world began with a big bang or a process of continuing creation.[1]

Beyond the lawn was the lake. In the depths of winter, it would gratifyingly freeze over, allowing ice-skating; in the sultry nights of midsummer, it would occasionally play host, as one veteran recalls, to a number of young RAF men, splashing about, nude and laughing. There were some geese that apparently felt rather proprietorial about the lake; one veteran recalled how some young women – clearly townies – were intimidated by the birds 'hissing at them'. There was also an abundance of frogs, which during the blackout were occasionally accidentally trodden upon.

The house had originally boasted a tennis court, which had to be removed to make way for the construction of a new hut. When Prime Minister Winston Churchill paid a visit a little later in the war, he was dismayed to learn that ball games were restricted to rounders alone; the PM authorised the construction of new tennis courts.

'Churchill was very horrified to find that the staff in the early days played rounders for exercise,' says Sheila Lawn, laughing. 'Churchill said: "This isn't good enough." And he is reputed to have ordered the tennis courts.' Indeed, in the years to come, the Bletchley Park Tennis Club was very popular. A surviving memo in the archives shows that its members were even permitted to use the Summer House as a temporary changing room.

By the side of the main house lay the ice house; beyond that, the stables and the cottages. In the earliest days of Captain Ridley and his Shooting Party, there was also a fine yew maze and a couple of rose gardens. But when the time came to start building the huts, these were sacrificed.

Reactions to the estate tended largely to depend on where each recruit had come from. For some young people, this was their first close-up view of a large, well-appointed property, and it thus acquired a sort of sub-Brideshead glamour; for other, posher recruits, it was nothing more than a nondescript provincial pile set just outside the most provincial of English towns.

According to Irene Young, the house was 'irretrievably ugly' and its style was a form of 'lavatory-Gothic'. In the view of codebreaker and, in later years, historian Peter Calvocoressi, it had 'a lot of heavy wooden panelling enlivened here and there by Alhambresque (Leicester Square, not Andalusia) decorative fancies'.

Later, an American recruit, soon-to-be-prominent architect Landis Gores, almost fainted with distaste. 'A maudlin, monstrous pile probably unsurpassed,' he said, 'though not for lack of competition in the architectural gaucherie of the mid-Victorian era . . . hopelessly vulgarised by extensive porches and solaria . . . inchoate, unfocused, and incomprehensible, not to say indigestible.'[2]

Even for the most delicate aesthete, however, the grounds gave few causes for complaint. And for some recruits, the gardens, with the backdrop of the house, had a slightly collegiate feel, although those recruited from Oxford and Cambridge would have found it several steps down in aesthetic terms from the beauty that they had left behind.

But in wartime Britain, particularly as the years went on – with all the rationing, the taped windows, the blackouts, the peeling paint, the fading, drab colour and, in many cities, the increasing number of bomb sites – Bletchley Park and innumerable other requisitioned country houses like it must have offered some kind of psychological respite. Certainly a number of the veterans recall that in the summer months, both the gardens of Bletchley and the countryside around acquired the most colourful and beguiling life.

As more and more young recruits came flooding in, the house and its immediate grounds seemed to reflect this colourful life. One veteran recalls that 'it was a village confined on the grounds . . . countless people passing in and out of the main gate, strolling, talking, and sitting around. There was a great seething of people – always movement – comings and goings. The whole thing reminded me of a bustling London railway terminus.'[3]

It was a railway terminus that bustled for twenty-four hours a day. Nigel de Grey remarked of the young new recruits fresh off the trains from Oxford and Cambridge that they were 'dropping in with the slightly unexpected effect of carrier pigeons'. Throughout the early 1940s, when the numbers of workers rose from hundreds to thousands, the shift system meant that people came in and out of the main entrance gates at all hours.

Inside the fences, recalls one veteran, were signs reminding the young recruits that this was no campus talking shop and exhorting them to the highest discretion at all times. But outside the fences, in the summer months, and well away from the brickworks that pocked the town's edges, there were shades of prelapsarian inno-cence about the green countryside around the house. Men and women would go for long bike rides along quiet country lanes. This, of course, was England before motorways. And in wartime, motor traffic was also extremely restricted by the strict rationing of petrol. 'Very few people at Bletchley Park had cars,' says John Herivel. 'Only the most important.'

So on leaving the house, perhaps at the end of a shift, and climb-ing on to a bike either to return to a billet or simply to get some fresh air among the fields, the young codebreakers, after only a few minutes' cycling, would have seen and heard a countryside that we would scarcely recognise today.

The fields would still have been small and manageable, as opposed to the vast industrial-farming prairies that are the hallmark of the contemporary English landscape. And apart from the buzz of insects, the lowing of cattle, distant church clocks, and faraway train whistles, the lanes would have been rich with a quality of quietness difficult to find nowadays within a 100-mile radius of London.

'I bought a third-hand cycle,' says Sheila Lawn. 'The second person who owned it, who worked at the Park, must have been very brainy, but somehow she could not learn to ride the bicycle. So I bought it. It was a very strong bicycle. I called it Griselda. I had it for years. And if I was on a day off, and I didn't have any people to meet, or any plans, I used to cycle.

'Of course the countryside around Bletchley was totally different from the countryside in the Highlands. It was a contrast. And I just loved it.'

These young recruits, as we have seen, were drawn from all across the country; many had left home for the very first time. The curious thing about the house at Bletchley Park, and the chalky lands around, was that they offered a calming backdrop to the deathly serious task in hand.

'I was very interested in natural history,' recalls Hut 6 codebreaker Oliver Lawn of some of the recreational pursuits that quickly took root at Bletchley. 'And there was bird watching, and butterfly collecting.' Of the brickworks immediately outside the town, says Mr Lawn, they 'gave a scent, a smell, to the place. With brickworks, you take the clay out and make the bricks and it leaves great holes in the ground. Some of those holes filled with water, naturally. Some of them didn't. The dry ones we used for shooting practice in the Home Guard. And the wet ones we used as swimming pools.'

And as the war went on, this oddly proportioned house was also to play a central role in some of the livelier recreational activities – nude outdoor bathing aside – enjoyed by the codebreakers.

5 1939: How Do You Break the Unbreakable?

From the day war was declared, the whole of Britain was, in a sense, mobilised. It was not merely the men waiting for their call-up papers. Everyone was set to do precisely as they were instructed by government officials, from giving homes to evacuee schoolchildren to taking jobs in factories. This sense of a total unity of purpose stretching across millions of people might seem a little difficult to imagine. What makes it easier is to bear in mind the very real, and acute, fear of invasion.

Austria, Czechoslovakia and now Poland had fallen to the Germans' unprecedentedly swift and shockingly ruthless military machine. The young people of Britain found it all too easy to envisage those same ineluctable forces crossing the 22-mile distance across the Channel. For many, the very idea was literally the stuff of nightmares.

It was quite simple, explains Ruth Bourne, who was to become a Wren at Bletchley and elsewhere during the war. 'More than anything else in the world, you didn't want the Germans to win. Particularly me with my Jewish antecedents – I would not have wished anyone remotely connected with the Nazi situation to win.'

And in those first few weeks – amid the darkly ominous quiet that

took hold in Britain during the so-called Phoney War – the directorate at Bletchley Park knew that one of the most urgent priorities
was to secure a break into the German navy's Enigma messages. The
prospect was a daunting one; that of cracking an enemy code system
that was universally considered unbreakable.

In times of conflict, an island nation becomes uniquely vulnerable; if the enemy gains mastery over the seas, it will swiftly find ways
to cut supplies of food and equipment to that island's shores. And
it was immediately clear that the German navy, with its U-boats,
would aim to strangle Britain's lifelines. It was for that reason that
Bletchley Park's director, Alistair Denniston, had taken the precaution of surrounding himself with so many of the cryptography
experts with whom he had worked since the First World War.

Commander Denniston was known by some as 'the little man'. A
literal (and unkind) nickname referring to his short stature, it also
obscured his many talents. He was trilingual; unusually, as a young
man, he didn't go to a British university, attending instead the
Sorbonne and Bonn University. Denniston had also been something of an athlete in his youth: he played hockey in the 1908
Olympics for the Scottish team. Judging by the many memos that he
sent in his time at Bletchley Park, and which have now surfaced in
the archives, he was also a man of uncommon patience, especially
when dealing with volcanic, quirky or short-tempered colleagues.

Perhaps in some ways Denniston was a little too diplomatic.
According to his son Robin, the establishment that Denniston
founded was brilliant, but he himself 'was not . . . a man who found
leadership easy. He lacked self-confidence. He was a highly intelligent self-made Scot who found it difficult to play a commanding
role among the bureaucrats and politicians with whom he had to
deal.'[1] Women's Auxiliary Air Force (WAAF) veteran Aileen Clayton
said that Denniston 'seemed more like a professor than a naval officer . . . I was immediately impressed by his kindness.'[2]

But there were those who saw how Denniston's quality of kindness could be misinterpreted. 'He was diffident and nervous,'

recalled Josh Cooper. 'A small fish in a big pond that contained many predators.'

Denniston had been an expert on cryptography since the start of the First World War, when, as a young man, he had been summoned to the Admiralty, the chiefs of which had been eager to use his German expertise. In 1914, the Admiralty realised the tactical value of decoding and translating German naval signals, before distributing them throughout the British navy to give the forces a chance of being a step ahead.

During the First World War, the cryptographers had gathered in the department within the rambling Admiralty building known as Room 40. As a naval concern, Room 40 was in a perpetual state of rivalry with its army equivalent. Between 1914 and 1918, Denniston and his Room 40 colleagues acquired skills that went far beyond languages. And the stupendous feats of logic which they deployed to break into coded signals were noted by a fascinated young Winston Churchill, then First Lord of the Admiralty.

A naval operation it might have been, but Room 40 also had an atmosphere of academic informality. This was deepened with the arrival, in 1916, of the ferociously intelligent – and in some ways, simply ferocious – King's College scholar called Alfred Dillwyn 'Dilly' Knox.

Knox was a classicist, but of an extremely unusual calibre: he was an expert on ancient papyri. This, ironically, provided him with the perfect flair and skill for codework. It would serve him especially well when squaring up to the challenge of Enigma.

Intriguingly, the First World War demands of Room 40 had dragged this irritable scholar away from deciphering one particularly beautiful and breathtakingly valuable papyrus found in southern Egypt: the 2,000-year-old *Mimiambi* of Herodas. Consisting of satiric dialogues only previously known by virtue of being mentioned in other Greek works, the discovery was wildly exciting to the academic world, much as if Aristotle's Second Book of Poetics had been found.

Over the space of many years, Knox had travelled between Cambridge and the British Museum in Bloomsbury, there to study the intensely complicated strips of papyrus. The nature of Herodas's dialogues was earthy, involving delinquents, brothels, slaves, sex-shops, flagellation and other such salty topics. But complications arose in deciphering such matters as where the speech breaks came, and indeed what was speech and what was not, and also in identifying errors of copying, since the papyrus may have been inscribed as a copy by an insufficiently attentive servant.

Then there was the question of how the crumbling text should be reassembled – how to ensure that the order was correct and that the pieces of the jigsaw were not out of place. This was a matter not merely of great classical learning or ability with language, but something of a cryptographical problem too. So when Knox was pulled into Room 40, the match seemed appropriate.

As soon as he arrived at work at the Admiralty in 1916, Knox bagged a room at the end of a long, untidy, undusted corridor; the room, arrestingly, also had a bath within it. This suited him extremely well; Knox was inordinately fond of hot baths.

And his department had an enormous early triumph: the decrypting of the so-called 'Zimmerman Telegram' – a message from the German foreign minister to the German ambassador in Mexico, urging that Mexico be encouraged into an alliance against the United States. It was this intelligence that brought America decisively into the First World War.

There was love (and laughter) in those dusty Room 40 corridors too; Alistair Denniston met his wife-to-be in the department. 'The camaraderie of the members of Room 40,' wrote Denniston's son Robin, 'all of whose names are inscribed on a silver salver which was given to Denniston and his bride on the occasion of their wedding in 1917, was borne out at the end of the war by . . . a pantomime, sung by all present. It was written by Frank Birch, himself one of the original cryptographers who left the secret service for the stage and for King's College.'[3]

In the interwar period, the Government Code and Cypher School (as Room 40, reduced to a small number of codebreakers, was now known) had moved to Broadway Buildings and devoted itself largely to dealing with Soviet codes. Dilly Knox was especially adept in this area. Bolshevism, together with Stalin's colossal ambition, was understood to be the most pervasive threat to the national interests. With Hitler's seizure of power in Germany in 1933, however, those geopolitical tectonic plates shifted very rapidly.

The German navy had been using Enigma since 1926. The machine itself – the basic model of rotating letter wheels with electric contact studs, keyboard and lampboard with illuminated letters, all looking a little like a typewriter – was adapted by German electrical engineer Arthur Scherbius from an earlier, simpler design.

Enigma had been on the market since 1923, when it was used by a few commercial banks to make sure their communications were kept secret. Too few commercial banks, though: the machine was a commercial failure. Curiously, in 1926 the British government purchased one model after the machine was demonstrated at the Foreign Office. The War Office felt, however, that it would be too ungainly for use in the field.

Once the German navy acquired the system, Enigma was completely taken off the open market, both military and commercial; the Germans then set about making a series of modifications that would make the machine's security very much tighter. Soon afterwards, the system was adopted by the German air force, and then by the army. The British War Office had been perfectly wrong about it. The machine was brilliantly portable; thousands were manufactured.

The principle of Enigma was that the machines both enciphered messages and, at the other end, deciphered them. The operator would type a letter on the normal-looking keyboard; a couple of seconds later, via an electric current sent through the rotating code-letter wheels, another letter on the adjacent lampboard would be illuminated. This substitute letter would be noted. And so on through all the letters of a message. The enciphered version would then be radioed in Morse to its intended recipient.

The recipient, with his Enigma machine set up in exactly the same way, would tap these encoded letters in, one by one – and one by one, the real letters would be illuminated on the lampboard.

'Although it would have been possible for one cipher clerk to carry out all the tasks of the enciphering procedure himself,' noted codebreaker Alan Stripp, 'this would have been a lengthy and confusing process; normally it called for a team of two.' Even with two, it was a time-consuming business. On top of this, the machine settings would be changed every twenty-four hours.

In 1927, GC&CS took the wise precaution of studying their basic, wholly unmodified Enigma machine. Hugh Foss – eventually to become a Bletchley leading light, brilliant at Japanese decrypts – was the man assigned to the job.

John Herivel later noted, in a tone of obvious admiration, the intricate innards of this aesthetically intriguing machine: 'the function of the [letter] wheels with their studs, pins, rings and serrated flanges, how they could be taken in and out of the scrambler, the function of the left-hand reflector drum' and 'the wonderfully ingenious way each of the three wheels was forced into the nearest of 26 equally spaced "allowable" positions where they were firmly held, yet not so firmly that they could not be turned by finger pressure on the flanges to any one of the 25 other allowable positions'.[4]

And so this neat machine of bakelite and brass was an irresistibly beguiling prospect for any mathematician or logician. Even if the machine settings were being changed daily, there surely had to be some means by which the device could be defeated?

But there was an extra difficulty. The new German version had what was known as a stecker-board, or plug board, which made the machine's wiring vastly more complex, and allowed for literally millions more potential encoding combinations. 'The Germans regarded the Enigma as a perfectly secure machine,' noted Stuart

Milner-Barry, who was at Bletchley in the early days of Hut 6. 'Proof against cryptanalysts however talented and ingenious they may be.'

Right from the start, though, Hugh Foss wasn't so sure about that. He wrote a paper saying that if enough could be gleaned about Enigma's internal wiring, then the machine just might be broken with the use of cribs – basically using guessed words or phrases to give a starting point into all the other letters. One crucial key to the machine was that any letter – say, 'W' – could never be encrypted as itself. In other words, no matter how often one typed in 'W', the letter would never be encrypted as 'W'. But this didn't make the task of breaking the machine much easier to contemplate. There were still millions upon millions of potential combinations.

By 1936, when it was increasingly obvious within Whitehall that Hitler's aggression would not be contained, GC&CS was applying renewed vigour to the Enigma problem. And in 1937, at the time of the Spanish Civil War, Dilly Knox devised a way into the earlier, unmodified version of the machine that was being used by Italy. He did this partly by means of 'rodding'; Knox's 'rods' were, in the most basic terms, a painstakingly calculated slide-rule style representation of the wiring and rotor position of the machine upon which cipher-text letters could be moved and rearranged.

And the British were not alone in these efforts. There was also invaluable aid from another source, for an early, slightly simpler German military version of the Enigma machine had been cracked as far back as 1932 by several gifted mathematicians in Poland.

The Polish triumph was extinguished a little later in the 1930s when the German army – now regenerated and strengthening, and keen to tighten its security – increased the number of code-letter wheels on the machine from three to five, thus increasing the huge number of potential combinations another tenfold. However, this setback was in part countered thanks to a valiant Frenchman called Major (later Colonel) Gustave Bertrand, who was working in close contact with the Polish mathematicians. 'I think we should acknowledge what the French did in the field of Enigma,' says Mavis Batey. 'And indeed how they really did work with us until the fall of France.'

In the early 1930s, Gustave Bertrand had been carefully monitoring Germany's development of Enigma and the machine's uses. Some years earlier he had made contact with a German spy (or traitor, as the Germans themselves would have put it) called Hans Thilo Schmidt. Schmidt supplied Bertrand with crucial Enigma documentation. He had come by such paperwork because he worked in the German Ministry of War.

This was not Bertrand's only success. 'When the Germans improved the plugboard of Enigma,' says Keith Batey, 'they sent out a manual. And the idiots actually gave a plaintext telling how one set up the machine and this manual gave you the answer. The Germans realised, and recalled the manual right away – but Major Bertrand got hold of one none the less. That's what gave the Poles the entry they needed.'

The Poles devised two cipher-checking methods. One was a manual method, using 'Zygalski sheets', named after their inventor, mathematician Henryk Zygalski. These, in essence, were a series of twenty-six thick sheets, one for each of the Enigma's possible sequences for the insertion of the machine's rotors. The sheets had specially prepared grids printed upon them, twenty-six by twenty-six, letters of the alphabet on the outer edges with holes punched or cut through the squares in certain combinations. The principle was based on what were termed 'females' – letter positions that would be repeated in an enciphered message. The sheets would be placed on top of one another above an illuminated surface, and moved and rearranged in carefully calculated sequences until the number of lights shining through the holes was reduced to one light shining through one section or square; this in turn would reveal the particular Enigma ring-setting. As a method, it was both wildly cumbersome and impossibly time-consuming. But before the Germans made further adjustments to Enigma, it worked. The principle was later to be expanded at Bletchley by John Jeffreys.

By the summer of 1939, as the Polish nation faced certain invasion, these Enigma experts, together with a small French contingent led by Bertrand, decided to share their knowledge with the British, in the hope that they might be able to help further. Conversely, the Poles had information that the British side needed very badly indeed. On 24 July 1939, British and French cryptographers went to meet their Polish counterparts at Kabackie Woods near Pyry, a few miles south of Warsaw. Among the British members of this party was Dilly Knox. With him was Alistair Denniston.

The meeting was vital. As Knox and Denniston would have been painfully aware, they had to get a serious head start before Britain and Germany were at war. In particular, there had been an unthinking assumption among many, before 1939, that Britain still enjoyed unchallenged global naval supremacy. It would soon become clear that this was no longer the case. Moreover, the German navy was even more security conscious than the army. While the army could use cables to transmit messages, ocean-going battleships were forced to use radio signals, all of which could be picked up by others. These signals had to be encrypted with real cunning.

By 1939, Knox had run into a dead end simply because of the internal wiring of the military Enigma – an extra dimension of difficulty, distinct from the code wheels themselves. The trouble was that the Germans could have used countless different combinations of wiring on the keyboard. However, on that day outside Warsaw, the Poles told Knox that the Germans had in fact followed the most obvious, alphabetic pattern: A to A, B to B – with, as Jack Copeland explained, 'the A-socket of the plug-board connected to the first terminal inside the entry plate, the B-socket to the second, and so on.'[5] This was by no means the solution to the Enigma problem – but it did provide a valuable chink of light.

To be told, after months of worrying away at the wiring problem, that the solution was in fact the most obvious one, apparently proved a little too much for the habitually unpredictable Knox. Initially, according to Denniston himself, Knox 'raged and raved' when back in the car to Warsaw, shouting that 'the whole thing was a fraud'. As Penelope Fitzgerald noted, however, for Knox 'it was a swindle, not because he had failed to solve it, but because it was too easy. Games should be worth playing.'[6]

In a letter written some years later, Denniston said: 'our position became increasingly difficult as even Bertrand, who knew no English, was aware that Knox had a grudge against the Poles who, so far as Bertrand knew, had only been successful where Knox had failed . . .' According to Hut 6 veteran John Herivel, too, Knox's temper could easily have had the most terrible knock-on effect. As he later wrote:

If Knox had continued to be in such a bloody-minded and intransigent mood, the conference would have been wound up, the French and British delegations would have returned home empty-handed, the further breaking of Enigma by the method of Zygalski sheets would never have taken place, and the Red Luftwaffe code would have remained unbroken, so that the Allied High Command would have been deprived of what Nigel de Grey termed 'the prime source of intelligence' for the most of the time from May 1940 until the end of the war.[7]

But the wild storm that Denniston seemed to recall must have passed very quickly. In a taxi on the way back from that forest rendezvous on the second day, Knox started cheerily chanting: 'Nous avons le QWERTZU, nous marchons ensemble.' And in a letter written at the time, he stated crisply: 'I think we may hand some bouquets to the Poles for their lucky shot.'

Luck or skill aside, the information about the wiring was vital. Knox telephoned the information through to Peter Twinn. It is said that by the time Knox returned to Bletchley, Twinn had worked out the wheel wiring from this information alone, and had set to work on a few messages sent and intercepted the year before.

'I was the first British cryptographer to have read a German services Enigma message,' recalled Twinn lightly, adding, 'I hasten to say that this did me little if any credit, since with the information Dilly had brought back from Poland, the job was little more than a routine operation.' And, he pointed out, 'of course, reading a few scattered messages [from] a single day in 1938 was a whole universe away from the problems that lay ahead.'[8]

The Poles also presented the British with a replica of the Enigma machine that they had built. 'Dilly always said that we owed a huge amount to the Poles,' says Mavis Batey, though she is equally adamant that the work of Colonel Bertrand should be properly celebrated. 'Bertrand really did a good deal, with his Pimpernel pinches [the acquisition of coding information from the Germans]. Until the fall, Bertrand had his own cipher bureau in Paris and we had constant traffic and all the correspondence, and whoever got the key out that day shared it. That went on right up until the fall of France.'

Elsewhere, Alan Turing had been quietly busy upon his own researches. And by December 1939, quite independently of Knox and his new Polish friends, he managed to break into five days' worth of Enigma material. Though this was, by itself, hugely encouraging, the messages Turing had worked upon were old – pre-war in fact. Neither he nor any other codebreaker had yet managed to crowbar their way into current German traffic.

In the deceptive quiet of those early weeks and months of the Phoney War, there was still time for theorising and experimentation. 'Some days it was actually very slack,' says John Herivel of his workload at that time. 'You wouldn't get that many intercepts in at all.' But as the season grew darker, even with all the clues and the help given by the Poles, the codebreakers knew they were facing an increasingly fearsome proposition.

It was not just the mentally exhausting prospect of facing, day after day, these groups of random-looking letters, trying to think from every conceivable angle of some logical formula that would bring order to the chaos and make the letters resolve into language. It was also the knowledge that they simply had to succeed.

The Italians provided a little succour. It was discovered that they were still using the earlier commercial version of the Enigma system, which although ingeniously complex, was known to be breakable. Dilly, with his rods and his fillies, was kept furiously busy in the Cottage, formulating means by which the Italian codes could be cracked by hand. At about the same time – the first Christmas at Bletchley Park, the ducks flapping in the freezing waters of the lake – Knox was also looking over Turing's plans for new 'bombe' machines – which were to prove revolutionary in their potential.

But another obstacle for Bletchley was the fact that the different arms of the German military used subtly different versions of the Enigma system. The army Enigma machine was already fearsomely complex; the naval Enigma, as the cryptographers knew, was quite a different proposition – more complex, with extra code-wheels and more disciplined settings, using strict tables. Denniston doubted it could ever be beaten. For some of the new recruits making their way in blithe ignorance to Bletchley Park in the early months of the war, this would be the overriding priority.

6 1939–40: The Enigma Initiation

From the start, one of the disorientating elements about Bletchley for a new recruit was the ambiguity of its status. It seemed to be neither a military nor a civilian operation, but – especially in its earliest days – a curious blend of the two.

In other words, this was not an environment of uniform, parade grounds and drill. And as work gathered pace, and the responsibility for breaking codes was divided between services – army, air force, naval – and sectioned off into separate huts, the place remained curiously self-governing and self-disciplining. If you worked in Hut 8 on the naval Enigma, for instance, you answered to the head of Hut 8 and seemingly no one else.

This vagueness of structure, combined with the nature of the personnel that Bletchley Park acquired, was the cause of some initial discomfort and bewilderment in Whitehall. As veteran and historian Harry Hinsley wrote of the organisation of the Park:

[It] remained a loose collection of groups rather than forming a single, tidy organisation . . . Professors, lecturers and undergraduates, chessmasters and experts from the principal museums, barristers and antiquarian booksellers, some of them in uniform and some civilians on the books of the Foreign Office or the Service ministries – such for the most part were the individuals who inaugurated and manned the various cells which sprang up within or alongside the original sections.

They contributed by their variety and individuality to the lack of uniformity. There is also no doubt that they thrived on it, as they did on the absence at GC&CS of any emphasis on rank or insistence on hierarchy.[1]

Lord Dacre, then Hugh Trevor-Roper, was attached to Intelligence at the time and quite often passed through the Park. He was reported as saying that the early years of Bletchley were marked with 'friendly informality verging on apparent anarchy'.

Perhaps the only parallel with the call-up to the military was that the summons for Bletchley was not questioned by anyone who received it. However, unlike the weeks of careful training that one received for military service – the weapons-handling, the exercises – Bletchley seems to have been something of a plunge pool. For the early codebreakers and linguists alike, there was an element of being parachuted straight in to their new lives with little in the way of instruction. There are those who recall short, intensive courses for beginners being held in a nearby school; according to others, there wasn't even that.

'It was all pretty quick,' says John Herivel. 'I think especially for those of us who arrived in the early days. I was shown the Enigma, and packed off to see Alan Turing and Tony Kendrick. They were, in a sense, my teachers.'

Oliver Lawn, who arrived a little later, found himself feeling quite gung-ho about the nature of the challenges that lay ahead. He recalls: 'These were basically mathematical problems and I had been trained as a mathematician, to spend my life doing these problems. This was just another form of problem.'

According to Mavis Batey the whole thing was more random than that. She recalls with some amusement the startlingly hands-off approach when she first joined Dilly Knox in the Cottage: 'We were all thrown in at the deep end. No one knew how the blessed thing worked. When I first arrived, I was told, "We are breaking machines, have you got a pencil?"

'And that was it. You got no explanation. I never saw an Enigma machine. Dilly Knox was able to reduce it – I won't say to a game, but a sort of linguistic puzzle. It was rather like driving a car while having no idea what goes on under the bonnet.'

Mathematician Keith Batey is amused to this day about his initiation to the new, esoteric world of Enigma: 'I arrived with two other chaps from the maths tripos. We were greeted at the Registry and were immediately given a quick lecture on the German wireless network. And I didn't pay much attention because I was focusing on these highly nubile young ladies who were wandering about the Park.

'Anyway, after twenty minutes of this lecture, which told us absolutely nothing,' continues Mr Batey, 'we were handed over to Hugh Alexander, who was the chess champion. He sat us down in front of what later turned out to be a steckered Enigma, and he talked about it. It didn't have a battery, it didn't work. And then we were just told to get on with it. That was the cryptographic training.'

Bletchley Park seemed an organic kind of institution. Perhaps, given the early, experimental nature of the work – so many minds attacking the problem of the codes in so many ways – there was little point in trying to give it an over-rigid structure. Nevertheless, in contrast to strict naval and military hierarchy, the place from the start seemed curiously self-disciplined. 'There were an awful lot of people who just used first names,' recalled one veteran, surprisingly given how socially formal the period was.

Meanwhile, Alistair Denniston's administrative difficulties were growing. There were problems involving accommodation for all the staff. An adjacent school – Elmers School – had to be requisitioned as more huts underwent construction.

Looking at these old huts now, one cannot help wondering why the authorities did not base the codebreaking activity in rather more comfortable, better-built space. One possible answer is that at that stage, no one anticipated the war lasting long enough for permanent structures to be needed. After all, even up until the summer of 1939, there were many who believed that Chamberlain's government would, of necessity, allow Hitler to get away with further acts of aggression throughout Europe. Perhaps another consideration was that it was vital that no unfriendly attention was drawn to the Park. Not only would extensive building work raise questions, it would also be more easily visible from the air by enemy reconnaissance pilots.

And so a series of huts were constructed and accorded separate functions, decided by the sorts of codes that were to be read. By the side of the house was Hut 4, which was to become the Naval Section hut. Hut 5 was to become the Military (and later, the Japanese) Section. Other huts, such as Hut 8, the home of the Naval Enigma operation, followed not too long afterwards.

Hut 3 – which, together with Hut 6, seemed to form the hub of the operation – was nominated in part for army/air intercepts and Intelligence work; Hut 6 was where air force keys were to be read. Hut 1 eventually came to house the first experimental Turing bombe deciphering machine. (And according to Mimi Gallilee, 'Hut 2 was for beer, tea and relaxation.')

From the very start, for the sake of security, the functions of each hut were kept as separate from each other as possible. Personnel were instructed that inter-hut discussions were forbidden. Absolute secrecy was a given. 'You just assumed,' says Keith Batey drily, 'that you'd be shot.' Recruits would be allocated to their hut and, during working hours, would be metaphorically hermetically sealed within. No one else, save the occasional messenger, would be allowed entry.

Even though the word 'hut' implies a cramped construction, these were long structures, with central passageways and rooms off either side. There were plain windows (shuttered at night for blackout purposes), floors of squeaky lino, basic desks and chairs. Green-shaded lights hung from the ceiling. A great many people worked side by side among plain filing cabinets; the rooms were suffocating in the summer sun, and draughty and cold in the depths of winter. As one cryptologist commented: 'Nothing . . . seemed less likely to house great matters than the ramshackle wooden building (its atmosphere nauseating at night when the blackout imprisoned the fumes from leaky coke-burning stoves) to which I reported . . .'

Heating was a perennial problem. Mittens were commonplace. Added to this was a faintly comical, Heath Robinson dimension: messages were passed between some huts by means of an extemporised wooden 'tunnel' and propelled by means of a tray with wheels on the bottom, and a long broom-handle.

John Herivel recalled the unique atmosphere in the ill-ventilated and sporadically heated huts. There were the big tables, covered with maps. Then there were the spartan lights giving out yellowish light on the simple desks and the bare whitewashed walls. Mr Herivel recalls that he was 'provided with a blackboard set on a low table' so that he could write while seated. And before him was a desk piled with intercepted messages.

The phrase 'need to know' was constantly evoked. Even for the young messenger girl, Mimi Gallilee, moving from hut to hut delivering the post and packages, entry was sometimes forbidden. Even though her older sister worked in Hut 10 alongside Josh Cooper, Mrs Gallilee recalls: 'I never knew what my sister did in Hut 10. I never even asked her. She wouldn't have told me anyway. She knew where I worked. Later, when I was promoted and moved into office work at the house, she never came to my department. I had to go to Hut 10 on a few occasions for my own department. I'd be asked to go over to Commander This or Squadron Leader That in Hut 10 and I'd see my sister sometimes.

'On the few occasions when I had to go over to her Hut, to talk to someone – if it was in the room she was working, I can remember seeing pieces of paper – not slips of paper but sets of figures. And so my sister would have been working on figures or letters, I don't know which.'

As the work of the Park continued to expand, so too did the demands for space. The Secret Intelligence Service had now, briefly, evacuated to Bletchley. They were occupying the upper floors of the house, though thanks not only to issues of space but also to straightforward operational concerns, they did not stay long. Meanwhile, in the early days, the ground floor played host to GC&CS, with the numbers growing daily. The corridors of the house were full of trestle tables. The telephone exchange was in the ballroom. The Naval Section, for a while, had to find a temporary home in the library.

For Dilly Knox, Alan Turing and Gordon Welchman, sanctuary was found in the Cottage. By this time, Turing, then just turned twenty-eight, was already at work on the design of his revolutionary 'bombe' machine.

In these first few months, the irascible Dilly Knox was beginning to take stock of the people that he had gathered around him. In a handwritten letter to Denniston, he reported of his young underlings: 'As you know, Joan H is a great personal friend of my family and myself. But as a secretary, she is frankly a flop.' Knox then gave his bullet-pointed appraisals of the others:

A few notes on senior staff:
a) Kendrick is quite admirable. It is a pity I have put him in the [Elmers] school since, tho' he has a lot to learn, he is the obvious second (or first?) in command.
b) Welchman is doing well and is v keen. I hope to get him back here [from Elmers School] to learn about the machines.
c) Twinn is still very keen and not afraid of work.

Knox's attitude towards the young Alan Turing was more ambivalent:

He is very difficult to anchor down.

He is very clever but quite irresponsible and throws out a mass of suggestions of all degrees of merit. I have just, but only just, enough authority and ability to keep him and his ideas in some sort of order and discipline. But he is very nice about it all.[2]

For a little while, there was some tension between Dilly Knox and Gordon Welchman. Knox as the senior cryptographer felt that the Cottage was overcrowded. So Welchman was exiled to the nearby temporarily requisitioned Elmers School (as the memo cited above indicates, Knox was keen that the exile should be short). The idea was that, rather than codebreaking, Welchman would be trying to crack the slightly different problem of 'traffic analysis'. This involved studying the origins of intercepted signals to work out where they came from, and thereby hopefully making deductions about military movements.

Welchman wrongly inferred from his exile that Knox had taken a dislike to him; as a result, he seemed to suffer slightly from wounded pride. It also seems to be the case that Welchman wasn't smitten by Knox himself. Years later, he wrote: 'He was neither an organisation man nor a technical man. He was, essentially, an idea-struck man ... By and large Dilly seems to have disliked most of the men with whom he came into contact.'[3]

Knox might well have smelled something to his distaste about the younger man; for very early on, Welchman was working on schemes to restructure and reorganise the entire codebreaking operation, in such a way that a great deal of power and authority would have slipped from Knox's hands.

Indeed, Welchman wasted no time at all during his exile. Mathematician John Herivel recalls one of the key innovations. Welchman was quick to form a strong working relationship with the most secret listening station – 'an old fort' at Chatham, Kent, on the Thames Estuary. It was through this establishment that, at that time, much of the German signalling traffic came.

Once the signals were picked up, the officers at Chatham would have bundles of intercepted coded messages sent to Welchman. These bundles would be driven from the coast to Bletchley, through the middle of the night and at harum-scarum speeds, often in the most atrocious weather conditions, by special motorcycle couriers.

The German rule was that no message should be more than 250 letters in length; if it was necessary to send a longer message, it should be split into multiple parts. This was designed to make life more difficult for codebreakers: the longer the message, the easier it might be for such a person to see patterns of letters forming among the apparent chaos.

But each Enigma message had a preamble and some operators used different discriminants (that is, groups of characters indicating the code set-up and reciphering key, and distinguishing the section of traffic) for the different parts. As Herivel noted, it was thus possible to work out any 'given key'. 'In this way,' he wrote, 'all the different German keys coming from Chatham – and later from France – could be identified, and every day, traffic could be divided into different bundles for different keys.'

The keys were then given different colours, to separate them out in the most direct visual way. To start with, the colours used were yellow, green, red and blue, respectively signifying the German Norway campaign, the army and air force codes, and separate air force training codes. The time and the frequency of each message would be noted down on vast sheets of paper, leading to an immediate strain on the Park's supply of coloured pencils. But the colour keys were a stroke of organisational genius – a vivid signifier that allowed everyone to identify each key with ease. Indeed, Welchman recalled in his memoir that one element of recruitment to Bletchley Park involved asking candidates 'if they were colour-blind'.

In our world of ubiquitous touch-screen technology, such a system smells of pencil shavings and glue and bits of string. But it worked. The avalanche of thousands upon thousands of intercepts – the numbers of which would multiply dramatically as the Phoney

War ended and the conflict intensified – had order imposed upon it. It could be deduced from which part of the German military they were being sent, and to which.

It soon became necessary to develop subdivisions for the keys (such as SS messages, and messages to do with German railways); before long every colour in the rainbow was deployed. When all available colours had been used, keys were named after marine life: birds; then elephants; and insects . . .

There were many occasions when a message could not be broken in its entirety, because words were missing or incomplete. As a result, a comment would be added with the words 'strong indica- tions', 'fair indications' or 'slight indications' to convey the varying degrees of the decrypt's reliability. But it was through the work of Chatham – and later other intercept stations such as Denmark Hill in south London – that Welchman began to understand about the different call-signs used by different operators, and what signs would be used for what sorts of messages.

Dilly Knox was also using the period of the Phoney War to get himself and his team ready for the onslaught of work that was to come. The difference between Knox and Welchman was Knox's apparent taste for pulchritude on his team, although now Mavis Batey laughs off – with a very faint edge of annoyance – any idea that she was recruited chiefly for reasons of glamour: 'Dilly was very firm. He said he did not want any debutantes who had got there by Daddy's knowing someone in the Foreign Office. Equally, he said, he didn't want a yard of Wrens who all looked alike and you could- n't tell one from the other.

'As for Dilly going around picking out girls, that is totally untrue. We were all interviewed by this dreadful Miss Moore, a fierce lady in the Foreign Office.'

There is another possibility too; that Dillwyn Knox had somehow found that women had a greater aptitude for the work required – as well as nimbleness of mind and capacity for lateral thought, they possessed a care and attention to detail that many men might not have had. This, of course, is just speculation; the other possibility, and one that seems likely considering the scratchiness of many of Knox's personal dealings, was that he simply did not like men very much.

As the war effort intensified, new recruits would be given a statutory three-week induction period to be taught the nuances of code-breaking. Later still, recruits were sent to Bedford for a few weeks, to sit in a dusty, anonymous office where they learnt the rudiments of Japanese, in order to be able to crack the Japanese codes.

But for that first wave of recruits, Bletchley Park as an institution had what some have described as a peculiarly English air of improvisation, of simply diving in and getting on with it. Perhaps there was no other way. For in the face of a challenge like the Enigma keys and without, at least at first, the technology to be able to attack them mechanically, the Park would need as many original, quirky, lateral thinkers as it could get, and then give them as free a rein as possible. This created a unique atmosphere that was to be remembered, despite the nature of the conflict in which they were so deeply involved, with the utmost fondness by everyone who served there, even if they were not allowed – under the strictest oaths of secrecy – to discuss even the smallest detail of it for decades afterwards.

7 Freezing Billets and Outdoor Loos

'This was Bletchley,' says one veteran. 'A very small railway town some fifty miles out of London. This town was expected to house all these people. And very few of these houses had baths.'

Even in the earliest days of Bletchley Park, before the crowds descended, it had not been considered practical or feasible to use the big house itself for accommodation. There had been a suggestion that the first wave of staff could somehow be housed in an underground shelter under the old headquarters of Broadway Buildings in London. The idea, as Alistair Denniston was swift to point out, was extremely unattractive; was it really sensible to cram people engaged in the most sensitive cerebral work together in this way? Though Alan Turing sometimes slept in the Cottage, Dilly Knox would make his way back to his own home in the Chilterns, while from the start senior personnel had been billeted in local hotels and inns.

As the new young recruits began making their way to the Park, it was clear that the townsfolk of Bletchley would have to put roofs over their heads. Some recruits made their way straight to rooms above inns; others to neat, terraced little houses; yet others to grander accommodation just outside the town. Perhaps this added a further dimension to the feeling that this was, in some ways, a university; all these students, classicists, mathematicians and boffins taking rooms in humble digs and doing their best to stay out of their landlady's hair. Before long, however, billets had to be found in all the villages and hamlets within a wide radius.

Baroness Trumpington had less than fond memories of the first place that she was sent. She recalled: 'My billet was with a chap who worked on the railways and I noticed when his wife showed me around, that there was no lock on the bathroom door. She said, "Oh you don't have to worry about that – when you're in the bath, my husband will be working on the railway lines." Well, I found differently on the very first night. So I changed my billet.'[1]

Another billet-changer was Keith Batey. 'My first landlady was a horror,' he says. 'I didn't stay with her for more than a month, I think it was. She wanted an assurance from the Park that I wasn't a conscientious objector. Well, she didn't ask again after that.'

This may have been quite a common problem for male Bletchley recruits. If a young man was not in uniform, and was still roaming around the place, then how was he to explain exactly what he was doing?

The experience of his wife Mavis, billeted on a local farm, was a little different. 'I looked after children, I babysat, I helped on the farm, I did my own washing,' she says. 'We did as much as we could and were always doing things with the children. But the landlady would insist on bringing us up a cup of tea in the morning. One day, she suddenly said: "I shan't be here next week, my aunt will be coming to look after you. Actually, I'm having a baby." We felt so awful that we had let her wait on us and we had no idea. She just laughed and said: "You know, you're not the only ones who can keep a secret."'

Keith Batey moved on to a rather more agreeable billet, as he recalls: 'I stayed at the house of Mrs Bidwell, much later. She was admirable. The widow of a metropolitan police sergeant – who knew how to feed men.'

Mr Batey adds: 'Tell you who was billeted with me: Howard

Smith. He became ambassador in Moscow and head of MI5. But the billet was a scandal really, in the sense of the strain that it put on Mrs Bidwell. As well as us, Mrs Bidwell had her mother living with her, and some invalid in a back room, and I suspect we had half their ration.'

For some lucky chaps at the start of the war, one's billet could also mean highly congenial access to beer and billiards. This certainly was the case for Stuart Milner-Barry. He wrote that he found himself installed 'at the Shoulder of Mutton Inn, Old Bletchley, about a mile from the entrance to Bletchley Park. Here Hugh [Alexander] and I were most comfortably looked after by an amiable landlady, Mrs Bowden. As an innkeeper, she did not seem to be unduly burdened by rationing, and we were able (among other privileges) to invite selected colleagues to supper on Sunday nights, which was a great boon.'[2]

Jane Fawcett MBE, who was later to head the Royal Institute of British Architects, was a little taken aback by the aesthetic prospect that awaited her in Bletchley. She says: 'I lived in a council house under the chimneys of the London Brick Company. It was a young family with two noisy boys. I couldn't sleep, especially after night shifts. And after about a year of this, my parents . . . became aware of the situation. Our family had friends who were at Liscombe Park. I was invited to stay there, in the staff wing.'

Angus Wilson, who worked at the British Museum with his friend and lover Bentley Bridgewater, had a head start; in 1939, he had removed himself from London to live in the relative bucolic peace of Bishop's Stortford. When he was recruited to Bletchley, he was billeted two miles away from the Park in a village called Simpson. He lived in a council house occupied by the local milkman and his wife, who would emit little coughs in order to try and discourage Wilson's enormous consumption of cigarettes. She was also on hand to save him from embarrassment when one day, he set off to work at Bletchley in his pyjamas.

But not everyone's domestic arrangements were quite so stable.

Sheila Lawn, who had never before left her native Scotland, recalls that throughout the war, she found herself being shifted around between homes quite a bit.

'When I first got to Bletchley, I was supposed to be put up in Newport Pagnell, which was eight miles away,' Mrs Lawn says. 'But when I arrived, they hadn't got a billet for me, and for three weeks, I was in the hostel. I met some charming girls there, delightful girls, a lot of them were secretarial, and they were so nice to me and they would come out with us in the evening. And then I was moved to my first billet, with people called Hobbs.

'It was delightful. They had a boy, Michael, bright as a bee, he was about twelve. And I was there for five very happy months. But unfortunately, Mrs Hobbs had leg trouble and the doctor said to her, "You've got to rest that leg." It was very painful and swollen. So I had to move on.

'And then,' Mrs Lawn continues, 'I went on to an elderly lady and her little dog. Quite obviously she wanted someone who would sit with her, and perhaps share in a little bit of knitting and that sort of thing. But we got on very well. In the end, though, she had to let the authorities know that she really thought it was too much. I was on shifts, a lot of them running from four p.m. to midnight, and midnight to eight a.m. And this lady was finding the pattern of the shifts difficult, in terms of me going in and out.'

The tough and rigid shift patterns of the Park caused problems in a great many households. Imagine, if you are the landlord, perhaps with small children, and your tenant is either coming back in well after midnight, or coming in just after 8 a.m. and needing to sleep throughout the day. Added to this, your tenant also requires food and drink. In a small, cramped house, and at all hours of day and night, such demands are not always easily met.

Sheila Lawn remembers her last billet. 'It was a very simple billet – outside loo, which most of us had, you know – but they were very pleasant people indeed, never asked me any questions. And they had a daughter of fifteen. She was a little bit of a tearaway. But they were so kind to me. I stayed there for the last eighteen months of the war.'

A fellow Scot, Irene Young, found billeted life rather more of a trial. In some ways, it appeared to have been rather a shock. Her landlady, a Mrs Webster, had 'a sharp nose' and 'a thin mouth' and her day-to-day clothing always involved 'a crossover apron'. Conditions in the small house were every bit as spartan as those encountered by Sheila Lawn. 'The WC . . . was outside,' wrote Irene, 'and I used to indulge in a small secret smile when, having crept out on a freezing night to the little "necessary house", I must needs sit facing an outdated calendar showing a picture of "A Sunny Haven."'

And if that wasn't bad enough, life indoors apparently verged on the Dickensian:

> I had a room to myself, but because fuel was rationed, there was no heating in it, and so in my time off I was forced to sit with Mr and Mrs Webster. He was a gentle man, happily dominated by his competent wife. I used to find my bed set at an angle from the wall and though I straightened it, it was always moved back into this odd position. Eventually Mrs Webster explained that she had had an evacuee before me who had 'breathed on the wall', and she did not want me to do likewise.[3]

For Captain Jerry Roberts, who joined the Park later to work on Colossus, the successor to Alan Turing's bombe machine, life in a billet meant that any romantic possibilities were frequently smothered with a cold, damp towel: 'It was difficult to be too social. In my billet, I had half the house. There were two bedrooms, and Mr and Mrs Wells had one and I had the other. There were two sitting rooms. They had the kitchen, if you like. And I had the parlour. Which they would normally never have used, they lived in the kitchen. Now it was not too easy to develop romances in that sort of situation. Not that that bothered me at that time, I have to say.'

*

In March 1940, the Bletchley Park authorities felt obliged to send out a stern memo on the subject of billeting:

> Any amenities provided by the householder are purely volun-
> tary. The householder is not bound by law to do more than
> provide breakfast, an evening meal, sleeping accommodation,
> and reasonable facilities for personal cleanliness.
>
> There is, for instance, no obligation to provide baths, fires, or
> allow those billeted to use the householder's sitting room. Nor
> is it at all certain that those billeted could insist on having their
> bedrooms cleaned, beds made, etc.
>
> A great many householders are, in fact, providing such
> amenities without extra payment and it is therefore incumbent
> on persons billeted to do what they can in these circumstances
> to make the householder feel that his or her co-operation is
> appreciated and not just taken for granted.[4]

This might have been particularly addressed to those who approached life in this small town from the more rarefied end of the social scale. One veteran recalls with glee the privations inflicted upon 'the debs', the glamorous upper-class girls drafted in through family connections and suddenly finding themselves having to live in suffocating little houses near a main railway line, 'where the occupiers kept their coal in the bath'.

'Let's not forget,' says Geoffrey Pidgeon, who was working with the signals intelligence Y Service at the time, 'you have the situation of "girls of quality" going into a room with a twenty-five watt bulb, and the instruction that they are to have only one bath a week. And there is lino everywhere.'

But one should never underestimate the fortitude, and indeed the impeccable manners, of that generation of upper-class 'gels'. Certainly, the Hon. Sarah Baring seems now to have fond memories of the scenario that she found herself in. 'We were very lucky, my friend Osla and I, we were billeted with a lovely old couple,' she says. 'In a village. We used to be driven backwards and forwards to work from the billet. And it was a nice house, a very pretty house near Woburn Sands.

'I think it was the manor house of the village. I'm not sure – we hardly spent any time there. We were either sleeping, or eating, or going off to work again. So we didn't really get to know the village very much. But our landlords were very good to us, very kind. They never complained, they just fed us, which was very decent of them. They had extra rations of course.'

Indeed, she only recalls one source of tension about her domestic arrangements, and that concerned one of her fellow billetees: 'We weren't the only ones, Osla and I. There was one of the cryptographers. We didn't like him very much, we thought he was frightfully pompous. So we weren't very nice to him.'

One other small problem, remembered by many other people during that period, concerned the simple business of getting out of bed on a dark morning in the depths of winter. 'It was always cold in the war,' says Sarah Baring. 'I can remember getting up to go on to day-watch and we just had a small electric fire. The cold! Getting out of bed! Freezing. Because no one had central heating, or anything like that.'

For the townspeople of Bletchley, it was not just this extraordinary collection of quasi-academics that had to be assimilated; there was also the occasional question of evacuated children to be dealt with. One such was 13-year-old Mimi Gallilee, later to work at the Park itself, who found herself fetching up in Bletchley quite unexpectedly. The town – and its collection of little shops and limited amenities – is still imprinted vividly in her memory.

'Before the war broke out, during the last couple of weeks in August – all the schools were on holiday – we were called back to school in Islington,' Mrs Gallilee says. 'We were talked to just in case there was a war and the parents had an opportunity to put their children's names down for evacuation.

'I was evacuated with the school, and we were sent to what was the lovely old Hemel Hempstead. Boxmoor Hill. It was beautiful there. But I was so homesick for my mother – I had only been there eleven days. And so she was sent to Bletchley. And she came and took me, found somewhere for me to live close by her.' But Mimi's mother had to find somewhere to work. Bletchley Park was where she ended up. Her young daughter followed a little while later, and remembers the town itself in those days:

'The first shops, such as they were, started beyond the railway bridge. And you had three or four little shops in a row. A fish shop. There was a jeweller and a WH Smith. Rustons the chemist. A sweet shop – well, it sold sweets when it actually had sweets in. A public house, the Duncombe Arms. There were two or three pubs. I didn't go in them, obviously, so I would never know what they looked like inside.

'I never quite realised at that age that the town was really rather small,' she continues. 'The library was within the local big school and all of the books were hidden from sight of the children in the classroom. They had shelves you could lock. I would go to the library a couple of times a week.

'There was the British Restaurant, where you could go and buy a meal at lunchtime. And no meal was allowed to cost more than half a crown. Half a crown was a very posh meal. That was a great deal of money.'

Some have less than fond memories of the town. During the pitch darkness of the blackouts, Jane Fawcett used to make her way to the Park with a hammer in her bag. 'You never knew who you might meet,' she observed crisply.

No one in Bletchley was immune from the depredations of rationing. Mimi Gallilee recalls how, for the women especially, the task of finding new or replacement clothing could turn into rather a quest. 'If you had to do shopping, you took the train to Bedford or Northampton and on a rare occasion, to Watford. That's if you wanted to buy clothes. Furniture was all on dockets and people didn't have the money anyway. You waited until your clothing

coupon ration came around, I think twice a year. You got twenty-six
at a time. A fully lined ladies' coat would cost you eighteen of those
coupons and you see from that how little you could buy.

'And a pair of socks or stockings would be one coupon. So you
couldn't have loads of anything. Shoes: if you had a hole, or if something started going, they were taken to the repairer, you didn't just
sling them out as you do now.

'Towards the end of the war,' she adds, 'a dress shop opened in
Bletchley. It was close to the Studio Cinema.' Beyond that, she says,
there was 'the butcher, the baker, the Co-op grocery store, and then
the department store. And if you could afford to buy things in *there*,
you were rich.'

And so it was that Bletchley and its inhabitants found itself growing steadily more populous as fresh young faces were drawn in from
across the country, and from a variety of different backgrounds. If
there was fervid speculation as to the provenance of these youngsters, the townspeople were good enough (and patriotic enough)
to keep it to themselves. Nevertheless, rather like that of the Park
workers themselves, this act of conscious mass discretion is one that
still surprises. To this day, many Bletchley veterans are lost in admiration not merely for the hospitality shown to so many of them, but
also for the fact that the people of Bletchley were careful never to
ask what exactly went on up at the Park.

In terms of security, this was obviously invaluable. As Sheila Lawn's
landlady indicated, it was obvious to the people of the town that the
Park was a secret establishment, and swarming with boffins. But to
stifle the urge to discuss, or speculate, seems to have become endemic.

As Mimi Gallilee explains, what now seems startling would have
come much more naturally back then. At the start of the war, it was
not merely the ubiquitous 'Careless Talk Costs Lives' posters; road
signs and railway station signs were taken down as a means of con-
founding potential spies and potential invaders. It was widely
understood, whether in the forces or as a civilian, that one should
discuss no more than necessary.

Given that, says Mimi Gallilee, one couldn't occasionally help wondering what was going through the heads of the townsfolk. 'What I marvel at is: what were the people who lived in Bletchley thinking? I don't ever remember anyone ever saying to me "What do you do there?" So I began to wonder. What on earth were they thinking about? What did they think was going on in the Park?

'Nobody said anything. The Bletchley inhabitants had no reasons to carry any secrets about with them. So it wasn't duty.'

Perhaps there is a slight class factor: that of the folk in the big house having automatic precedence over the townspeople overlooked by the estate. Regardless of their youth, the largely middle-class intake of recruits to Bletchley Park were of a higher social station than the townsfolk. And the townsfolk simply had no business asking them about their affairs.

Even though households throughout the country were presented with so many extra tenants, there were some who were able, by dint of special pleading, to keep their houses and bungalows free of interlopers throughout the war. In general terms, the system involved inspectors first visiting likely properties, and asking the occupants what room they could provide, if any. The more quick-witted, privacy-loving homeowners became adept at spinning yarns concerning elderly relatives and available living space. There does not seem to have been any such reluctance at Bletchley.

As staffing levels at the Park ballooned, living arrangements were provided at the stately home of Woburn Abbey, among other locations. Woburn was quite a different proposition from that of the Bletchley billet. But one of the most evocative – and pivotal – of all billets was that occupied by mathematician John Herivel. In his memoir, he wrote:

I returned each evening to my billet close by in one of a long line of terraced houses in the road sloping down from the level of the Park towards the railway bridge. I had been given a sitting room in the front part of the house, and when the landlady –

alias the lady of the house who had been required by an all-powerful wartime government to give ME board and lodging in HER house – had cleared away the supper dishes, said Good Night – I hope I stood up as she did so – and closed the door, I was then totally cut off from the outside world except for the occasional faint Proustian sound, through the tightly drawn curtains, of the shuffling feet of some lost soul toiling up or down the hill in the deep snow outside – for the winter of 1940 was an exceptionally severe one.

As for me, each evening I was soon installed in a very comfortable late Victorian or early Edwardian armchair before the fire, always hissing and spitting as it really got under way, backed up by a full scuttle of coal, enough to see me halfway through the night.[5]

It was in this exact room that John Herivel was to make the psychological leap that helped to break the Enigma codes.

8 1940: The First Glimmers
of Light

So, with practically nothing in the way of ceremony – or indeed, in some cases, of more than rudimentary training – the young recruits squared up to their extraordinarily complex, gruelling, grinding tasks. As Keith Batey has recalled, the nature of the work often had very little to do with mathematics and everything to do with patience and concentration.

The working day would be split into three shifts: 4 p.m. to midnight, midnight to 8 a.m., 8 a.m. to 4 p.m. It was the Air Section, under Josh Cooper in Hut 10, that started the 24-hour watch system quite early on, and the routine was quickly replicated across the establishment. Among codebreakers – and later, the Wren bombe operators – the shift most disliked, quite understandably, was midnight to 8 a.m..

But the intention was to speed up the decoding and translating work. With the enemy's code settings being changed on a daily basis, the amount of signals traffic to be worked through could not be delayed in any way.

Keith Batey remembers that the nature of the work was not almighty intellectual effort: 'I wouldn't describe the work as hard slog. More tedious,' he says. 'In fact, the work I was doing to begin with in Hut 6 didn't even require a mathematician. I told Gordon Welchman that any of the girls could do it.'

Sheila Lawn equally recalls the unromantic and often unexciting nature of the tasks before her. 'I just did what I had to do. It wasn't exciting. I got these messages, I translated them, I decoded them, and simply got through them. They got a lot in. From the radio stations and gun emplacements along the Dutch, Belgian and French coasts. And some in the Mediterranean, but I never distinguished that, and didn't ask too many questions. It was sightings, weather reports, sightings of ships, sightings of aircraft, anything peculiar.'

For the Hon. Sarah Baring, the notion of a work ethic was already firmly in place before her arrival at Bletchley, thanks to her stint at the plane factory near Reading. Physical labour was one thing though: the concentration required for translating duties at Bletchley was another.

'It was the hours,' she says. 'You were translating German decrypts. And you really got to know how to do them pretty quickly. If you had the lingo, that is.' The shift system also took a little getting used to, as she recalls: 'If you turned up for work in the day, hopefully night shift had got through a bit of the messages. It depended on what was going on. There was always plenty to do.

'But night-watches were hell,' she adds. 'You do get a bit tired, but then suddenly you're woken up by a signal that is so important that you sort of become alive again. It's not just routine. You suddenly get terrifically excited about where such and such a U-boat is, or where the *Graf Spee* is. You've got something really worth it.

'And the sleep patterns! They were awful, because we changed every week, from day watch to night watch. That was hell. But everyone did it, of course. Soldiers, sailors, everyone.'

No one in the huts, according to Ruth Sebag-Montefiore, looked their best after so many nocturnal hours of ferocious concentration. 'Individually, these backroom boys, with their original minds and brilliant brains, could be described as interesting looking,' she recalled. 'Seen collectively, as they poured out of their huts for a breather or en route to the dining hall, with their gesticulating arms, unkempt hair and short-sighted eyes peering through thick spectacles, they looked like beings from another planet.'[1]

The actor Sir Anthony Quayle – who according to some spent a little time himself at Bletchley later in the war – was deeply, and helplessly, in love with a married actress called Dorothy Hyson. At that time, Hyson was a byword for theatrical West End glamour. The night work that awaited her now was of a different order. Hyson had been summoned to work at the Park while Quayle was out in Gibraltar serving with the forces. Once, when he was on leave, Sir Anthony recalled, 'Dot, the essential reason for my return to England, was not even in London; she had gone to work as a cryptographer at Bletchley Park. I went to see her there and found her ill and exhausted with the long night shifts.'[2]

Many decades on, cryptographer William Millward found himself pondering the side-effects of the punishing shift system. He wrote:

> We worked in shifts on a pattern allegedly recommended by the medical authorities, its aim being to avoid painful changes in the circadian rhythm. It meant in practice destroying this rhythm . . . I worked these shifts for two and a half years with one week's leave a year, and have sometimes wondered whether working thus, with all the excitement and dedication which it involved, was perhaps a cause of the bad insomnia which hit me some dozen years later.[3]

Some female veterans recall that occasionally, a night shift in a hut could have an uncomfortably quiet, 'spooky' quality. Then there was the difficulty of moving around outside in the thick darkness, with few effective torches. One recalls that she found herself subconsciously memorising where the potholes in the roads were.

'I have a memory of looking out of the first floor window of the house,' says another veteran, 'just as a night shift was switching over. Some people would be coming in to start work, others going home.

And I seem to have this image, of seeing, down by the lawn and the lake, all these people, milling around in the dark.'

Sheila Lawn, however, recalls the upside of the system. 'Because we were all young, we were very adaptable. I think now the shift system would be a big shock to *my* system. But no, we were very adaptable, we just accepted this. And there were advantages and disadvantages. A more flexible day. Sometimes you had to work at night, of course, but you had part of the day to yourself.'

Another veteran is equally phlegmatic: 'When you changed rota, your sleep pattern would change and that gave you an awkward day or two. But this is how it was.'

But it was not just a question of sleep. The ever-pressing need for one hundred per cent accuracy meant that the pressure in the small hours could be unusually intense.

Keith Batey offers an insight into the intricate yet repetitive nature of the work, talking of the simple-sounding yet fearsomely complex 'rodding' system invented by Dilly Knox. 'They assumed that there was a word likely to appear in the message. Six or more letters. And you could select places worth looking at by checking for what we called "clicks". In other words, you set the assumed plain letter against each section of text and look for settings on Dilly's rods where you got the same twice – charts were made to pick out all the "clicks" quickly. When you got a double "click", you set the rods up to see if it would work. Very often it did – you didn't set out to work on each code seventy-eight times.'

As well as Dilly Knox's system of rods, there was the 'Zygalski sheet' system devised by the Poles who had originally broken into Enigma, and updated and modified at Bletchley by John Jeffreys, Alan Turing and Gordon Welchman. The updated versions were known as 'Netz' or Jeffreys Sheets.

Of great help to Bletchley was Dilly Knox hitting upon the principle of what were termed 'cillis'. These were defined by Sir Harry Hinsley as 'procedural errors by Enigma operators combining (1) a recognisable instead of random choice of message setting, and (2) failure to alter the wheel position much, or at all, before sending a message'. Sir Harry added that this insight was thought to have been named after a German operator's girlfriend, called Cilli. The operator, using his girl's name as a message setting, had shortened it to 'Cil'.

On top of this, there had been, according to Alan Stripp, another chink in Enigma's armour: the 'indicator setting'. After following instructions for that day's wheel order, ring-setting and cross-plugging, the German Enigma operator would turn the three wheels to a random starting point. Then, as part of the preamble to the messages the operator sent, he would twice key in 'his own randomly selected choice of text-setting', as Stripp noted.[4] This choice might be FJU. He would then tap the setting out again as confirmation, and it would appear as encrypted letters, say PORCDQ.

'The operator had to give an indicator for the chap at the other end,' says Keith Batey. 'But because of the possibility of Morse error, it was repeated, so you got two of these three-letter things. So that you knew that there was a repeat.'

Once Bletchley had worked out the nature of the six-letter preambles, they instantly provided a slender means of working back through the rest of the code by days and days of calculation (though of an intensity that would still be utterly beyond most). 'But then,' adds Mr Batey, 'the Germans suddenly began to realise that this was bad.' Once the Germans became aware that the practice – originally instituted for extra security – ironically made their communications very much less secure, they put a stop to it in May 1940.

And this had only ever applied to military and air force traffic; the German naval Enigma was never so straightforward to catch out. From the start, it was a very great deal tighter and more labyrinthine in its theory and use. Its operators had far less personal leeway, and thus, the chance of the operators making mistakes were virtually eliminated.

The work was thus not simply a matter of clever young people in Fair Isle sweaters gazing blankly at apparently random letters; it was these same young people using tiresome though necessary means to test and test and test again, against such regular messages as enemy weather reports and call-signs, the language of which were presumed straightforward and repetitious enough to help produce some kind of a crib.

In the coming months, when successful attacks upon Enigma had resulted in a specific codebreaking methodology, the huts were to become extraordinarily intense places to be, not only for cryptographers but also for translators. 'When the codebreakers had broken the code,' explained Peter Twinn, 'they wouldn't sit down themselves and painstakingly decode 500 messages . . . by the time you've done for the first 20 letters and it was obviously speaking perfectly sensible German, for people like me, that was the end of our interest.'[5]

The messages would then be passed on to the Machine Room, in which British Typex code machines had been rigged up to act as Enigma machines. Here, operators, normally women, would set the machines up using the decrypted keys, sit down and start typing. If the code was correctly cracked, what they typed would appear in German.

Then there was the matter of translation. As historian and codebreaker Peter Calvocoressi recalled:

The Watch in Hut 3 sat around a horseshoe table. Their function was to translate the deciphered Enigma material from Hut 6, interpret it and transmit it abroad. What the Watch received was a stream of slips of paper the size of an ordinary Post Office telegram, or on two or more such bits of paper.

The letters were in five-letter groups and ideally they made German words. A dozen people sat around the semi-circular table with the head of the Watch inside the semi-circle and facing his colleagues who were scribbling away or scratching their heads. They all knew German as well as they knew English.

Schoolmasters were ideal for the job, as they were meticulous. If not satisfied, they would throw back a translation at even

an eminent professor. It reminded me of Chief Examiners at 'A'
level who would send back scripts to an Assistant Examiner to
re-mark.[6]

Once the messages had been successfully decoded and translated, there was the organisational horror of the cross-referenced
card system to be faced. And this, it seemed, was a problem that
required a rather more upper-class sort of girl to take on. Oliver
Lawn recalls: 'The intelligence people could of course read the messages. They could decide what information, if any, to pass on to
whom. And they were supported by a huge card index.

'Let's take as a random example someone called Bruno Schmidt.
As the subject of a previously decoded message, he would have been
entered into the card index. And from this, one could pull him out
in the future when he turned up in other messages.

'One could ask: "Ah yes, this chap is a rocket chap, he's to do
with rockets. He is being moved from A to B. Why?" And this information came about because of the accumulation of the card index.
That was the information side. Now the index used to be put in a
section which was locally called "The Deb's Delight".

'This,' Mr Lawn continues, 'was because the debutantes, and
ladies from high society, were regarded as suitable for doing this
indexing work. Ladies – a few with rather modest brains – very well
connected, and very loyal and security conscious.'

As a result of the 'sheet' system and the 'cillis', and thanks to the
crucial involvement of the Polish codebreakers, Bletchley Park's
first break into current military Enigma traffic – as opposed to old
messages – came in January 1940.

Alan Turing had been sent to Paris to confer with the Poles about
such matters as wheel changes in the Enigma machine, taking with
him some of the Zygalski sheets. In those few days, they managed to
crack an Enigma key via this method. One of the Polish mathematicians, Marian Rejewski, remembered his dealings with Turing:

'We treated Alan Turing as a younger colleague who had specialised
in mathematical logic and was just starting out in cryptology.'[7] At the
time, he was not aware that Turing had quietly been making some
astounding cryptographical leaps off his own back. Nevertheless, the
Polish contingent based in Paris – even with their scantier
resources – were still brilliantly helpful to the Bletchley operation.

Very shortly after Turing returned to Bletchley Park, the momen-
tous breakthrough came. The veteran Frank Lucas recalled: 'On a
snowy January morning of 1940, in a small bleak wooden room with
nothing but a table and three chairs, the first bundle of Enigma
decodes appeared. The four of us who then constituted Hut 3 had
no idea what they were about to disclose.'[8]

In addition to their factual content, these decodes produced an
important psychological boost. In the days of the Phoney War, tension was high. No one had yet managed to stop the German army.
All knew that Nazi territorial ambitions were virtually limitless.
Along with the desperate scramble to rearm and train her forces,
Britain was in a furious struggle to gain an advantage in intelligence. That first break into the army code of the previously
unbreakable Enigma machine was a source of some relief.

Perhaps the weight of the unrelenting pressure was behind an
explosive row between Dilly Knox and Alistair Denniston. For reasons of security, Denniston had been extremely reluctant to let Alan
Turing travel to Paris with the Zygalski sheets; Knox, on the other
hand, felt that aid and assistance to the Polish and French cryptographers was a promise that the Park was honour-bound to keep.
The argument came to a head when Knox wrote Denniston this sul-
phurous letter, opening 'My dear Alistair':

[The statistics] must be handed over at once . . . My personal
feelings on the subject are so strong that unless they leave by
Wednesday night, I shall tender my resignation.

I do not want to go to Paris but if you cannot secure another
messenger, I am actually at the moment completely idle.[9]

Of course, Turing went, and Denniston bowed to Knox. But there were to be further outbreaks of ill-temper and seething resentment between the two old friends.

And the pressure to achieve results was only to grow. It was Gordon Welchman who, even at the earliest stages, saw that Bletchley would have to be moved into what might be termed 'mass production' – especially when the first regular, daily breaks into Enigma were made, for then they would have access to thousands of intercepted messages daily – and that numbers at Bletchley Park had to increase dramatically. And it was Welchman, rather than the veteran Knox, who made representations to Alistair Denniston and his deputy Edward Travis. Welchman was also helping Alan Turing with the development of the bombes. He was clearly a young man with a colossal amount of energy and enthusiasm.

The early months of the war had given the operatives at Bletchley a terrific head start. For although the fighting on land had yet to begin, hostilities at sea were under way, allowing the codebreakers a period of time in which to hone their skills on German traffic. 'The exercise gave us invaluable practice,' says one cryptologist. 'And it provided us with a battery of cribs of which we were able to make use when the war became real.'

Bletchley Park, and by extension the entire military machine, was relying upon human inspiration. The circumstances in which it came were quite extraordinary.

9   1940: Inspiration – and Intensity

On a week of damp, chilly nights in February 1940, at a point when the Germans had further changed the settings of their military Enigma machines – and in the days before the arrival of Turing's bombes – the young John Herivel was in the sitting room of his billet, in his customary position before the fire, 'always concentrating on the encoded messages,' as he wrote, 'and always totally without any glimmer of progress.

> Then suddenly one night something very strange happened; I may have dozed off before the fire – a dangerous thing to do as I often smoked a pipe and might have burnt a hole in my land-lady's carpet, or worse – and perhaps I woke up with a start and the faint trace of a vanishing dream in my head. Whatever it was, I was left with a distinct picture – imagined of course – in my mind's eye, of a German Enigma operator.
>
> This was the trigger that was to set off my discoveries . . . I seem to have taken Aristotle's advice, that you cannot really understand anything thoroughly unless you see it growing from the beginning.
>
> In this case, the beginning would be early in the morning

when the wretched operator would have to wake or be wakened and set up the new key of the day on his machine.[1]

What he was describing came to be known as 'The Herivel Tip' or 'herivelismus'. Loosely, Herivel's insight concerned Enigma's ring-setting, and how the machine's operator might, for various reasons ranging from laziness to tiredness to panic, choose as the new day's setting the letters already in the machine's window from the day before.

Herivel went on to calculate how such an error might be detected – and how the subsequent messages could be decoded. 'I don't think that I slept much that night,' he now says lightly. It is not an exaggeration to say that it was one of the most startling breakthroughs made at Bletchley Park. Gordon Welchman was quick to assure young Herivel that he 'would not be forgotten'.

The working-through of his insight was mathematical brilliance, but the original vision, that of the operator himself, was a flash of psychological genius – an understanding of human nature, rather than calculus. And this intuitive approach seems to be a recurring theme in the story of Bletchley Park, as had been seen with Dilly Knox's use of 'cillis', or 'Dilly's Sillies' as they were sometimes known. As Gordon Welchman wrote: 'Unbelievable! Yet it actually happened, and it went on happening until the bombes came, many months later. Indeed . . . it seems to me that we must have been entirely dependent on Herivel tips and Cillis from the invasion of France to the end of the Battle of Britain . . .'[2]

One other non-scientific element helped the codebreakers, and that was the occasional foul language used by the German operators as they sent out multi-letter test messages. 'The German operators with their German words were just oiks being oiks. Ask a chap to think of a word with four letters . . .' says Keith Batey.

His wife Mavis points out the chilling converse of this. 'Enigma would never have been broken but for those procedural errors. If, on the other hand, the German operators had all done exactly what they were told to do . . .'

But now the theoretical work at Bletchley Park was about to face the test of real firepower. Early in 1940, both the Allies and Germany had their own designs upon Scandinavia; the Allies realised that Hitler would want to grab bases in Norway in order to protect the safe sea-passage of iron-ore supplies from Sweden. Prime Minister Chamberlain was determined that British forces should land on the coast of Norway and take control of the iron-ore mines themselves.

However, while the Bletchley operatives were still trying to find ways of speeding up the decoding of Enigma, it appeared that the Germans had managed to penetrate the British code system. Informed of the secret British plans for Norway, Hitler urgently ordered the invasion of both Norway and Denmark. Though both countries had previously declared themselves neutral, this meant very little either to Hitler or to the Allies who had planned to come to their defence. For many in British High Command were convinced that a German attack on Britain was not far away.

Hitler's invasion of Norway ironically gave the codebreakers another boost. It was at this time – when the number of intercepted messages had leapt upwards – that they broke the Yellow key, that used for the German campaign in Norway. The breakthrough provided a satisfying amount of intelligence about German movements, even if the Yellow key itself was only used for the duration of the Norwegian campaign. Much was learned about organisation and supplies. It was intelligence that had no immediate practical use, but the mere fact that such intelligence could be obtained was vital in itself. Moreover, the speed at which the messages were being decrypted was far greater than had previously been the case. Some could be cracked within an hour of being received by a transmission station.

There was, however, one immediate setback: no one at Bletchley Park or in the government departments knew exactly what to do with all this information. No one, it seems, was 'equipped to handle the decrypts efficiently'. That meant that no one knew in what form to transmit the information to British commanders in the field. Nor did anyone know how to explain to the commanders the significance of the information, without divulging exactly where it had come from.

Already, the question of security was paramount. Should the senior ranks of the general military be allowed to know the provenance of this rich seam of intelligence? The problem was that the more people who knew, the more chance that the Germans might learn of it too.

Something of this tension is revealed in an earlier letter written by Alistair Denniston to Commander Saunders of the Royal Navy. It began: 'Dear Saunders – I am about to speak bluntly', and continued thus:

> I wish to have it made quite clear that all matters cryptographic are to be dealt with by GC and CS.
> To take specific instances:
> 1) Why was it necessary for [your forces] to copy out the portion of the German Air Code salved at Scapa Flow? It turned out to be a portion of the code used by the German Air Force which had been broken by the Air Section of GC and CS. It required expert handling to obtain full value and a certain amount was lost by being handled hastily and stuffed into tight little envelopes.
> 2) Why are notebooks from prisoners not sent at once to GC and CS for first examination? . . .

The memo continued, rather saltily:

> If your staff have not enough to do on their legitimate work, it might seem that you are overstaffed . . . It is being asked here, in the event of the Enigma machine being captured, why you would consider it your duty to investigate it before it reached Knox and his trained staff.

Such a situation would become intolerable and I do hope you will exert yourself to stick to your own job which you are doing so well and not butt in on the jobs of others who are obviously better qualified to carry them out. We have the means of a very efficient co-operation and I do not propose to let any personal sentiments spoil it.[3]

Even though the Park had done very well in principle by breaking the Yellow key, the fact was that none of the intelligence it gathered was used in any form throughout the Norwegian campaign.

And, in these early days when codes were broken 'by hand', there was already a certain amount of resistance among high-ranking officers not in the know; they were concerned about this seemingly miraculous stream of information, and whether or not it could be trusted. With the nature of Bletchley not being mentioned to anyone – especially in the early months of the war – it had to be assumed by military commanders that information was being supplied not by codebreakers, but by spies on the ground. And spies, however useful in some sense, were also notoriously unreliable. As the conflict unfolded, there were to be instances when vital tips picked up at Bletchley Park were dismissed by senior officers simply because it was felt that the information had been gleaned from untrustworthy quarters.

'The German strategy,' wrote codebreaker Jack Copcland, 'was to push Britain towards defeat by sinking the convoys of merchant ships that were Britain's lifeline, bringing food, raw materials, and other supplies across the Atlantic from north America.'[4] Throughout 1940, those U-boat 'wolf packs' succeeded in sinking hundreds of ships. Yet there had been a further turn in Bletchley's fortunes in February 1940. In the dark waters of the bitterly cold Firth of Clyde, near Glasgow, a German U-boat – U33 – was detected as it was laying mines in the mouth of the estuary. HMS

Gleaner, a minesweeper, detected the craft, and released depth charges which brought it to the surface. Its crew, stranded in the open, freezing waters, were forced to surrender. On board the submarine was an Enigma machine. In the pockets of one of the submariners were three of the machine's code wheels.

Bletchley thus discovered that the naval Enigma was using a choice of eight code wheels. The Hut 8 codebreakers, led by Alan Turing, realised that they faced several colossal problems. Not only were the naval Enigma operators more disciplined than their counterparts in the army, tending to make fewer mistakes such as repeated call-signs, or the use, for test purposes, of girlfriends' names that provided codebreakers with invaluable cribs. Now, with this latest discovery, the number of potential combinations of wheel settings – millions of them – was hugely increased.

There was a further complication. The sender enciphered each message, then super-enciphered it – once by using the Enigma and the second time by hand, using bigram tables. These tables set out substitutions for pairs of letters; and the tables were changed day by day according to a very strict calendar. The task of cracking this was going to be the most formidable challenge the Park faced.

Of course, the other Huts also faced the problem of getting regular breaks into Enigma keys. While work proceeded painstakingly on Alan Turing's reinvention of the Polish 'bombas' – machines that could check off hundreds of combinations at top speed – the terrible pressure on senior individuals remained. The growing tension is perhaps illustrated in a lengthy and emotional draft resignation letter written by Dilly Knox sometime in the spring of 1940.

Knox's health was not good, which may have contributed to the angry tone of the letter. In it, among many other things, he gave as his reasons for wanting to go slights that had been perpetrated before the start of the war. Although there is no indication as to whom the letter was finally to be addressed, it was clearly someone higher up than the Director of Bletchley Park. Indeed, given Knox's long-standing friendship with Alistair Denniston, his view of his work is astonishingly intemperate:

> In Commander Denniston's view, research is wholly unimportant in the sense that all able workers are constantly snubbed and reprimanded and that little or no money or staff or accommodation can be obtained . . . When a cipher is out, Commander Denniston is willing to parade superiors round sections of whose work he understands literally nothing and to assume credit for achievements his mismanagement nearly ruined.
>
> In contrast at the moment, Mr Turing and I are faced with two vital pieces of research. The staff available to us consists of Mr Twinn and three women clerks.

And the last few paragraphs of Knox's letter contained an eyebrow-raising burst of anger:

> During the last week, Commander Denniston has envisaged a system whereby Mr Turing, if successful in finding methods for a solution of German Naval traffic, should work 'under Mr Birch'. The very suggestion, which would subject the Enigma section to the mystic hierophancies of an inexpert, is so absurd and unworkable, so clearly a breach of all previous agreements and arrangements, that I could no longer remain in your service to work with its proposer.
>
> In my opinion, Bletchley Park should be a cryptographical bureau supplying its results straight and unadorned to Intelligence Sections at the various ministries. At present, we are encumbered with 'Intelligence officers' who maul and conceal our results, yet make no effort to check up on their arbitrary corrections.

Yet he had still not finished. The most unpleasantly acidic sentiments were saved to the very last:

Two things remain to be said. As to my right to criticise, I need only remind you that I am a Senior Cryptographer. At the end of the Great War, Commander Denniston (with a staff of about 30) was administering one of the German Fleet Cyphers and I (with a staff of three) another. If memory serves me at the end of the war, the smaller unit was supplying copious and accurate information, while the larger remained silent ... I need only say that neither Commander Denniston's friends, if any, expected, nor his many enemies feared that, on the outbreak of war such responsibilities should be left in hands so incapable.[5]

The document is now held in the archives and there is no marking on it to suggest that it was sent; or if it was, how it was received. Knox stayed at Bletchley Park until his ill-health made it impossible to remain; he was, on the occasion of this letter, clearly talked down from the parapet. Alistair Denniston's son Robin was later to brilliantly understate the fraught relationship between Knox and Denniston: 'Dilly Knox, the most brilliant of all [the staff] had not the same collegiate attitude to management.' Knox, he said, was also 'difficult to manage'.

But under such pressure, it was perhaps inevitable that frustrations would be vented volcanically. The fascinating thing is the senior staff seemed to succeed in not taking it out on the younger people working for them. We must remind ourselves that when it came to his own team of girls, Knox was never anything less than generosity and consideration. In August 1940, he was concerned about the amount of money they were getting and wrote in a memo:

Miss Lever [now Mrs Batey] is the most capable and the most useful and if there is any scheme of selection for a small advancement in wages, her name should be considered ...

Miss M Rock is entirely in the wrong grade. She is actually

4th or 5th best of the whole Enigma staff and quite as useful as some of the 'professors'. I recommend that she should be put on to the highest possible salary for anyone of her seniority.[6]

But the really impressive thing about this, and other leaps forward made with Colossus, the successor to the bombes, was that they were made in such incredibly demanding circumstances.

The months between September 1939 and the spring of 1940 had given Bletchley Park the advantage of a quiet run-up; but once Britain was caught up wholly in the conflict, this luxury was gone. From the need to try and anticipate bombing raids, to the later stalking games being played in the north Atlantic between the convoys and the U-boats, information provided by Bletchley was crucial. And the demands for it were intense. So how did the younger codebreakers deal individually with such a crushing weight of expectations? In the case of one particular Bletchley couple, it was with remarkable coolness.

As Mavis Batey says, 'At the time, you took it as a matter of fact . . . we'd be given the message, with the instruction "jumbo rush" which meant absolutely all out, no one do anything else, get it through. It was all about an invasion.

'But we had no idea where the invasion was going to be until we turned on the radio in the morning and heard that we had landed in North Africa. And we'd think, "Oh, that's what we were doing, was it?" But we never felt terribly "aren't we clever" or anything like that.

'The authorities were very sensible about that,' adds Mrs Batey. 'Just imagine that the codework in front of you is a crossword. If you had someone breathing down your neck and saying: "You've got to get it done in five minutes," it wouldn't help at all.'

'It wouldn't have done any good to get worked up about it,' says her husband Keith. 'And you got used to doing it. When you have been in a situation before, you get less worked up about it. I dare say if you were just plonked down and told that there was a war going on, you would get bothered about it. But given that you have been at it for several months, years . . . we got hardened, I suppose.

'Some people may have got stressed but I don't know anybody who did. Whether the senior people got worked up, though,' he adds, 'they could have done.'

In fact, Dilly Knox was not alone in getting 'worked up'. Angus Wilson, who joined Hut 8 in the early 1940s, is now one of those Park figures who evokes the fondest and most vivid memories, even in people who did not work directly alongside him. This is probably because Wilson (like Alan Turing) made few attempts to disguise his homosexuality, or to tone down his colourful manner. 'Angus Wilson was as queer as a coot,' says Sarah Baring, herself not inclined to tone it down. 'And he was always losing his temper, you know, like a child.

'I remember once, he came out of one of the huts. You know the big pond in front of the house? Well he was in a sort of state, a real paddy. Someone said to him, "Do stop it, Angus, otherwise we'll put you in the lake!" And he said: "Don't worry, I'll do it myself!" And he did. He threw himself in, and he had to be pulled out.'

Wilson clearly found the Park extremely difficult; the lake episode is described by some as a serious attempt to drown himself (although it should be pointed out that there are pictures of Wilson surrounded by hut colleagues and Wrens and looking perfectly happy, while his portrait, which hung in the National Portrait Gallery, was painted by another Bletchley Park veteran, Ann Langford-Dent). There were other Technicolor outbursts, including one occasion when he is said to have thrown a bottle of ink at a Wren.

And he did seek professional psychoanalytical help. According to his biographer Margaret Drabble, during his time at the Park, he had bad dreams about drowning in icy seas. Indeed, Wilson became a source of such concern to the Park authorities that he was offered a stay in a grand mental institution in Oxford, although he wisely declined. It is easy to see that for a man already as tightly wound and temper-prone as Wilson, the sensation of being hemmed in, doing utterly vital yet at the same time dreary work, and living in a featureless town, must have been maddening. Whatever the case, Wilson suffered a nervous breakdown just after the war and it was while he was recuperating that he began writing short stories.

Wilson is perhaps the most perfect emblem of the stresses that could be suffered at the Park, but he was not alone. 'There were some codebreakers who had nightmares,' says one veteran. 'It really all could be that intense.' And Gordon Welchman's own account includes a telling detail:

> Josh Cooper and Colonel Tiltman were not only heads of expanding sections, they were both distinguished cryptanalysts. I was far too wrapped up in my own work on Enigma to know about the breaking of other codes and ciphers under these two experts. I remember, however, being told by Josh Cooper that his work was an almost intolerable strain.
>
> Success so often depended on flashes of inspiration for which he would be searching day and night, with the clock always running against him.[7]

Despite the strain that he felt personally, Josh Cooper was an object of admiration even to those from outside the Park. 'He was one of the most unforgettable people I have ever met,' recalled WAAF signals intelligence operative Aileen Clayton, who at that time was based at the Kingsdown Y-station. 'A brilliant mathematician, and much younger than he appeared to be at first sight, he was the archetypal absent-minded academic – slightly deaf, incredibly unkempt in his dress, dark hair flopping over his face, hair which he constantly brushed back with a vaguely irritated gesture, often thereby dislodging his thick spectacles. Yet one was aware of an inner brilliance.'[8]

Clayton went on to describe how, just as she entered his hut, Cooper was starting to go through some scraps of paper – not encrypted messages, but odds and ends from the pockets of a German bomber shot down over East Anglia. In the manner of Sherlock Holmes – and before the widening eyes of young Miss Clayton – he began to assemble, from old tickets and a cigarette packet, the pilot's exact movements on the continent prior to his mission.

It was not merely an intellectual exercise. The more information one could glean, the more the bomber's interrogators could startle him with their apparent knowledge of his comings and goings – and in so doing, startle him into giving away further information.

'Nowadays,' recalled Aileen Clayton, 'we are blasé about detective stories, seeing them so often on the television – but to me, then, it was quite fascinating to see how, from such little things, so much information could be gleaned.'

So while the pressure was obviously intense, in another sense, the game was also afoot. And for others at Bletchley Park, this was precisely the reason why they seemed not to become quite so highly strung. For instance, Alan Turing's biographer Andrew Hodges throws intriguing light on the way that many of the 'boffins' may have viewed this branch of war work:

Nor was there any pretence at heroism in Bletchley circles. It was not simply that Intelligence traditionally represented the most gentlemanly war work; not simply that the unspoken agreement was that of doing one's bit while making as little fuss as possible. For at the higher levels, the cryptanalytic work was intensely enjoyable.

Being paid, or otherwise rewarded, seemed almost a curiosity. It was also something of a holiday even from professional mathematics, for the kind of work required was more on the line of ingenious application of elementary ideas, rather than pushing back the frontiers of scientific knowledge. It was like a solid diet of the hard puzzles in the *New Statesman*, with the difference that no one knew that solutions existed.[9]

For the young codebreakers, working in hermetically sealed departments, under the strictest instructions not even to talk to one another about their work, there was another factor that rendered it sometimes a little abstract. Josh Cooper, in a rare moment of disclosure intended to raise morale, once praised a young codebreaker's work by saying that it was 'helping to save lives in the Atlantic'. But information was generally almost non-existent. 'What you didn't know was the effect that this was all having upon the war,' says Oliver Lawn. 'You see, we knew no more than the public news bulletins, which were obviously censored.'

Very occasionally, there would be a shockingly vivid reminder of what was going on outside. 'The only time I actually realised what we were doing was when I was shown a notebook,' recalled Gwen Watkins. 'It had just been captured and rushed to Bletchley from a captured plane, and of course we had no plastic envelopes or anything then, the poor thing was just given to me as it was. And I was horrified to see a huge bloodstain on it. The blood round the edges was drying, but the blood in the middle was still wet.

'And I realised then that somewhere there was this German. This German air-crew bleeding, still bleeding while I was decoding. That did bring the war very close.'[10]

But these moments were vastly outnumbered by the sense of simply getting on with it, working almost in a void – a feeling to which the nature of the shift system itself contributed. Veterans recall starting a shift, with perhaps a pile of intercepts waiting either to be cracked or to be translated. Segregated in different huts, and under strict instructions never to discuss their work outside the Park, when the shift came to an end and it was time either to go back to a billet in town, or even for a bicycle ride in the countryside, there was little else one could do but pass the baton to those coming in on the following shift. And try to forget about it all, as indeed they were instructed to do.

'I don't think it was particularly intense,' says Keith Batey, drily. 'Well, mathematicians tend to be phlegmatic.'

The mathematicians stayed so. But as the war progressed, elements of friction and stress within the organisation of the Park itself would come to the fore and be felt by all. Before that, though, came Bletchley Park's magnificent moment of technological breakthrough – the introduction of the bombe machines.

10 1940: The Coming of the Bombes

Secret service officer Frederick Winterbotham described the bombe as 'like some Eastern goddess who was destined to become the oracle of Bletchley'.[1] The machine's origins were more prosaic, although inspiration had its place in their development.

Alan Turing had, among other attributes, a tremendous gift for building things from scratch. When it came to electrical experiments, he was the master of what popular fiction authors always describe as 'lash-ups'. Even in the years that followed the war, with all the technological progress that had been made, Turing's devices tended to fulfil the stereotype of the mad scientist's invention: a labyrinth of wires trailing everywhere, held together with sticking plaster. Prior to his premature death in 1954, his home in Manchester was filled with extraordinary and sometimes pungent chemical experiments.

Turing had fixed upon the idea of a 'Universal Turing Machine' in the 1930s; the inspiration had been provided by a mathematical problem posed in Cambridge, concerning the provability of any given mathematical assertion. Turing had the idea of developing a machine that could carry out this task.

When first trying to envisage the form of such a machine, Turing thought of typewriters, how they were built to carry out a certain sort of function. According to his biographer Andrew Hodges, he had in his head an idea of a super-typewriter: a machine that could identify symbols; that could write, but could also erase. A machine that could be configured in many ways to carry out many tasks, and yet would be automatic, requiring little or no intervention from a human operator. His argument was that any calculation that a human could perform, a machine could perform as well.

The bombes were not Universal Turing Machines. Far from it. Nor were they an extension of the Polish 'bomba' machines, from which their name was taken. The British bombe was quite a different thing.

In one sense, it was a philosophical response to the nature of Enigma. Despite the daunting number of combinations thrown up by Enigma, it none the less worked via a mechanical process. Thus, reasoned Turing, Enigma could also be thwarted mechanically. If Enigma, with its rotors, and wiring, and steckerboard, could encrypt, then surely an electric system involving circuits could decrypt.

As many veterans have pointed out, this wasn't an entirely mechanical affair. For a bombe to work, it would require the push-start of a crib; that is, a series of words or a phrase, guessed at by hand and offered to the machine – which would then run through all the different letters and combinations to see if the crib would unravel the encoded text. In other words, such a machine would still require the initial power of human lateral thought. Nevertheless, in an era in which electronic telephone exchanges and television signals were brand new science, the notion of a machine that could take on the exhausting task of checking endless combinations at a speed beyond even an army of codebreakers was revolutionary.

When the young mathematician Oliver Lawn was recruited to Bletchley Park by Gordon Welchman, he found himself being diverted into the business of creating a bombe that would be effective. Construction took place in Letchworth, where Lawn oversaw this delicate and confidential work. In a technological sense, it was almost like being present at the construction of the first nuclear device. Certainly the impact that Turing's codebreaking machine would have on the course of the war was immeasurably as profound.

'Turing was a theoretician, Welchman was the practical chap,' Mr Lawn says. 'And the two put together their brainpower and evolved this machine which was made in large quantities in Letchworth by the British Tabulating Machine Company, as it was then called. In my early months, the first machines were being made.

'I and several others used to go over and stay in a hotel in Baldock near Letchworth and work with the engineers on the making of the machine. The engineers had their engineering skill, we had none of that, but we had the mathematical skill. And we worked with the engineers – the chief engineer was Harold Keen, known familiarly as "Doc" Keen because he used to carry what looked like a doctor's bag in his hand. He was a very bright engineer.

'Because the Germans had devised new ways of encrypting, we had to find new methods to break the codes,' he adds. 'Eventually we got on to using cribs, guessing bits of messages, and testing them on the bombe machines which Turing and Welchman together had conceived. Then when the design of the machine was more or less settled, 'they got on with it and more were produced. We weren't needed after.'

The first bombe was called 'Victory'. Given the months of painstaking work that had gone into its creation – and the acute sensitivity of the job that it was required to do – there was some debate on how the machine should be physically transported with maximum safety, and secrecy, from Letchworth to Bletchley.

Some felt that such a vital device needed all the security that it could get, and that it would have to be taken with a full convoy of protection. However, if there was enemy undercover surveillance about, such a convoy would make obvious the strategic importance of both the machine and its destination. And that could not be allowed. So, perhaps surprisingly, Victory was transported in an open lorry, with no escort of any kind.

The one-ton machine was installed in Hut 1 on 18 March 1940. It did not immediately prove to be the answer to Allied prayers; indeed, it achieved very little in terms of key-setting results. The essence of the machine was that, like a giant calculator, it cycled through every possible combination of the three Enigma code wheels. When the machine hit the menu provided to the bombe operator by the cryptographer it would hit a 'stop'. There would be good 'stops' and bad 'stops', which would all have to be checked.

There would be little unintentional outbreaks of assistance from the Germans, examples of idleness that provided invaluable clues. There were Enigma operators who ended each message with the proclamation: 'Heil Hitler!' and others who started each communication with a list of names for which it was intended. However, the first breaks into a new key were very difficult.

Alan Turing's friend – and briefly, fiancée – Joan Murray worked specifically on naval Enigma and made much use of Victory early in 1940. The messages that were decoded turned out not to be of much direct value, but they did allow intelligence to build good background information about the navy itself. The work was gruelling; Joan and Turing often had to go through each of the possible 336 wheel orders.

Soon, however, a crucial breakthrough was made in the design of the bombe machines. This time the credit went to Gordon Welchman, as Andrew Hodges described in his biography of Alan Turing: 'on studying the Turing bombe design, he saw that it failed to exploit Enigma weakness to the full . . . Welchman not only saw the possibility of improvement, but quickly solved the problem of how to incorporate the further implications into a mechanical process.' It required only a piece of electrical circuitry – soon to be called 'the diagonal board . . . the following of implications could still be achieved by the virtually instantaneous flow of electricity into a connected circuit'. Hodges continued:

Welchman could hardly believe that he had solved the problem, but drew a rough wiring diagram and convinced himself that it would work. Hurrying to the Cottage, he showed it to Alan, who was also incredulous at first, but rapidly became equally excited about the possibilities it opened up. It was a spectacular improvement . . . With the addition of a diagonal board, the bombe would enjoy an almost uncanny elegance and power.[2]

On 9 April 1940, the Germans landed in both Denmark and Norway with 15,000 troops, catching the British completely by surprise. Indeed, only four days beforehand, British ships had set sail in order to lay mines in Norwegian waters, prompting Neville Chamberlain to prematurely declare that 'Hitler has missed the bus.'

The following month saw the German invasion of Belgium, Holland, Luxembourg and then, with astonishing and appalling speed, France – a full-scale offensive every bit as brutal as that against Poland. The British Expeditionary Force was encircled and nudged back towards Dunkirk. Prime Minister Neville Chamberlain resigned, and the government collapsed beneath him.

On 10 May Winston Churchill became Prime Minister, heading a National Government. Although the French had been under the impression that the British would leave a force behind, he immediately ordered the evacuation of British forces across the Channel. Then came the fall of Paris; and if one reads the many British Mass Observation diaries now, one is left in no doubt that the British were convinced that they were next.

The country was in a state of agonised suspense. From Mass Observation to the diaries of society figures such as Harold Nicolson, there is a sense of an almost dreamlike mental state; London and the larger cities were undergoing nightly bombing raids. The Nazi war machine appeared utterly inexorable.

But before the extraordinary and exceedingly fortunate retreat at Dunkirk, Bletchley made another vitally important breakthrough.

In a further triumph for the Herivel Tip, it broke the 'Red' Enigma key. To have a way into the German air force messages was a glittering prize. 'The Red became of vital importance immediately,' commented one veteran of Hut 6, 'and remained so all the way through the war and in all the main theatres of war except Africa . . . The Red was the great standby that kept Hut 6 going. I cannot remember any period when we were held up [in decoding] for more than a few days at a time.'

From that point onwards, the Park was able to read, on a daily basis, every single Luftwaffe message – something in the region of one thousand a day. The messages also gave vital clues as to the movements of land troops. The latest setback was that the messages were also filled with technical jargon: abbreviations, equipment terms, out-of-date map references. In the short term, the intelligence yielded was of no use whatsoever to the thousands of British troops gathered on the French beaches at Dunkirk, awaiting the deliverance of the little ships. But in principle it was a fantastic breakthrough; and the difficulties would be overcome with time and experience.

There was an important psychological point too, one that would have been relayed to Churchill; in the midst of all these decrypts, it was obvious that the main German concern at that moment was the successful conquest of France. There was no mention at that stage in May 1940 of plans to invade Britain. Not one of the thousands of decrypts had suggested that there was going to be an incursion from across the Channel.

By June 1940, however, the decrypts were throwing up intelligence concerning the refit of the Luftwaffe, which strongly suggested that a bombing campaign against Britain was imminent. 'Enigma gave general warning of the approach of the Battle of Britain,' wrote codebreaker Sir Harry Hinsley. 'The fact that Enigma had now been producing intelligence for some months on the German Air Force's organisation, order of battle and equipment was also of great strategic value.'[3]

Indeed, thanks to Bletchley Park – the information was described as 'heaven-sent' and 'apparently sure' – Air Intelligence and the RAF gained a much more realistic idea of German bomber strength, and was given a vital boost of confidence; the enemy forces were not quite as multitudinous as had been first thought. On top of this, the cumulative effect of listening in to so many messages had the effect of bolstering Churchill's determination. Thanks to the decrypts, he knew that he and the British had just a little extra time.

In fact, on 16 July 1940, with the German subjugation of France consolidated, Hitler issued Directive no. 16, involving preparations for 'a landing operation against England'. The plan was called 'Operation Sea Lion' a phrase that, ominously, was picked up with increasing frequency thereafter by the decrypters – and an initial air offensive was to begin on 5 August.

This then was the background to the Battle of Britain – that extraordinary moment when, as Bletchley veteran Captain Jerry Roberts now puts it, 'one tiny blob to the north of the map of Europe' stood its ground while all others around it fell. Even though Bletchley could not be of practical assistance to British planes as the battle was fought, the help it had provided beforehand was immeasurably valuable.

And in the midst of the national anxiety, there was one other small, but vital fillip for the Chiefs of Staff: they had learned that the Germans could be outwitted. Their sheer physical force may have seemed unbeatable but to have advance notice of plans and manoeuvres made their threat, at last, surmountable in theory.

Initially, the bombe machines were operated and serviced by specially picked RAF technicians, headed by a Sergeant Jones. After weeks of frustration during which Victory produced endless false stops, as Sergeant Jones wrote later, 'it was realised that some radical change was still required . . . So the theorists, the cryptographers, the engineers, professors, doctors, got together and decided what was needed.'

It was the first sign of serious friction at Bletchley Park. While it could hardly be said that the three services – army, navy, air force – were in competition, the fact was that some codes were being broken with reasonable success whereas others – the German naval codes – were still proving resistant. As a result, it was felt that the British navy was not getting the vital intelligence it needed.

Although during the Battle of Britain in mid-August, the emphasis was very much on air force intelligence, Frank Birch, head of the German Team of the Naval Section at Bletchley Park, wrote a memo to Edward Travis, Deputy Director of the Park:

> I'm worried about Naval Enigma. I've been worried for a long time, but haven't liked to say as much . . . Turing and Twinn are like people waiting for a miracle, without believing in miracles . . .
>
> Hut 8 has not produced any results at all so far . . . Turing and Twinn are brilliant, but like many brilliant people, they are not practical. They are untidy, they lose things, they can't copy out right, and dither between theory and cribbing.[4]

There might have been something in Birch's complaints – Jack Copeland later stated that Turing was extremely bad at making himself understood – but in a wider sense, the complaints were unfair, as would become clear as the months progressed. Thanks to the stringency with which naval Enigma was employed, including the use of bigram tables, it was far harder to break than the military and Luftwaffe Enigma codes worked upon in Hut 6. The only reasonable chance Turing and his Hut 8 team had of cracking naval Enigma would be if one of these books of tables were to be captured.

In the meantime, there was yet another breakthrough. Turing and Welchman saw that their 'diagonal board' feature could allow for simultaneous scanning of all the possible twenty-six plug-board settings for an individual wheel setting. 'Agnes' – an abbreviation of its real name, Agnus Dei, the sister machine to Victory – made her debut in August 1940 in Hut 11. Once both machines had been fitted with the diagonal boards, they were truly operational. One veteran recalled: 'The bombes were bronze-coloured cabinets about eight feet tall and seven feet wide. The front housed rows of coloured circular drums – the naval colours were dark blue, black and silver.'

'After the first two, a large number of machines were made to a fairly standard form,' says Oliver Lawn. 'It proved its use. Altogether about two hundred were made. The first ones were located at Bletchley itself, in what is now called the Bombe Room, which still exists. But when the numbers grew bigger, they had to use other places, and as the war went on, most of them were put at two locations in north London – Eastcote and Stanmore. They had roughly a hundred machines each, run by a large company of Wrens in both cases.' The reason for the multiple locations was simple: the threat of bombing. To have such precious and irreplaceable machines working in a single location would have been unthinkably risky.

The very first Wrens, eight of them, made their appearance at Bletchley Park in 1941. They were there to see if it was possible for young women to work the bombe machines. Some senior men held the view that 'it was doubted if girls could do the work'. They were not merely being sexist; it was perfectly reasonable to wonder if such young people would indeed be up to the remorseless, ineluctable pressure of the job. However, clearly the Wrens were up for it. And as throughout the war the number of bombe machines crept up to a total of 211, so too did the numbers of Wrens. One estimate suggests that by 1945 there were 1,676 bombe operators. The effect of the work on those early Wrens, though – and indeed, among the many who were to follow – was often deleterious.

The work was very hard for the young women who were drafted in to carry it out. To operate a bombe properly took all one's concentration and focus. Accuracy was of the highest importance. One young Wren recalled: 'The back of the machine defies description – a mass of dangling plugs . . . and a multitude of wires, every one of which had to be meticulously adjusted with tweezers to make sure the electrical circuits did not short.'

According to Ruth Bourne, herself a Wren, the effect of this on individual women could sometimes be distressing. There were instances of the strain getting too much, of girls collapsing and having to go for periods of extended rest. Medical attention was sometimes needed. Bourne also recalls that bombe operating was unforgivingly harsh in less obvious, more psychological ways.

'It was very pressurised because of the working hours. It was very intensive. You did an eight-hour shift – you only had thirty minutes off in the middle of the shift to rush across from the place where you were working to the place where you were eating, queue up for the food, eat it and go back. Then the person who was working with you, called your oppo, went and had her thirty minutes. And the reason you worked together was because you alternated.

'One night you were standing up operating the bombe for seven and a half hours. On the next night you could sit down for most of the time operating a checking machine, which was not very hard to do. Stops didn't need checking that often. Maybe you would get four or five stops a night, which wasn't arduous. The only time you worked together was plugging in the back of the bombe because it was so complex. But there was the noise, and it was smelly. And many people got what they called burnout.

'I had it for a short period of time. You'd go to the sick bay and say "I don't feel well." They'd say "What's the matter?' and you'd say "I don't know," and maybe you'd just cry or something.

'And they'd put you to bed for about four and a half days – with a big jug of water. All you'd remember is wandering in and out of bed, drinking water and sleeping. After about four and a half days, you'd wake up, and that's what happened with me.'

The other difficulty of the bombes was that they were so intricate to set up. Ruth Bourne recalls: 'You had to be accurate as a bombe operator. You didn't have to be a crossword puzzler or a Greek scholar, but you did have to be incredibly accurate. Because with all these little wires on a wheel – one little group of wires must not touch another. And if you were putting in twenty-six pin plugs, you mustn't bend the pins. Anything you did wrong caused a short circuit.

'And every fifteen minutes,' Mrs Bourne adds, 'the machine stopped and some of the wheel orders had to be changed. So you'd have to check those wheels with a tweezer and put them back on the rack. You'd put on the new ones, check the old ones, and if there were a lot of wheels, you might have only just enough time to check them before the run was finished. At the end of fifteen minutes, you'd start again with another lot of wheels.'

Ruth Bourne recalls in particular looking at the women who were just coming off a week of night shifts: 'All their faces were terribly pale. I remember when I first went there, I saw all these scarecrow pallid women coming off their shift. And I thought, "My God."'

Tellingly, about a year into the bombe operation, one Dr Gavin Dunlop, of Newcastle Street, Worksop, Notts, sent a concerned letter to the Bletchley Park authorities concerning one of his Wren patients:

Dear Sir,

Miss Adele Moloney is late on leave on account of the high temperature which is the cause of my keeping her in bed. This is not the first time that the same thing has happened when she has been on leave, and as there is no physical reason that I can find for this being thus, I wonder whether there is anything about the nature of her job to account for it.

Miss Moloney has hypertrophy of the conscience to such an extent that she will not divulge the smallest detail of what she does, even though it is against her own interests. As I find it difficult to believe that this young girl is on work which is so important that her doctor must have his hands tied by lack of knowledge, I thought I would write to ask for your comments.

It was a perfect illustration of how, at every conceivable level, the work at Bletchley was kept absolutely secret. Just a couple of days later, Commander Bradshaw sent a reply:

I am sorry to hear of Miss Moloney's indisposition. There is in the ordinary way nothing that we know of in the work that she does that is in any way likely to be prejudicial to her health. The same work is done by a large number of other girls, none of whom so far as we know have suffered in any way. The hours are not abnormally long and except that a good deal of standing is involved, it is not physically exhausting.

Bradshaw went on to add, with pointed understatement:

. . . there is nothing peculiar in her silence. That is perfectly correct in her behaviour – in fact it is highly commendable. I think I have only to point this out to you to prevent you pressing her further on the subject. The sick return from the Section in which she works is exactly the same as all other Sections, where the work varies considerably, and the staff varies in age . . .

I think, therefore, that you will have to look elsewhere . . . to account for her indisposition unless it be that Miss Moloney finds the work a mental strain and worry. She is perfectly at liberty to say so if she does . . .[5]

It scarcely needs to be added that, even without the background of the war, this was not an era in which concerns about workplace health were given a sympathetic hearing or researched in any depth. From shipbuilding yards, to deep coal mines, to deafening factories filled with potentially lethal machinery, the discomforts of manual occupations were simply part of the burden that working men and women were expected to accept in return for their wages. Indeed, in industrial terms, there is something about the image of the bombes, ticking and clicking and spraying oil in unison, that puts one in mind of Fritz Lang's film *Metropolis* – the image of small people tending to vast, inexorably functioning, demanding machines.

Occasionally, the bombes could be downright dangerous. According to one account from a technician: 'A Wren operator was prettying herself using a metal mirror which slid across two large electrical terminals. There was a bright flash, the mirror evaporated, and her lipstick shot across her throat. I was working nearby. The scream made me look up. I thought she had cut her throat!'[6]

For others, though, like Jean Valentine – a young Wren who later went on to break Japanese codes in Ceylon – the thing was simply to take a deep breath and get on with it. 'I was sent to Adstock, living in a village called Steeple Claydon, and started working on the bombe. We worked shifts, or "watches" as they were called, eight in the morning till four in the afternoon for one week; four in the afternoon till midnight the following week; and then midnight till eight on the third week. Then we went off duty at eight in the morning and were back on at four till midnight, so we did sixteen hours that last day. Once you had learned how to [work the bombe], it was OK. It wasn't all that complicated.'

Jean Valentine says that – speaking for herself – she saw few signs that working on these great machines was more stressful than any other part of the war effort. 'Yes, there was a call for accuracy, but that was discipline. You disciplined yourself to do it because you were being disciplined. There was nothing serious done to us but it was the expectations on us as youngsters.

'When you're younger, your fingers are very flexible, you can do things much more quickly. And the brain works quicker.'

On top of this, many have testified to the unendurable noise of the bombe machines working hour after hour. Again, Jean Valentine remembers slightly differently: 'I don't like noise. But to me, it was like a lot of knitting machines working – a kind of tickety-clickety noise. It was repetitive but I can't say I found it upsettingly noisy. In fact, the bombe reconstruction in the Bletchley Park Museum sounds a lot noisier to me than a room full of five of them.'

One other side-effect of the work, says Jean Valentine, was apparent when she went home. And it was another indicator of the general discretion of the time that this did not prompt more questions: 'My mother never questioned anything, but she did say to me once: "What are you doing to your shirt cuffs?" I used to take my washing home and the cuffs would be all black. It was the fine spray of oil, which you couldn't even see so you didn't know it was happening, a spray coming off the bombes.

'So I just said, "Oh, it's the work I'm doing." And my mother didn't pursue it.'

11 1940: Enigma and the Blitz

'Ultra never mentioned Coventry,' commented Air Section head Peter Calvocoressi. 'Churchill – so far from pondering whether to save Coventry or safeguard Ultra – was under the impression that the raid was to be on London.'[1]

The German raid on Coventry on the night of 14 November 1940 is still the cause of debate and controversy today. Thanks to a pointed reference by Captain Winterbotham in his pioneering book on Ultra, the theory that Churchill allowed the Midlands city to burn – in order that the Germans wouldn't suspect that Bletchley had broken into Enigma – has continually reappeared. And even though most Bletchley Park veterans firmly believe that the theory is nonsense, a few are not so sure. But in order to get a better idea of the searing events of that night, it is necessary to explain a little of the background, and of the increasing value of the intelligence that Bletchley was providing, through the Battle of Britain and beyond.

Back in the summer of 1940, huge numbers of people in Britain had been bracing themselves for what seemed the inevitable. The Germans, triumphant in France and the Low Countries, would, it was popularly believed, now turn to Britain. There was little belief that in the event of an invasion, Hitler's forces could be successfully fought off. Such pessimism would very rarely be heard out loud; one wouldn't want to be reported for damaging morale. Nevertheless, to read contemporary diaries, and to hear contemporary accounts, it is clear that a great many people were sick with anxiety about what they saw as Hitler's coming victory.

Little wonder; nothing like the German war machine had been seen before. Added to this was the calculated sadism, together with the way that any conquered nation would be subject to the paranoia of informers and curfews, the terror of random public executions. News of what had been happening in Poland had come back to London. To listen to Churchill's speeches now, one simply hears the growl of inspirational defiance. But as Mimi Gallilee says, whenever she went to bed after a day's work at Bletchley, she would 'pray first, and pray hard'. She and countless others lived in real fear of a lightning invasion.

Secret preparations were made for such an eventuality. Among them was the recruitment of the 'Scallywags', outwardly passive-looking men such as clerics, writers and intellectuals, trained in techniques of subversion and assassination, with the aim of starting as much mayhem as possible. But when would Hitler invade? From the Cabinet and MI6, down to the saloon bar debaters in the Anchor and Crown, it was a subject of intense speculation based upon little more than guesswork.

In August, in preparation for Operation Sea Lion, the Luftwaffe launched a ferocious concerted attack from the air upon RAF airfields and radar stations. Yet in the succeeding weeks, during what became known as the Battle of Britain, the RAF pulled off astonishing repeated triumphs in its airborne skirmishes with the enemy. The image is ceaselessly evocative; that of the people of Kent looking up into a wide, pale blue sky to see, far above, the tiny forms of Spitfires firing upon the encroaching enemy, and of German planes spiralling downwards, their bailed-out pilots floating down on parachutes.

The end of August brought the conclusion of the Battle of Britain, and with it not merely a sense of relief but also a valuable raising of spirits. Churchill now gave the command for an air raid on Berlin. This in turn led Hitler to order the Luftwaffe to begin an even stronger attack on London. The unforeseen side-effect of this German strategy, however, was that it relieved pressure on the RAF airfields which previously had been the Luftwaffe's main targets.

As mentioned before, Bletchley Park could offer little in the way of practical help to the air force at this time. However, come September, one particular decrypt was of great tactical importance. The message ordered the dismantling of air-lifting equipment on Dutch airfields. Its meaning was very swiftly deduced by the Chiefs of Staff: Operation Sea Lion was to be postponed.

In other words, the Few had succeeded brilliantly; the Luftwaffe having been repelled, there was little chance, with the season of storms now upon the English Channel, that the Germans could launch an effective troop landing. Hitler, the Chiefs calculated, would have to shelve preparations for the winter. It was precisely this sort of information, provided by Bletchley, that gave the forces what was termed a 'crystal ball'. 'So efficient did Bletchley become in handling this material,' wrote Aileen Clayton, 'that there were even cases where, during poor conditions for reception, the German recipient of a signal was obliged to ask the sender for the message to be repeated, whereas our listening stations had recorded it fully the first time. This placed British Intelligence in the position of knowing the contents of a signal before the intended recipient.'[2]

By late September, Hitler was starting to turn his attentions east, towards his projected invasion of Russia. Although the Luftwaffe had lost a great many men and planes throughout the Battle of Britain, however, this did not stop their aerial bombing campaign.

The Blitz started on the afternoon of 7 September 1940. Dread-filled Londoners gradually became aware of a distant muffled roar, like thunder, approaching from the east as 350 German bombers darkened the horizon. The RAF, expecting an assault on their bases, had missed the attackers. Within minutes, the German planes were flying over the vast docks and warehouses of east London. As they dropped their incendiary bombs, the warehouses, filled with imported sugar, molasses and timber, went up in a series of blossoming yellow and blue infernos.

The daylight raids were not to continue, for too many of the German planes were picked off on their way back to base. But nightly bombing soon began, and even though the darkness hampered much of the Luftwaffe's accuracy, the result was still devastation, and a population forced to seek shelter and sleep far underground in Tube stations. It was, and remains, unimaginably relentless – in the following months, some 19,000 tons of bombs fell on London alone.

But with the coming of that ferocious onslaught to London, the cryptographers at Bletchley made a further breakthrough. Crucially, the Germans sent information about their bombers' navigation beams – the beams that were supposed to keep them on course – via radio. These radio signals were picked up by the Y Services. And on being passed on to Bletchley, a new colour of Enigma decrypt – 'Brown', for this section of the Luftwaffe – was assigned to the specific cracking of such messages.

The operatives of Hut 6 rapidly succeeded in doing so. Within days the Air Ministry was receiving vital information concerning potential raids and the numbers of bombers that might be involved. Thanks to Enigma, as Oliver Lawn explains, the Air Ministry also had the wherewithal to 'bend' the German navigation beams, thereby causing the planes to drop their loads in the wrong places: 'One of the things the Germans used the Enigma machine for, in the early stages of the war, was directing their bombing of British cities – beam bombing. That's an aeroplane going along a beam and another beam being set to cross it. And that was the point at which they dropped their bombs, over the centre of the city.

'Now, there was a code which set the angles of the beams. And if you could break the code, clever engineers could bend one of the beams so that the crossing point was over green fields, and not over cities.'

London, of course, was not alone in bearing the brunt of the nightly assaults; British industrial cities from Birmingham and Liverpool to Manchester and Glasgow lived in expectation of receiving hits. The information Bletchley supplied was never conclusive, but they were able to identify squadrons and call-signs and thus report on numbers. However, Bletchley Park was not able in 1940 to accurately identify disguised place names in messages. For that, what would be needed was not a bombe, but a physical codebook, for aliases are simply impossible to guess at.

Thus the war acquired a new and terrible urgency. The deployment of British troops in foreign lands was one thing; the targeting of ordinary citizens in large cities – in other words, total war – was another. Although much was made at the time of the claim that 'Britain can take it!', the true effect upon morale, especially among the East Enders whose houses and streets were being flattened on a nightly basis, was more difficult to gauge.

British government psychologists were extremely concerned about the possible effects upon large urban populations of subjection to Blitzkrieg of the kind suffered in Spain and Norway. Mass panic was predicted, along with a breakdown of law and order, and the development of a sort of collective psychosis. In fact, those first Luftwaffe raids upon London had demonstrated something quite different; a tangible sense of defiance among all the smouldering bricks and the shattered houses. But London was a vast city. What would be the effect in a smaller, perhaps more tightly knit community?

The RAF campaign against German cities stepped up. That autumn, British bombers aimed for Munich and for arms factories in Essen; they also bombed Hamburg. In response, German bombers started roving more widely across Britain. And in November 1940, one particular raid led to a conspiracy theory involving Bletchley Park that has persisted to this day.

The story, according to 'end-of-war' reports from Bletchley itself, seemed to go like this: thanks to a 'Brown' message decrypt from Enigma on 11 November 1940, the Park was able to tell Air Intelligence that there was to be a very heavy raid. The codename given to this raid was 'Moonlight Sonata'; the reason for the name was that it was apparently to take place at the height of the full moon. The German planes would be led by navigation beams. And there was a list of four potential targets, each of which had been given codenames. One of the codenames was 'Korn'.

Just earlier, a German prisoner of war had told his interrogators that a heavy raid was planned on Birmingham or Coventry. On 12 November, a 'Brown' Enigma decrypt seemed to give navigation beam bearings showing that three of the potential targets were the heavily industrialised Midlands cities of Birmingham, Wolverhampton and Coventry. The date for the raid was most likely to be the 15th.

And so with this information, gleaned from Bletchley, Air Intelligence reported to the Prime Minister on the morning of the 14th, telling him that the target was possibly London – given the sheer size of the raid planned – but could also either be Coventry or Birmingham. After all, no one could know what the code word 'Korn' signified. Both Midlands cities were likely targets, as both had high concentrations of manufacturing plants directly involved with the war effort. In the case of Coventry, many of these factories were within the bounds of the city centre. As targets on a brightly moonlit night, they could hardly be easier.

By 3 p.m. that day, radio signals finally made it clear that Coventry was to be the target, and that the raid was to take place that night.

This is where the conspiracy theory begins. Why, it goes, were the people of Coventry given no warning? Why was no attempt made to stop a raid that loosed thousands of incendiaries and tons of high explosives, creating a hellish blaze that destroyed almost everything within the radius of a quarter of a mile, even the city's cathedral? In other words, why was the old city of Coventry sacrificed in this conflagration?

The reason, say the conspiracy theorists, is this: that to have deflected the bombing by sabotaging the navigation beams – or allowing RAF fighters to defend the city from the air – Churchill would have been effectively telling the Germans that he had access to their most secret transmissions. The Prime Minister, this theory goes, was therefore faced on 14 November with a hideous dilemma. Could he step in with this foreknowledge and order that Coventry be given full protection from the onslaught – but by doing so alert the enemy to the fact that its messages had been read? Or instead, should he allow the city to be put to the sword so that the secret of Bletchley remained unguessed at?

In fact, the entire premise is flawed; but it none the less emphasises a wider truth about the work of Bletchley. For as soon as Enigma was broken, it became utterly vital that the Germans should never suspect that this was the case. As many veterans have pointed out, if German Intelligence suspected that its communications had been breached, they would instantly have been rendered much more complex and potentially impenetrable.

There was the later occasion, for instance, of the sinking of the *Bismarck* in 1941. The truth of the matter was that the German warship had been tracked after Bletchley had succeeded in cracking certain codes. But for the Germans not to suspect this, a pantomime was necessary. And so, hours before the ship was sunk, the RAF arranged for four reconnaissance planes to conduct a survey of that area of the ocean. When one of the planes 'spotted' the *Bismarck*, it was spotted in turn by the ship's crew, who alerted High Command. Thus it looked as if the vessel had been located by chance. A number of Bletchley's other intelligence tips also had to be made to look like the inspired sleuthing of spies and agents on the ground.

But the theory proposing that Coventry was sacrificed omits certain essential details. First, Churchill had left London for the country that afternoon before getting the message. When he was told that there might be a vast raid on London, his car turned back to the city. It was only when he returned to Whitehall in the evening that it was confirmed that the target was to be Coventry.

Moreover, the jammers of the navigation beams were apparently set to the wrong frequency, an error that was not corrected until the following month. It also happened to be the case that Coventry did have anti-aircraft defences. But in the face of such an onslaught, such defences would always be of only limited use. 'Coventry could never have been evacuated in time,' recalled WAAF Y Service operative Aileen Clayton. 'It would certainly have been a physical impossibility to get all the guns and searchlights needed for defence, as well as the fire engines and other equipment, moved from other places to the target zone . . . with the information that was available to us, there was no way in which the city and its people could have been saved from that suffering.'[3]

And so the centre of Coventry was consumed in flames, the molten lead of the gutters pouring hissing into the streams, the cathedral transformed into russet-glowing ruins. Some 558 men, women and children were killed, and thousands more were injured.

It is a subject that occupies Bletchley veterans to this day. Oliver Lawn – who, it should be remembered, worked on decrypting messages concerning German bomber flight paths – still thinks there is some ambiguity about the issue: 'You will find people going on both sides of that argument. Now that's a typical case. But there are other cities where the codes were broken in time and the bombs were diverted. Coventry is still controversial.

'The head of our section – Stuart Milner-Barry – felt that it was Churchill,' adds Mr Lawn. 'Milner-Barry felt it was *not* a delay in breaking the code.'

Another who took this view was Captain Frederick Winterbotham, who was there on the afternoon when it became apparent that the city would be bombed, and wrote that there was still a chance that a decision to evacuate Coventry could be taken:

There were, perhaps, four or five hours before the attack would arrive. It was a longish flight north and the enemy aircraft would not cross the coast before dark. I asked the personal secretary if he would be good enough to ring me back when the decision had been taken, because if Churchill decided to evacuate Coventry, the press, and indeed everybody, would know we had pre-knowledge of the raid and some counter-measure might be necessary to protect the source which would obviously become suspect.

It also seemed to me, sitting in my office a little weary after the sleepless bomb-torn night before, that there would be absolute chaos if everyone tried to get out of the city in the few hours available and that if, for any reason, the raid was postponed by weather or for some other reason, we should have put the source of our information at risk to no purpose.

I imagine the Prime Minister must have consulted a number of people before making up his mind. In any case, the RAF had ample time to put their counter-measures into action, such as jamming any of the aids to navigation that the Germans might be using. In the event, it was decided only to alert all the services, the fire, the ambulance, the police, the wardens, and to get everything ready to light the decoy fires. This is the sort of terrible decision that sometimes has to be made on the highest levels in war. It was unquestionably the right one.[4]

Oliver Lawn still finds himself musing on the subject: 'There were others who took other views. We will never know.' Perhaps so. But this was not the only instance in which Churchill and Bletchley Park were suspected of having connived to withhold information. Years after the Japanese launched their devastating surprise attack upon the US base of Pearl Harbor in Hawaii in December 1941, thus bringing the Americans into the war, it was suggested by some sources that Bletchley Park, through its work on the 'Purple' Japanese codes, had decrypted vital messages concerning Japanese military intentions. The allegation was that having seen such intelligence, Churchill ordered it to be suppressed so that the Americans would gain no advance warning, thus ensuring that the attack would bring the USA into the conflict.

In fact, British intelligence was anticipating an attack upon Malaya – there was no forecast of any strike against any American base. And there is one further point in the defence of Bletchley and the Prime Minister. During bombing raids carried out on British cities in the early months of 1941, the business of meddling with Luftwaffe navigational beams was much more successful; one night in May, twenty-three German fighters were brought down on Humberside. And a ferocious attack on Derby – planned to be on the same scale as Coventry – was largely thwarted.

Even so, in such situations it was often a matter of bluff and counter-bluff. According to a recent work by Rebecca Ratcliff, there were times when the cryptographers would receive irrefutable evidence of forthcoming bombing raids in certain locations.

During the Blitz of 1941, they worried in particular about air-raid counter-measures. Ordering the Air Raid Precautions (ARP) for the correct target well before the Luftwaffe bombers appeared in the sky would reveal foreknowledge of the bombing raid and jeopardise the intelligence source. The Hut 3 analysts directed that all ARP orders be postponed until the Germans began their raid preparations and turned on their radio guidance beams.

These beams led the Luftwaffe planes to their targets . . . In addition, the analysts suggested that ARP measures be ordered not only for the target revealed by Ultra but "in [other towns] also, preferably situated along the line of the . . . beam". Then, if the Germans heard about the ARP measures, they would assume the British had been warned by the beams, rather than by Enigma messages.[5]

Finally, Bletchley veteran Roy Jenkins – later Lord Jenkins of Hillhead and biographer of Churchill – observed that the attack on Coventry, while 'shattering its monuments and shops', ironically 'did less damage to its aircraft factories'. He also pointed out that a raid that took place over Birmingham barely a week later was far more lethal, resulting in 1,353 deaths.[6]

The same hideous moral dilemma implied in the treatment of Bletchley's information about the raid on Coventry was to apply throughout the war. By the spring of 1941, the Blitz was largely over, as Hitler turned his full attention east towards Russia. But there were still those in British Intelligence who believed that a Nazi invasion of British shores was imminent, and it suited German Intelligence to give such false indications to divert attention away from genuine plans.

It has also been said that Churchill and the British government knew of the systematic extermination of the Jews which by 1941 was gathering horrifying pace, with vast numbers of men, women and children being sent in cattle trucks to Auschwitz, Dachau, Treblinka and Sobibor. In August 1941, there were seventeen decrypts, over the period of eight days, of German police messages; they concerned the shootings of thousands of Jews.

In a radio broadcast given on 25 August, Churchill said: 'Whole districts are being exterminated. Scores of thousands, literally scores of thousands, of executions in cold blood are being perpetrated by the German police-troops upon the Russian patriots who defend their native soil. Since the Mongol invasions in the 16th century, there has never been methodical, merciless butchery on such a scale, or approaching such a scale . . . we are in the presence of a crime without a name.'

So why did Churchill not mention the Jews? The reason was that to have done so would have been to reveal to the Germans, once again, that their messages had been intercepted. It was all Churchill felt that he could do to let it be known – at last – that the Allies were aware of the multiplying atrocities, and would do everything in their power to stop them.

A little later, Bletchley was able to break into the codes dealing with German railways – the same railway lines that led to the concentration camps. To a certain extent, they were able to glean from these messages the forced deportation of waves of thousands upon thousands of people, the lines leading inexorably to these places of death. As some have seen it, railway lines are easy targets for bombers – they glitter in the moonlight. Should the Allies not at least have tried to cripple this infrastructure, to try and bring the deportations to an end?

The answer, it seems, was the same: nothing could be done that would betray the Bletchley secret. In any case, such efforts would have been little more than a temporary hindrance to the Nazis; a railway line can be easily repaired. It was more fruitful to aim for larger military and industrial targets. The only way that the horror could be halted – no matter how fine and detailed the intelligence – was by halting Hitler himself.

All this demonstrates Bletchley Park's fearful responsibilities. From 1942, the Abwehr section of Bletchley Park found itself decrypting tables which turned out to be SS returns on the numbers of people entering and dying in the camps; mass extermination reduced to chilly, efficient bureaucracy. To know exactly what the enemy is planning – to know just how many hundreds, thousands of lives will be extinguished, to know such things in advance from secret messages – now seems a burden too great to imagine.

Most of the codebreakers, of course, possessed no such knowledge, at least on a day-to-day basis; they dealt with fragments, fragments of fragments, random messages from hither and thither, before handing on the baton to the following shift. Nevertheless, they knew well the import of what they were doing. And for the senior codebreakers, and those who ran Bletchley Park, it must, at times, have been almost unbearable. As Josh Cooper's son Michael was later to recall of his father: 'His was the heroism of the long, hard slog and the burden of ugly, painful secrets.' We might also see traces of this strain in the terrible illness later suffered by Dilly Knox.

In domestic terms, given the sheer number of German bombing raids above central England – and the sheer profusion of railway lines around Bletchley at the time, pointing north, south, east and west – it seems something of a miracle that the Park itself only received two German bombs throughout the war. Both came on a single night – the same night, by coincidence, that Coventry was bombed for a second time, 21 November 1940.

The adjacent site of Elmers School, which had once housed Gordon Welchman, took a direct hit on the building's telephone exchange and typing room. Another bomb from the same drop came down between the house and Hut 4, and was said to have lifted the naval Enigma hut off its foundations. In truth, it may not have taken that much of an explosion to achieve this.

And another bomb landed in the stable yard, just yards away from the Cottage, where Dilly Knox and Mavis Lever were at work on the Italian naval Enigma. This bomb, however, failed to go off. A couple of others apparently fell and failed to go off as well. They are still somewhere in the grounds of the Park, though no one is quite sure where . . .

It has been noted by some that even though Bletchley was utterly secret, and therefore there was no specific reason to bomb it, the place was still incredibly lucky; for any returning bomber who still had some load to discharge might, on a cloudless night, have been drawn by the silvery lines of the rails running through the town, and used those as a target. Indeed, given Bletchley's geographical centrality, it is astonishing that it – and its associated signals stations across the county – weren't simply targeted randomly.

As a postscript, Sheila Lawn has a haunting memory of the nights a little later in the war when the Luftwaffe once more turned its attentions to London. It was one such night that made her realise just how blessed Bletchley was to have escaped such a furious onslaught.

'I do remember that the bombing of London resumed in 1944. That was when I was billeted with this elderly lady in the village. Now, I had a very nice bedroom and it looked over fifty miles, to London. And when they resumed the bombing, I could watch, at night, what looked like an amazing firework display. Flames leaping up and explosions in the sky. And I thought, the people who are there, how brave they are. What are they going to find in the morning? If they are alive in the morning.'

The disconcerting truth was that by the autumn of 1940, any progress made by Bletchley Park – no matter how ingenious – was still frustratingly slow. While there had been some success with military and air force codes, a way into the naval Enigma remained agonisingly elusive, as the German U-boat wolf packs threatened the convoys in ever more serious numbers. But the part the decoders had played in the Battle of Britain was merely a taster; as the work went on, it was not too long before Bletchley's contribution to the war effort started to have a lasting, definitive impact on the course of events.

12 Bletchley and the Class Question

'If you had a day off, you scurried up to London by the train,' says the Hon. Sarah Baring. 'Boyfriends or friends would be back from the war, and we'd always manage to keep in touch. And I tell you who used to do it for us. There was the most lovely man called Gibbs, who was the head hall porter at Claridges. And he knew exactly where all our boyfriends were. He used to say. "Hullo Miss, so-and-so is back, he was in yesterday." That's how we kept in touch.'

It is an image that one cannot help relishing for its cheering incongruity; in the middle of the blackout, the doorman of London's smartest hotel is still keeping the glittering gay young things informed of the whereabouts of their peers. It also prompts one to wonder how such blithe carryings-on were regarded by friends and colleagues of different backgrounds.

The personnel of Bletchley Park were initially drawn either from the intellectual or the social elite; young Cambridge mathematicians working alongside girls in pearls. According to Josh Cooper, some of the very first pearled girls were not at all suitable: 'There was an elderly and very imposing typist secretary whom the Section immediately nicknamed "Queen Mary". And a younger and rather promising recruit who made her position impossible, scandalising her Bletchley billetors by saying to all and sundry that the only friends she had ever had were Germans.'[1]

Of course, owing to outbreaks of Mitford foolishness in the 1930s – plus the recurring suspicion that certain members of the royal family were not quite so anti-German as they ought to be – the upper classes had more cause than most to be sensitive to other people's feelings on that subject. Generally, though, the first wave of titled girls and debutantes, including Sarah Baring, were staunch, occasionally flinty, patriotic in every degree and determined – possibly even more determined than anyone else, with a sharpened sense of noblesse oblige – to do their very best. Sarah Baring herself has lost none of that sense of the duty she felt she owed.

They also brought some rather colourful distraction. There was the example of Maxine Birley, later to become the Comtesse de la Falaise, who according to one Park veteran held 'unmissable parties . . . I remember her giving a party at which we all had to be very French.'

As numbers at the Park began to expand, a draft recruiting document (now in the archives) was drawn up for new staff. The intention was to send it out to 'all regional controllers' who had access to the Central Register. Not only does it give a fascinating insight into the way the Park was portrayed for security reasons, it opens an unintended window on to all sorts of thorny questions about class, and about how upper-class recruits should be treated:

We have been approached about vacancies for Temporary Assistants of the executive type in a branch of the Foreign Office in a country district of Bucks. The work is secret and particulars of its exact nature cannot be given. In the main, recruitment could in the first instance be limited to young women, but young men who are unfit for military service should not be excluded . . . candidates should be alert and distinctly above average in intelligence, and capacity for concentration and sustained effort is essential . . .

There may also be some people on the register who because of their social position would find it difficult to settle down in an ordinary office. This difficulty should not arise in the present instance and, while it may appear to be snobbish to have regard to considerations of this kind, the fact must be faced that those already in post in the establishment in question belong to a certain social grade and people who move in the same circles would more easily fit themselves into the present organisation.

Although the work is arduous, we are informed that the living conditions are comfortable and that the social amenities are pleasant.

As soon as the document crossed his desk, Alistair Denniston was swift to countermand it: 'The question of social status can now be disregarded as we have people from every type of life.' He added, perhaps as a slight giveaway: 'I should not like to stress our social amenities, though great efforts are made to help people pass their spare time as pleasantly as possible in such a place as Bletchley.'[2]

The Hon. Sarah Baring's own recollection is that in the Park at least, the different social classes rubbed along quite happily: 'Perhaps before the war, debutantes were never asked to do anything serious,' she says. 'When you land yourself in a place like that, it's pretty overpowering. There were people from all walks of life There were Wrens, there were girls like me, people in uniform, army, navy, air force and later on, of course, Americans. All classes were represented. Especially among the Wrens.'

She remembers the outburst of excitement that rippled outwards when her title was discovered: 'In terms of class tension, there was absolutely no trouble about that whatsoever. I'd been there about a year and a half at least when it got out that I was an Honourable. And I was frightfully embarrassed about this. Somebody came up to me and said: "Sarah! You're an Honourable!" I said, "No, I'm not really, I'm very dishonourable."'

In what might be a reference to the Mitford girls, Sarah Baring recalls thinking about the way that she was vetted for working at the Park: 'I presume that they must have done a little bit of work on one's background. Make sure that you weren't a . . . Because there were a lot of young girls at that time who were mad about going to Germany and thought that Hitler was really rather wonderful. Silly girls. I think they probably wanted to know that we weren't like that.'

If the community of Bletchley Park was ever taken as a cross-section of young British society of the day, then it does offer up some fascinating insights into the class structure of the time. These days, it is widely assumed that the end of deference, and the declining power of the old school tie, only began to manifest itself in the late 1950s and early 1960s. Yet there was clearly a humorous scepticism directed towards the ruling classes long before that. In the 1930s, P.G. Wodehouse's aristocratic dilettante Bertie Wooster was hugely popular among a wide readership, not because his readers wanted to doff their caps to him, but because he fitted precisely the popular perception of the upper-class idiot. The 1930s had given rise to an expanding middle class, and their intelligent children were now at Bletchley Park, exploring the shifting contours of this new class landscape. The posher ladies tended to end up doing some of the most fundamentally unglamorous and unstimulating work.

But, says middle-class Oliver Lawn, social status was not a subject that impinged greatly: 'I was not aware of it at all. I think a number of people – girls in Hut 6 – whom I got to know were probably of fairly high-class social standing. One or two of the people I worked with were probably towards the debs' class. But I wouldn't have known except that it is likely that they would have come in through that sort of influence or channel.'

Yet the opulent lives of the upper classes continued to exert – possibly against their will – a certain glamorous fascination, even if it was not consciously acknowledged. 'I was with a girl whose father was a lord or something but she was just one of us,' says Jean Valentine. 'Yet you did meet people from both above and below you, as it were, and it was OK. One girl had been evacuated to America at the start of the war, but when she reached eighteen, she came back in order to join up.

'There were others who were clearly a little more working-class. On the whole, it was a pretty middle-class society.'

That was not always the case. There was the extremely rare instance of social mobility, and at breakneck pace: this applies especially to MI6 agent Hugh Trevor-Roper, who often had dealings with Bletchley Park. A few years ago, in an interview, Trevor-Roper conjured an amusingly irritating image with his account of his visits to the Park: 'I went on hunting right through the early years of the war. Occasionally, when I had a staff car, I found it compatible with my conscience to make my visits to the Code and Cypher School at Bletchley Park coincide with my hunting days with the Whaddon.'[3]

In Bletchley, class tension did occasionally make itself evident. As Marion Hill records, one deb was particularly bemused by the class of girls who were sent to her for secretarial duties. 'I was given four or five girls as copy typists. One said when I was interviewing her, "Well, me name's Maudie, but I like being called Queenie. I did used to work at Fletton's but then I thought I'd better meself so I threw up the brickworks and went into the Co-op."'[4]

Balancing that was the occasional outbreak of what can only be described as jolly-hockey-sticks behaviour. One incident still makes the Hon. Sarah Baring laugh.

'At that young age, you do get very mischievous, I'm afraid,' she says. 'Specially when you're doing something which you think is a bit dreary at the time. We had a great friend called Jean Campbell Harris, who is now Lady Trumpington, she's in the House of Lords. She was always up for some merry larks and one night shift, we didn't have very much to do.

'The signals used to arrive in enormous laundry baskets. And we'd taken them all out and got them pretty well finished, but the Watch wasn't quite over yet. So we said: "Jean, get in the laundry

basket now it's empty and we'll give you a ride down to the loos."
They were at the end of this terrible passage.

'And so she got in,' she continues, 'and of course, we lost her
because she was quite heavy, darling Jean, and she went straight
down this long corridor, straight into the gents' loo. The embarrassment! Though I think it must have been much more
embarrassing for the gentlemen.'

Having said that, she emphasises that high jinks went hand in
hand with a deep seriousness of purpose: 'We really were conscious
of what we were doing, we knew how important it was. We were
pretty good actually. I'm making out that we were silly little girls. But
actually we weren't. We did work incredibly hard.'

Elsewhere, for some at the Park, outward appearances were
important, although not to the same degree as they are today. 'We
were never scruffy, we kept up appearances, and that was true of
everyone during the war,' says Mavis Batey. (Not quite: the men,
such as Turing and Cooper and Knox, were allowed all sorts of sar-
torial transgressions, from intense scruffiness to the wearing of
pyjamas in the office. One Bletchley contemporary recalls Turing
looking 'like a tramp', with trousers held up not with a belt but a
striped necktie. His grooming too was on the neglectful side: he
had a permanent five o'clock shadow caused by his reluctance to
shave with anything other than an old electric razor; his fingernails
were chewed to a point where small scars would be left on the very
tips of his fingers; and even though he did not smoke, he none the
less contrived to have yellow teeth. Angus Wilson in contrast had
his blue shirts and apricot bow-ties, as well as artistically long hair;
quite the thing in raffish Hampstead, where he had lived for a
while, but the cause of a little local consternation in this small
country town.)

But how exactly did Mrs Batey and all those other women keep
themselves looking presentable and respectable? Bletchley was a
small town – frock shops and hairdressers were extremely thin on
the ground.

When it came to matters of hair, a salon called E. & G. Wesley, of High Street, Woburn Sands (several miles away), was rather cunning about cornering the Park market. After a period of correspondence with the Bletchley authorities, they set up a new branch of the salon in Hut 23.

It was open 'weekdays 10 a.m. – 5.45 p.m. (not Wednesdays)'. Men could have a simple haircut, or a shampoo too, for one shilling. For women, there was the choice of a simple trim, a "shampoo and set", or a "Trim, shampoo and set", which would have cost four shillings and sixpence for civilians, and three shillings and ninepence for those in uniform.

Customers, however, had to provide their own towels. 'The position regarding towels is very serious,' wrote Mr Wesley to Commander Bradshaw. 'The shortage being very acute.'[5]

Hairdresser Mr Wesley presumably had to undergo security vetting as thorough as everyone else. But the idea of bringing such a service into the Park was ingenious; even the nearest salons were scattered around the countryside, and in towns such as Bedford which were a step or two too far away.

Everything, of course, was in short supply, especially clothes. Mimi Callilee recalls with horrified vividness the occasion on which she borrowed her older sister's smart frock, hoping to be able to put it back afterwards without her sister realising that it had gone. This turned out to be a forlorn hope – Mimi had to deliver a message to Hut 10, where her sister worked, and her sister saw her wearing it. The ensuing row was volcanic. Given that clothing was so severely rationed, and that the coupons barely bought synthetic stockings, let alone dresses, the possessiveness is quite understandable.

There was something levelling about 'make do and mend', at least in theory – though the girls from more privileged backgrounds had more material to work on in the first place. Nevertheless, many of these upper-class girls were keen not to be seen as ostentatious; they wanted people to see that they could hunker down with everyone else and accept their duties – and attendant privations –

without complaint. It was a fine national moment of class cohesion – or at least, as close as Britain would ever get to it. For as soon as the war ended, the change was astonishingly rapid.

One might argue that in Britain at any rate, the Second World War was the last high tide of the aristocracy. From the young Princess Elizabeth joining up with the ATS and getting under the bonnet of a truck, to the double-barrelled young ladies with pearls quietly going about their administrative duties at Bletchley and in the Admiralty, this was a time when family name and connections opened every door imaginable. That is not to say that this does not happen now; of course it does. But one would very rarely now hear such privileged people being described anywhere as 'the quality', and one would also rarely hear that they were noted for their abiding sense of duty and loyalty to the nation.

In questions of politics, as in many other things, Bletchley Park seemed a microcosm of the nation as a whole. Change was clearly in the air. Evelyn Waugh's *Brideshead Revisited* (1945) was a cry of mourning for the passing of an aristocratic way of life. The opening chapter of that novel saw Charles Ryder returning to a house that he had once seen in very different, rather more gracious circumstances, and which was now requisitioned by the army. In real life, this was the case up and down the country. Yet there was still a smart set. And unless one was born into it, one on the whole never caught sight of it.

Similarly, most of the young people who worked at Bletchley would only ever have read about the aristocracy. Certainly they would have been highly unlikely in any other circumstances to meet such rarefied creatures, while the smart 'gels' who volunteered their services would only have had the patchiest idea about the lives of those alongside whom they were now working.

But Bletchley represented the last gasp of the notion of the smarter set and their sense of mucking in and doing what one could, just as it represented in miniature the oncoming triumph of the middle classes: the classes for whom the old snobberies were being cast aside, not merely in the interests of the nation pulling together, but because they had read Orwell and Priestley and understood the terrible privations suffered by so many in the 1930s, and were determined that a better country should come of this.

When Captain Eric Jones was put in charge of Hut 3, everyone who worked with him could not help remarking on his Cheshire vowels and indeed the source of his wealth ('. . . His qualifications for the post were not immediately apparent. He was a wholesale cloth merchant from Macclesfield,' wrote William Millward. Peter Calvocoressi thought that he had been 'something in biscuits') – but, crucially, these same people stressed how brilliant he was in the role. All who worked with Captain Jones (later to become Sir Eric) were full of praise for his strong principles and the strength of character that enabled him to deal smoothly with 'tiresome intrigues and controversies', as Millward put it.

The point they seemed to be making – only slightly patronisingly – was that Jones's background was an indicator of quiet strength, and that he was the reverse of a chinless wonder. And in contrast to the pre-war Foreign Office days, when recruits tended to be plucked from the more privileged classes, Jones was one of the men who was to form the post-war establishment, going on to head the successor to Bletchley Park, the Government Communications Headquarters (GCHQ).

Even if they could not have known it, these young cryptographers, from the minor public schools and the grammar schools, and their peers, were set to become the dominating voices of the new age. And by 1941, the nature of the conflict was changing, intensifying further; for Bletchley, it would prove a crucial year in which Britain's fortunes were ever more vulnerable. For all those who worked at the Park, it was a time of both exhaustion and occasionally elation.

13 1941: The Battle of the Atlantic

As the war widened and unfolded, the importance of Bletchley Park's work – and the concomitant pressure to get every tiny detail absolutely right – increased accordingly. In 1941, during the Battle of the Atlantic, German spies in various ports reported back to German High Command that a vast British convoy, comprising thirteen cargo boats, four tankers and ships carrying innumerable aircraft parts, was sailing off the coast of Africa. This message to Hitler was sent by radio – meaning that it was also picked up by British Signals Intelligence. It was decoded at Bletchley perhaps even before German High Command got to read it. As a result, the British convoy was alerted to the imminent German danger and was able to take evasive action.

The nightmare dangers that the Atlantic convoys faced were all too easy for those back home to imagine; the vessel ruthlessly stalked by U-boats, torpedoed, with countless crew and sometimes civilian passengers perishing in the dagger-cold ocean waters. Anxiety over the peril to supplies was matched by the ache of sympathy for the men out on those seas. So a naval victory of any sort always proved to be an effective morale booster back in Britain.

There was an important lifting of spirits at sea in March 1941

thanks in great part to Mavis Batey, who had been working with Dilly
Knox in the Cottage on the Italian Enigma. Mrs Batey recalls with
a smile how Knox was brilliant at getting people to look at problems
from unexpected angles. 'Dilly would ask: "Which way do the hands
on a clock go round?" One might say clockwise. But Knox would
reply that that would depend on whether one was the observer, or
the clock.'

And this lateral approach was applied to Enigma. Mrs Batey still
has the 'rods' that were used to work out the order of the wheels
inside the machine, and the starting position of those wheels for the
message being cracked. But the rods were not much use unless the
person employing them had a lively intelligence; and it was deep
into one September night in 1940 that Mrs Batey had first found
her way into the code, by guessing that the first word of a particular message, for which they thought they had the letters PERX, was
in fact PERSONALE – 'personal'.

That gave her a start, yielding up two or three more potential letters within the message. A night's worth of infinitely patient and
extraordinarily focused work later, and Mrs Batey had identified the
wheel order and the message setting. It was a brilliant feat of inspiration and perseverance.

Now, in the spring of 1941, it was this same light-touch but
inspired approach that cracked a message to an Italian naval commander; 'Today 25 March is X–3.' As Mrs Batey says now, 'If you get
a message saying "today minus three", then you know that something pretty big is afoot.'

It was. Subsequent, more specific messages came in. Mavis
worked through shift after shift, not leaving the Cottage. And then:
'It was eleven o'clock at night, and it was pouring with rain when I
rushed, ran, absolutely tore down to take it to Intelligence, to get it
across to Admiral Cunningham.'

After some work, intelligence analysts deduced from the message
that the Italian fleet was planning to attack British troop convoys
sailing from Alexandria to Piraeus in Greece. Admiral Cunningham

was in charge of the operation that explosively ambushed four Italian destroyers and four cruisers off the coast of Sicily. From the point of view of the Italians, the British had sailed up out of nowhere.

It was a spectacular coup, as Admiral John Godfrey, Director of Naval Intelligence, was keen to tell Bletchley Park. He rang with a message: 'Tell Dilly that we have won a great victory in the Mediterranean and it is entirely due to him and his girls.'

Mrs Batey illustrates vividly how, when something of vital importance was going on, the codebreakers would not budge until their job was done. 'Finally,' she says, 'the work was finished in the middle of the night after three nights.'

Mrs Batey is modest about her pivotal role. 'It was the Italians' errors that gave the game away,' she says. 'Our eyes were so used to picking things out. I got a long message and it didn't have a single "L" in it. The Italians only ever sent out a few telegrams, so the very idea that they were sending messages out automatically gave you the signal that they were going to do something for a change.

'And so they sent out dummy messages all the time so it would look like a uniform transmission. And of course, what this Italian chap had done was just to sit with his finger on "L", smoking a fag, the biggest crib there ever was.

'A message that long that contained only "L"s! That actually broke one of the wheels of the Italian Enigma machine.'

Another 1941 sea battle of some significance to Bletchley took place inside the Arctic Circle, and featured a British attack on German ships. The real target was a trawler called *Krebs*; for it was known that on board this vessel was an Enigma machine, which could prove invaluable for breaking into those almost impossible German naval codes. The German captain, sensing the danger, threw the Enigma machine overboard into the freezing ocean, but he was killed before he had a chance to destroy his coding documents and bigram tables. The vital documents and tables were retrieved, eventually taken back to Bletchley and pieced together.

Then, even more brilliantly, came the episode of the U-110. This was the U-boat that had, in the first few days of the war, caused widespread public horror by torpedoing and sinking the passenger ship *Athenia*. Now the U-110 was itself depth-charged and captured in the Atlantic. The captain, Julius Lemp, was unable to prevent the British from seizing vital Enigma material, including bigram tables. These in turn were rushed back to Bletchley. The submarine was being towed to Iceland when it sank; the crew who had torpedoed and drowned so many sailors were now themselves lost. But it was from these courageous naval operations that grew Bletchley's outstanding achievement – the breaking of the notoriously unbreakable naval Enigma.

Even back in 1940, Alistair Denniston had remarked to Head of Naval Section Frank Birch that 'You know, the Germans don't mean you to read their stuff, and I don't suppose you ever will.' However, from these tables, and other data, Alan Turing calculated a new method into the codes, which became termed 'Banburismus' – in essence, as his Hut 8 colleague and sometime fiancée Joan Murray recalled, it involved 'punched holes on long sheets of paper, made at Banbury'.

Often on the night shifts, recalled Joan Murray, 'around midnight was a particularly interesting time, since the German Naval keys changed at midnight, but results of analysis of most of a day's traffic began to reach us before then.'[1] The result, she recalled, was that very often people were too absorbed at the end of the shift – like Mavis Lever – to even think of going home. Instead, they preferred to stay on and carry on working with the following shift.

And the effect it began to have on the course of the war was almost incalculable. In the first few months of 1941, U-boat attacks on the convoys had meant that Britain was facing a catastrophic shortfall of imported food; if the submarines could not be thwarted, there would literally not be enough to feed the population. On top of this, there would not be enough imported oil for war production to continue. Now, according to Jack Copeland, convoy re-routings 'based on Hut 8 decrypts were so successful that for the first twenty-three days [of June], the north Atlantic U-boats made not a single sighting of a convoy'.[2]

In the midst of these events, Joan Murray gave a short description of Alan Turing, and his own gentle abstraction. 'I can remember Alan Turing coming in as usual for a day's leave,' she wrote, 'doing his own mathematical research at night, in the warmth and light of the office, without interrupting the routine of daytime sleep.' Another veteran recalls Turing's abstraction when being congrat-ulated for his work by a senior ranking officer, while later, Hugh Alexander was to say of Turing's role that 'Turing thought it [naval Enigma] could be broken because it would be so interesting to break it . . . Turing first got interested in the problem for the typi-cal reason that "no one else was doing anything about it and I could have it to myself."'[3]

No better example then, of the partnership between unfettered mathematical inquiry and the national interest. For much of that summer, Bletchley was able to read the majority of German naval Enigma messages, and in so doing could provide protection beyond value to British shipping. In the days before either America or Russia had joined the conflict, and when Britain was standing quite alone, this feat could easily be counted as one of the decisive points in the war.

There were other examples in 1941 of just how vital the work at Bletchley was. It was entirely thanks to the decoders that the British were forewarned of the German intention to target not Malta – despite the false impression the Germans were trying to give – but Crete. In spite of this advance warning, Crete was to fall, but the warning did perhaps help with the evacuation of some 17,000 troops. Elsewhere, similarly, amid the generally dispiriting progress of the war in Africa, an Enigma decrypt concerning the size and for-mation of Rommel's forces at the Halfaya Pass on the Egyptian border offered at least the consolation prize of enabling the British forces to escape being crushed.

There was also the fantastic coup of the *Bismarck*. In May 1941, this mighty and formidable battleship, commanded by Admiral Lutjens, had sunk the British vessel HMS *Hood*. Out of the crew of 2,500 men, only three survived. A few days later the Royal Navy had, with the help of Bletchley, tracked the position of the *Bismarck*. In an effort to conceal the fact that the signals had been intercepted, it was arranged for the air force to fly two or three reconnaissance planes over the area, to give the *Bismarck*'s crew the impression that this was how they had been spotted.

In fact, the Bletchley Park intercepts had been the result of a certain amount of serendipity. Jane Fawcett MBE was there as the scenario unfolded. She recalls:

'I was in Hut 6 and on the occasion of the *Bismarck* codes, I worked a 24-hour shift all the way through. We intercepted a message from one of the senior military commanders in Berlin – he was asking German High Command for the whereabouts of the *Bismarck* because his son was on board. His message went: "Where is my son?" And the message back told him. The *Bismarck* was at Brest.' Interestingly, in 1974, the late Diana Plowman made an inscription for the benefit of her family in her copy of Frederick Winterbotham's book. In this inscription, she gave a miniature portrait of life at the Park. And at the very end – again, solely for the benefit of her relatives – she wrote: 'But the Bismarck was my own special piece of luck.'

After the message was intercepted, a ring of British warships attacked the *Bismarck*. In all, 2,300 of its crew drowned. The mighty symbol of the strength of the German navy was scuttled. The effect in Germany was serious. One senior Reich figure observed: 'The Führer is melancholy beyond words.'

The activity prior to this great triumph had been similarly intense in Hut 4. One veteran recalls cots, or small camp beds, being moved in so that the personnel concerned would never be far from developments. One codebreaker, Walter Ettinghausen, spent forty-eight hours in the hut; he eventually emerged, 'unkempt and unshaven', and announced to his colleagues that 'the *Bismarck* had finally been chased down'.

Perhaps appropriately, given the centrality of the conflict at sea, there was now a distinctly naval flavour to the personnel at Bletchley Park. This chiefly took the form of the Women's Royal Navy volunteers, the first of whom were just starting to arrive. Ruth Bourne was such a young woman, although pleasingly, she was a little less impressed with the central notion of Bletchley than her commanding officers seemed to be.

'When we were called up, we had to go to training camp,' she says. 'And even though I lived and volunteered in Birmingham, we were sent all the way up to a castle called Balloch, outside of Glasgow. And there was what had been a farm called Tallyhewen and this farm was turned into a Wrens' training camp.

'And that's where we spent the first three weeks doing naval training – salutes, square bashing, cleaning out the ablutions. Organising concert parties, whatever you wanted to do in your leisure. Then at the end of that period, there was a mustering process and people were told what they were going to do.

'A group of us were told we were going to do SDX – and that was connected to joining a 'ship' called HMS *Pembroke* 5, which was later on shortened to P5. Anyone who was P5 was doing bombe operating and codebreaking and so on. But we didn't know that then.

'Eventually when we were brought in to see the Petty Officer, we were told that this was highly secret work – if we entered into it, we would not be able to leave it.'

There was that one tiny opportunity to back out if the idea seemed utterly uncongenial. 'At that stage, we could have opted out, but no one ever did,' says Ruth. 'And then when we'd been told that, we were taken somewhere else and asked to sign the Official Secrets Act and then we were taken into what was known as B-Block, which was a huge block eventually where we finished up. My strongest memory is of the Chief Petty Officer saying "We are breaking German codes" with a kind of triumphant smile.'

As Diane Payne recalled in an essay, it was often difficult to explain to loved ones exactly why one wasn't on board a ship, as one had signed up to be:

> My pay amounted to thirty shillings a week as an ordinary Wren, rising to £4 10s when I later became a Petty Officer. We had no category badges, and were supposed to say, if asked, that we were just 'writers'. Sometimes it was very difficult having so little to say about one's life, and this explanation did not always satisfy relatives and friends, so my wartime activities were considered unimportant and something of a failure.

By now, the numbers working at the Park were expanding as the decrypting grew steadily more successful and reliable. As historian and codebreaker Asa Briggs succinctly put it: 'I'd never seen so many women in my life!'[4] Often, when looking out from her office on the first floor of the house, over the lawn and the lake, recalls Mimi Gallilee, one could see, at shift changeover time, 'a great sea of bodies. All these people going to and from the coaches that would ferry them to their billets in the outlying villages. Countless people, all milling about – it was a magnificent sight.'

Around this time, Bletchley was using so-called 'Hollerith Machines', mighty efforts that processed punch-cards, another logic-based means into some of the codes. And it was obvious that it would be better to have these machines operated by people who knew how they worked. One such group were very loosely termed 'The Lewis Ladies'.

The Park authorities had, in their search for Hollerith personnel, turned to the retail firm John Lewis; it used similar punch-card machines, and had women specially trained to use them. Making a plea via the Ministry for Labour and National Service, the Park interviewed fifty of these young women, and selected ten. To the fury of the Park authorities, the Ministry suddenly withdrew the offer and allocated the John Lewis women to land work instead. Vinegary memos passed back and forth. One read: 'The John Lewis episode is a disgrace.'

The fight between Bletchley Park and the monolithic bureaucracy grew so rancorous that eventually Churchill got to hear of it. As recorded in one Park memo, 'the shortage of personnel reached the ears of the PM who directed Ismay to render an immediate report on the shortage of female personnel.'

It was a significant problem, as another memo from September 1941 makes clear: 'We have had some very considerable difficulty in recruitment, especially women clerks, and we are now considerably underborne with the result that some very important jobs are being held up.'

Some women – even if headhunted for positions – seemed most reluctant to do their bit. This letter, from a Whitehall acquaintance of Denniston's, concerning a potential female recruit, illustrated the problem vividly: 'the lady didn't want to go to BP as she thought the specialised work there would not fit her, particularly for administrative work after the war . . . Waterfield [the recruiter] is in a rage and is apparently calling for the lady again to tell her it must be BP or nothing.'[5]

The lady concerned might have had a point. Some of the females who did make it to Bletchley seem to have initially regretted doing so. Certainly, the massive influx of Wrens into the town created an enormous amount of strain. One Superintendent E. Blagrove wrote: 'There were many difficulties in the early days in the struggle to live. Ration cards failed to appear, the bath and laundry situation caused many headaches, medical and dental arrangements had to be organised and the problem of billets was always cropping up.'[6]

The conditions of the work could seem at first rather heart-sinking too. Codebreaker Diana Plowman recalled: 'The Hut next to mine was flanked on each side by great flanks of teleprinters manned by Wrens. Tho' I wasn't supposed to see. Security was so great we might have been in a prison camp.'

However, as Superintendent Blagrove reported, a rather more positive frame of mind began to become apparent among the girls: 'There was a magnificent spirit among these pioneers and wherever they turned they found great co-operation and many helping hands. The stimulation was the knowledge of the essential work on which they were employed.

'Their keenness to do well and their enthusiasm was the inspiration for all who came later. These ratings were destined to be the future officers and chief wrens of their section.'

14 Food, Booze and Too Much Tea

If an army marches on its stomach, then it would also seem to be the case that the most absent-minded and eccentric of boffins and linguists decrypted on theirs. One of the subjects that seems to cause the sharpest polarisation in views of Bletchley Park is neither the pressure of the work, nor the tension of keeping it secret – but the quality of the food (and indeed of the drink) that was on offer.

And this is perhaps not surprising. In a time of severe rationing, it was only natural that young appetites would be sharpened. And the taste, smell and texture of food is one of those things, like scents, that have the power to bring old memories sharply into focus. Just as Evelyn Waugh's son Auberon recalled that an intense feature of his post-wartime childhood was the very occasional manifestation of bananas, so Bletchley Park veterans now find themselves amused to think back to the food that they were served up on both day and night shifts. One might think that in such a rarefied, cerebral atmosphere, that food would be low on the list of daily concerns. But it wasn't.

'The food was *disgusting*,' declares Sarah Baring. She elaborated vividly in her personal memoir of life at the Park:

We thought a lot about food. Night watches were especially vulnerable to rumbling tummies and usually forced us to go down to the canteen at 3 a.m., where the food was indescribably awful. It is a well-known fact that to cater for so many people is difficult, and particularly in wartime . . . but our canteen outshone any sleazy restaurant in producing sludge and the smell of watery cabbage and stale fat regularly afflicted the nostrils to the point of nausea.

One night I found a cooked cockroach nestling in my meat, if you can dignify it by that name, the meat not the beetle. I was about to return it to the catering manageress when my friend Osla, who had the appetite of a lioness with cubs, snatched the plate and said: 'What a waste – I'll eat it!' How she managed to eat so much – minus the insect – and stay so slim I never knew, because any leftovers on any nearby plate were gobbled up by her in a flash.

Oliver Lawn recalls differently, though his endorsement does not quite add up to faint praise: 'Andrew Hodges, in his biography of Turing, talks about the "poor food" at Bletchley Park. Which I didn't agree with. I thought it was all right: wartime food, rationing, all the rest of it. But it wasn't as bad as he has painted it.' Another veteran said: 'A lot of people complained about the meals but I thought they were wonderful.'

When the war began in 1939, meals were taken in the house itself; the then head of SIS, Admiral Hugh Sinclair, arranged stylishly for a professional chef to be brought in from the Ritz, and there was waitress service at the tables, as Mimi Gallilee remembers well, since for a short time her own mother was one such waitress.

Even then, however, there was no such thing as a free luncheon. In October 1939, the first of many nit-picking internal memos concerning catering arrangements and tea breaks was circulated to staff. 'There is no obligation for anyone to take lunch at the war

site,' the management memo stated. 'But those who do must understand that the rates charged apply for the whole month.'
Furthermore, 'all GC and CS personnel are requested to pay their
lunch money to Miss Reid, room 38.'

And that unusual and generous bonus of exquisitely prepared
food was not sustainable. In the first place, the Ritz chef in question
was a troubled soul who tried to commit suicide. He did not last
long at Bletchley Park. Second, as numbers at the Park steadily grew,
this method of catering was less and less practical; although another
Bletchley veteran, Jean Valentine, recalls that the ground floor was
used for quite a while for 'self-service cafeteria' purposes – quite a
novelty to a young Scots girl unacquainted with such modern ways.
Later there was to follow a large purpose-built canteen, the wares of
which were to divide opinion sharply.

Given the shortages of meat, of butter, of sugar, of practically
everything, it would have been a tall order to expect the canteen
staff to produce works of culinary genius. But reactions might also
have had a little to do with one's upbringing: for instance, if one
hailed from the north of Scotland, where the food tended towards
the plain and hearty and filling, then there may have been some
comfort to draw from the Bletchley efforts.

For instance, one wartime dish, Woolton Pie – named after its
inventor, Lord Woolton, and involving substantial amounts of potatoes, turnips and other bland vegetables – was rather popular with
some of the Bletchley Park veterans. It might have been plain and
tending towards the tasteless, but it was also gratifyingly filling.

One Scottish lady who was not so impressed was Irene Young,
who recorded these views in her memoirs: 'The food was not particularly appetising – I remember with especial distaste the packeted
pastry fruit pies which we called "cardboard tarts" – but then, few
expected delectable food in wartime.'

Just because it tasted of nothing didn't lessen demand, however,
as she wrote: 'Some people, though, were very hungry, and second
helpings were not allowed. I recollect one girl putting on dark

glasses as a disguise in the hope that she would be luckier than Oliver Twist. She was similarly rebuffed.'[1]

An admonishing official memo from the Park authorities to all personnel put the issue in sharp relief. 'Everyone should collect their own helpings from the counter, one course at a time. No second helpings can be given,' it declared, going on to explain the parameters of what constituted a helping. 'A Welsh rarebit or cheese dish with vegetables or salad is classed as a main dish.'[2]

And yet it wasn't all cheese dishes and cardboard tarts. Bletchley Park did have more access to meat – local, it has been suggested – than many other establishments. The same was true of vegetables – even though, as one memo from Alistair Denniston pointed out plaintively, 'competition from the railways and the factories has increased our difficulties' in terms of getting fresh produce. Jean Valentine recalls: 'The food was great at BP. I am open to correction. But I think there was a vegetable garden just over the stone wall. Whether they still grew vegetables there I don't know, but that is certainly what happened when the Leons owned the house.'

And Sheila Lawn found herself comparing it favourably with the competition on offer in the town: 'One day, I went to see a film, and then, I was hungry, so I went into what was called the British Restaurant. And I thought: "This isn't half as good as our canteen." I thought it was a terribly dull meal.' But one might also see that a week of working night shifts would turn tastes, as well as sleep patterns, upside down.

The canteen itself is remembered by many for its egalitarian atmosphere. Diana Plowman observed: 'There was a huge cafeteria where one could eat breakfast (exhausted) with an Admiral on one side and an American Colonel on the other.'

There was a lounge area within the house in which anyone could take a quick break of tea or coffee. Happily there were fewer complaints about authenticity on this front. One veteran said: 'We got real coffee – it came in those sealed tins. Lyons, I think.' Yet the subject of tea, and tea breaks – those perennial marker buoys of all things British – proved a reliable source of controversy at the Park. Quite early on, a peevish memo was sent out to all personnel: 'It is regretted that owing to losses, it is no longer possible to provide service crockery for morning and afternoon teas . . . those wanting tea must provide their own gear . . . all service cups, saucers and spoons are to be returned to the kitchen by Tuesday 13th Feb.'[3]

Among his many eccentricities, Alan Turing was known to chain his tea mug firmly to a radiator. According to Andrew Hodges, people would then pick the lock and steal the mug to tease him. Hodges claims that Turing's logic was impeccable; such mugs during the war were in short supply. So why not take good care of your only good one? This memo places Turing's mug in its proper context. Clearly he was anxious that it would otherwise be removed by officialdom.

But crockery friction did not end there. Captain Ridley sent out another memo in which he practically levitated with indignation. 'The breakage and loss of tea-cups, tumblers, knives and forks is taking place on a fantastic scale. The rate of loss is no less than five times that normally experienced in a man-of-war. Tumblers, cups and plates,' he added crossly, 'have been found pushed away into the shrubberies and left about in offices, many of them broken.' Only the most extreme measures would do. 'The watchmen have orders to stop anyone carrying government crockery away from the dining room.'[4] Despite this, Mimi Gallilee remembered of Josh Cooper: 'When he had his coffee, he used to amble along, in old grey suits, all loose, his hands going in his hair. He would go round the lake, finish his coffee there – and then throw the cup into the lake.'

The wastage of crockery was not the only problem. Tea breaks also raised a matter so serious that a memo came from Alistair Denniston. 'A considerable time is wasted every forenoon and afternoon by persons congregating in the dining hall for the purpose of taking tea,' he wrote. 'Heads of section should arrange that one junior member of their sections is sent to collect jugs of tea, milk etc.'[5]

His strictures may have caught attention for a while but a year later, the Park's senior men were forced to return to the subject. 'Owing to the time taken in collecting afternoon teas,' one memo went, 'arrangements are being made to obtain a limited number of tea urns which will be supplied to heads of larger sections . . . these urns,' the memo added, clearly for encouragement, 'have a capacity of about 70 cups.'

For a teenager like Mimi Gallilee, there were other food priorities, which the war made extremely difficult to satisfy. She recalls: 'Everything was rationed and you couldn't walk into a sweet shop unless you had some of your sweet coupons left – and need I tell you, mine would go in the first week! That was the month's worth.'

A couple of veterans recall that in the later stages of the war, a NAAFI van would periodically turn up at the edge of the Park – its arrival would especially be noted by those within the house – to be greeted with enthusiasm similar to that of six-year-olds crowding round an ice cream van. This one, however, specialised in such delicacies as chocolate and cigarettes, both very rare commodities at the time.

Cigarettes were especially sought after; this was a more innocent age in which most adults smoked. The scarcity of tobacco led some to try other brands, sometimes American; but these were deemed inferior to more familiar products such as Black Cat and Passing Clouds.

Eschewing the allure of the canteen, Gordon Welchman would often duck into the town of Bletchley for some fish and chips, which he recalled as being especially good, although thanks to shortages, one sometimes had to provide one's own newspaper in which to wrap them. Bletchley caterers offered other lures: one could, apparently, procure ox heart at the Station Inn, though it was 'very pricey'. The railway station itself boasted a buffet – 'a gloomy place, almost a replica of the film set for *Brief Encounter*', said Irene Young. And the coffee was akin to snake venom.

Back at the Park, there were comforts other than food on offer. Beer was available from Hut 2. Staff on their breaks could come here and indulge in general (never work) chit-chat – or indeed anything else that might break the knot of tension. In the early days, people also went to Hut 2 for afternoon teas and coffees, while a tiny library was also provided. According to one veteran, as staffing levels at the Park crept up, so Hut 2 became almost intolerably popular: 'There were times when if one wanted to move down the central corridor, one had to shuffle sideways.' Eventually, the tea operation was moved to the purpose-built canteen, and the library inside the big house.

Occasionally there were transgressions, such as the time when Alan Turing established a barrel of cider in the corner of Hut 4, and was informed in unambiguous terms that it was not to stay there. Others managed to secrete barrels of beer in their billets and spend summer evenings consuming it by the jug. On top of that, the men tended to favour the very many local pubs in the vicinity, though even here there was rationing and shortages. One veteran recalled how whisky became a rarity and thirsts had to be slaked with sherry instead, a most unsatisfactory substitute.

Sarah Baring vividly recalls how she was introduced to alcohol at Bletchley Park:

There was the Recreation Club. My friend Osla and I were too shy at first to apply for membership, but eventually plucked up courage, hoping to be treated to a glass of beer when as applicants we were considered suitable. I am sure everybody was welcome, but we didn't know it at the time. It was in this Recreational Hut or Beer Hut as it was commonly known that I was first introduced to alcoholic spirits.

It was something called Dutch Gin, a pale yellow oily looking liquid. I practically burst into flames at the first sip, like a volcanic eruption, but as it sank lower into my system, my stomach produced a warm glow and I promptly took another swig . . .

The night shifts proved to many to be the most wearing, not only in terms of work but of refreshment. Tea was stewed until bright orange – and milk was often of the 'dried' variety, which tended to produce big, unappetising lumps. There were also digestion issues after eating cheese and piccalilli or even prunes in the middle of the night. Jean Valentine found that working to such a strict rota had unexpected side-effects. 'It's the disturbing of your stomach. When you wake up in the morning, normally you have breakfast. But after a night shift, you wake up and have your evening meal. In other words, you come off at eight, go to bed, and when you get up at five or six, it's the evening meal that's laid on, so you are having an evening meal for breakfast. Most people suffered slightly bumpy tummies.'

But she adds: 'The food was very good – and compared to what I got later on a boat over to Ceylon [codebreaking in the Far East], it was magnificent, laid out in cafeteria fashion which we had never come across until then. If you went out for a meal, you sat down and somebody served you. Here, you went and served yourself, which I had never seen before. It was a whole new world. Everything was different.'

And whatever the complaints, there was a bright side. Since the war, it has been proved time and again that whatever the privations, and no matter how irksome the shortages of butter, sugar and meat were, the wartime diet was possibly the healthiest that the British have ever consumed.

15 1941: The Wrens and their Larks

As the numbers of Wrens at the Park grew from hundreds into thousands, their increasing presence also subtly changed the atmosphere of the place. Photographs of these girls in uniform, taken on what seem to be perpetually sunny days in Buckinghamshire, show not only a freshness, but also a good-humoured, no-nonsense expression in so many of their faces.

Despite the discomforts and privations and the relative lack of freedom – or perhaps because for many working-class girls, this life actually presented *more* freedom – there seemed a general sense of satisfaction, the knowledge that they were fundamentally doing their bit.

For Jean Valentine, who grew up in the Scottish town of Perth, and who turned eighteen in the later years of the war, joining up was a matter of patriotic duty, although she believes that her own recruitment for work on Turing's bombes was an administrative mistake; for crucially, at just over five foot, she was, according to Bletchley guidelines, too short (indeed, when Jean's work on the machines began – once she knew the secret, there was no question of opting out – she had to use a special stool to reach the highest drums). Like so many young women during those years, she was acutely aware of the need to contribute in the most solid and practical way possible. It was not enough to stay at home. She now recalls:

'I got to be eighteen and I thought, if I don't hurry up and do something positive apart from a bit of firewatching and working in a soldiers' canteen . . . then I might end up in a munitions factory. Or on the land. Neither of which was my cup of tea.

'So one day, I was going down to Carnoustie, near Dundee, to visit my aunt. I had some time to spare so I wandered off into the city. I saw an office which was a recruiting centre for the navy, so I popped in. They gave me an intelligence test and said, "You'll be hearing from us."'

Like linguist Sheila Lawn, Jean Valentine had never before left her native land. Her upbringing was comfortable, middle-class – her father had businesses in Perth, one of which, Valentine's Motors, is still remembered fondly by the townspeople today. Jean was aware that she was signing up for a life radically different from the one she had known. Thanks to that administrative mix-up, she was heading into a career of helping to crack the Enigma codes. Her rude introduction to that life, however, was a head-spinning culture shock.

'I got a summons and a railway warrant to go to Tullichewan Castle in Dumbartonshire, which at that time was a training centre for Wrens. And I spent a fortnight there learning to do what you do – marching, saluting, that sort of thing.

'We were told the castle had just been vacated by workmen. The place was filthy. It was disgusting. There were filthy greasy tables. And the washing facilities, to put it mildly, were primitive. They were huge concrete huts with a concrete floor. The loos did have doors, but there was no lock. And I can't tell you what the smell was like.

'There was a bit where people could have a shower – a row of showers on a wall. I was an only child and I wasn't used to stripping off in front of people and washing myself, but I did it. Some of them kept their swimming costumes on because they were just too embarrassed to strip down to the buff.'

But after these privations – perhaps deliberately spartan – a rather more attractive prospect for some Wrens started to loom. Jean Valentine recalls: 'On the last day we were all called into a room – forty or fifty of us – and told to sit there, and we would be called one at a time and be told where we were going, what we'd be doing. So when I was called in, I did what I was told, sat down in a chair in front of three or four officers sitting there. "We don't know what we're going to be asking you to do. But we have been told to look for people like you. So tomorrow you will go to London."'

After a short interlude of excitement in the capital, the work in hand soon beckoned. But there was still a little bewilderment to come. 'Then I went to the Bletchley outstation site in Eastcote, Middlesex,' says Jean. 'And I was introduced to the bombe machine.'

However, before long Jean Valentine had more serious concerns, which were to do with the nature of the work opportunities that she could pursue during the war. For any woman who might have been even a little ambitious, working on the bombes seemed a little like factory work. 'Only Wrens worked the bombes. I assume it was because the boss was naval and veered towards his own "gels".

'But we couldn't get any promotion. I think the theory was that the humbler we looked, the less that anyone from outside would think that we were doing anything of great importance. We were told, if people asked us what we were doing, to say that we were "confidential writers" – or secretaries, in other words.'

The lack of prospects may have been put in place by the military hierarchy as opposed to the Bletchley Park authorities. Unlike the Wrens, the Hon. Sarah Baring did achieve promotion – she was sent to work at the heart of the war establishment in the Admiralty, her role to be a go-between representing Bletchley Park to the naval establishment. 'I was seconded up to Admiralty from BP at the beginning of 1944,' she recalls. 'The Bletchley Park authorities opened an office there, underneath that hideous monstrous building on the Mall. The Citadel, the one that's a mass of concrete that people used to call "Lenin's Tomb".

'We got all the Park decrypts concerning the navy,' she continues. 'It would come up to us, and we would have to decide what to do with it. So really I was doing the same work as in BP but just in Admiralty. It was Bletchley Park all in one tiny room.'

And the story of the Wrens can also be contrasted with the experiences of female codebreakers Joan Murray and Mavis Batey, who were treated with a respect that was perhaps a little unusual for the time.

Yet not all the Wrens sent to Bletchley were deemed to come up to scratch. In a rather crisp memo to the Admiralty, concerning the quality of the personnel being sent to him, Alistair Denniston addressed the cases of several individuals who had been brought to his attention:

Wren Kenwick is inaccurate, very slow and not a bit keen on her work, not very intelligent . . .

Wrens Buchanan and Ford are unintelligent and slow and seem unable to learn. Wren Rogers suffers from mild claustrophobia and cannot work in a windowless room.

There seems to be some mistake in regard to Wren Dobson, we have never so far as I am aware complained of her work which is satisfactory, and now that I have informed her that she cannot have a transfer, she appears to have the intention of putting her back into the job, in which case she may well equal our best.

The remainder of the Wrens are doing most excellent work, none of them have so far given the slightest trouble.

Denniston concluded pointedly:

I think perhaps you might ask the Deputy Director to impress upon the selectors the importance of the work on which these

Wrens are employed and not to send us too many of the Cook and Messenger type.[1]

Of course, the Wrens were not the only women drafted in. Also present were six WAAFs whose task it was, from the beginning, to man the telephone exchange. Then there were thirty-six WAAFs who were there to run the teleprinters, with their communications chattering in and out of the Park.

For a lot of the girls who signed up, this life threw up a number of surprises. Felicity Ashbee, of the WAAF, kept sporadic diaries. She recalled signing up and being sent to the nearby town of Leighton Buzzard where she and other WAAF girls were put through parade paces by a male sergeant, who was mortally embarrassed by the whole thing.

They were told that maths and science were not essential subjects for the girls to know about. Miss Ashbee was then posted to Stanmore, where she recalls meeting a lesbian ballet photographer. She did not seem tremendously shocked.

She also recalls the routines that so many hundreds of young women had to get into; in terms of leisure, this meant a sparse diet of books, knitting and chess. The egalitarian spirit of the post-war world was still some way off; even in the WAAF, ranks were discouraged from fraternising with one another. Miss Ashbee recalls having debates in the early 1940s about whether the 'Commies' were actually worse than the Nazis.

She was then sent to Bletchley for a while, and had sketchy memories of Josh Cooper, and the disorientating mix of uniforms and civilian dress that mingled around the place. Miss Ashbee recalled just 'one café' and (perhaps because she was not tremendously popular) 'no social life'. She recalled a show being staged there, called *Blue and Khaki*, part of which involved a Cossack song.[2]

A number of Wrens were housed in Woburn Abbey, once a splendid private house and after the war to become one of the country's premier visitor attractions. For those who now watch the Channel 4 reality show *Big Brother* and marvel at how complete strangers can live in such close proximity for so long, it's worth having a look at the life that was led at the Abbey. Given the gruelling nature of the work and the slog of the hours, this rhyme from one dormitory – entitled 'Martha's Prayer' – rings an amusing chord:

> God bless Marie and grant that she
> May not drop things and wake me
> And grant that Marjorie's heavy feet
> May not disturb my slumbers sweet
> And when they go to bed at four
> Oh God, don't let them slam the door.[3]

There might also have been an element of Malory Towers about the set-up. Some of the women recalled listening stations high up in the Abbey's tower room, and a continual problem with bats, which would cause a great deal of high-pitched panic.

Woburn Abbey was also reputedly haunted. According to Jack Lightfoot of the RAF, the young women were talking about the ghost of the 'Flying Duchess' – Mary, Duchess of Bedford, who was born in the Victorian age but conceived a fancy for the new pursuit of aviation at the age of sixty-one. But the house also reputedly was haunted by a monk, and there were stories of doors that would not stay shut at night.

There would not have been a lot of time for nocturnal spectral activity though – Bletchley Park, of course, was a 24-hour operation, and workers were transported to and from their shifts by special buses after midnight and before 8 a.m.

There were also Wrens posted a few miles away in a small village called Gayhurst. There, writes Diane Payne,

> . . . another 150 Wrens lived and worked on the premises . . .
> cold rooms, no transport and, I am told, swallows nesting in the

house and flying in and out of the broken windows. There too, mice abounded, and one lunchtime a dead one turned up in the gravy boat.

It was a beautiful place dating back to 1086, and Sir Francis Drake owned it in 1581. The Wrens used the old church in the grounds every Sunday, and my friend remembers dutifully pumping the organ.

Highly virtuous! And something, I feel sure, that would have captured the imaginations of many of the male service personnel of Bletchley. As indeed would the stories concerning Wrens sunbathing topless on the roof of Gayhurst Manor.

If for the codebreaking civilians in the huts, the bounds of knowledge seemed limited, then for a Wren they were more limited yet. It was not just the mechanistic nature of the work of bombe operating; it was the commute back to the dormitories. Jean Valentine only realised, upon returning some decades later, how very little of the Park she had ever seen in that brief period during the war. She recalls: 'Everything was so brilliantly compartmentalised.'

And the restrictions were not purely physical – the methodology of the work was equally hermetically sealed. 'I worked in that bombe room,' she continues. 'And when we got an answer from the machines, we went to the phone, to ring through this possible answer to an extension number. It wasn't until all these decades later that I realised we were just calling Hut 6 across the path.'

If they had done their jobs properly, the encrypted message would be typed in and a length of tape would come out in German. 'Then that went to the pink hut which was just opposite to the entrance of Hut 11, not six steps away. There the translators changed it into English. And the analysts decided who was going to get this information. This was all happening in this tiny little square. I saw nothing of Bletchley Park except that grass oval in front of the mansion.'

There was also an element of culture shock produced for many by being transplanted right into the centre of what was still largely rural England. She recalls: 'We used to go to the village hop on a Saturday night if we weren't working. The whole village used to turn out for this hop. To my absolute horror, one evening, a woman, there with her baby, took her bosom out and stuck it in her baby's mouth. Now, I had never seen a baby being fed in my life before, and certainly not at a village hop.

'But it seemed to be the norm. No one else seemed to think anything about this woman casually producing a breast and feeding her baby.'

Sheila Lawn considers that 'Eighteen-year-olds then were younger than 18-year-olds now in terms of attitudes.' But this is perhaps something to do with regional divides; it is reasonably well documented, for instance, that in the 1920s and 1930s, people who lived in small communities in the English countryside were more relaxed about such matters as premarital sex than their town counterparts. Even there, many children born out of wedlock were swiftly subsumed into the larger family – the child in question being told in the occasional case that its mother was its 'sister'.

Regardless of how young the Bletchley recruits felt themselves to be, however, it was obvious that passion – and, indeed, love – were always going to find a way in such intense circumstances. But there was another sort of intensity at Bletchley too – a steadily growing sense of friction caused in part by the ballooning expansion of the Park's activities, and by the sheer numbers of its personnel. There were to be moments midway through the conflict – in Britain generally, as well as throughout Bletchley Park – when it seemed that morale could not sink any lower.

16 1941: Bletchley and Churchill

> He's the grand old man
> For us he's doing all that he can
> Britain's guiding star
> Known near and far
> Wearing his famous bulldog grin
> And smoking his big cigar

It's difficult to listen to Max Miller's chirpy 1941 ditty now without wincing just a little. Enthusiasm is one thing, but sugary show-business sycophancy? Yet this song, 'The Grand Old Man', was something of a hit at the time; not merely because it was a less cynical age but because a colossal number of people felt, as soon as he took over in May 1940, that Britain was extremely lucky to have Churchill's leadership. (Very few people, for instance, would have agreed with Evelyn Waugh's later assertion that Churchill was wrong about most things and surrounded himself with crooks.)

For many years after the war, it was asserted that the most common dream had by British people was that of the Queen unexpectedly dropping round for tea. In a similar way, the figure of Winston Churchill loomed very large in the minds of Bletchley Park operatives, and not merely because they found him an inspirational figure. The psychology seems to run deeper than that. Is it possible to hear, through various accounts, a yearning for proper recognition?

Gordon Welchman recorded the day in September 1941 when Churchill paid a visit to Bletchley Park. Welchman's account, in his book *The Hut Six Story*, appears to have a pleasing dimension of wish-fulfilment to it:

> Winston Churchill himself came to visit us. Travis took him on a tour of the many Bletchley Park activities. The tour was to include a visit to my office, and I had been told to prepare a speech of a certain length, say ten minutes. When the party turned up, a bit behind schedule, Travis whispered, somewhat loudly, 'Five minutes, Welchman.' I started with my prepared opening gambit, which was 'I would like to make three points,' and proceeded to make the first two points more hurriedly than I planned.
>
> Travis then said, 'That's enough, Welchman,' whereupon Winston, who was enjoying himself, gave me a grand schoolboy wink and said, 'I think there was a third point, Welchman.'[1]

Winston, indeed! Not to mention the 'grand' schoolboy wink, which seems to have the effect of placing both men on the same level – a level above the officious-seeming Travis. Welchman added, more appropriately: 'We were fortunate in having an inspiring national leader in Winston Churchill, whose oratory had a powerful effect.'

But Churchill's relationship with Bletchley Park was of the greatest importance. It was not simply a question of the grand old man granting the codebreakers extra resources for machinery or staff, or even bestowing upon them a fresh tennis court. It was a crucial question of respect. Respect that, one senses occasionally through various accounts, the Park was not necessarily receiving in other parts of Whitehall, or from the intelligence services.

Churchill had been fascinated by the business of cryptography, and indeed of secret intelligence, since before the First World War. He had seen ingenious espionage ploys and counter-ploys in action during his youthful exploits in different parts of the Empire; he had a hand in the setting up of the Room 40 cryptography division at Admiralty; in the 1920s, he took a keen interest in the intelligence agents who could glean most information on the Soviets.

So naturally, when he at last became Prime Minister in May 1940, just two weeks after Bletchley Park broke into the German air force Enigma, Churchill had no doubts how vital the operation was. From the moment he arrived in Downing Street, he insisted on having a daily buff-coloured box of intercepts sent on to him – a box that was sometimes delivered personally by 'C', the head of the SIS, Sir Stewart Menzies. The key to this box was kept on Churchill's key-ring.

Only a handful of other people – military and civilian – were permitted to know from where these decrypts emanated, and if ever they should have cause to refer to them, they used the obscuring term 'Boniface'. Churchill himself sometimes referred to these bundles of intelligence as his 'eggs', a reference to the Bletchley 'geese that never cackled'. For everyone else – generals and ministers alike – the source was, to all intents and purposes, a number of fictional spies. It was only in 1941 that the intelligence produced from the decrypts started to be known by the term 'Ultra'.

This intense secrecy could prove a source of vexation to other government departments such as the Foreign Office, and indeed to the military top brass. The Prime Minister was 'liable to spring upon them undigested snippets of information of which they had not heard'. Added to this irritation, from the outset of the war there were those high up in military command who were sceptical of the extent to which Bletchley Park could provide serious, usable, useful information. These tensions grew as the Park expanded its remit and started producing intelligence, as opposed to simply raw decrypted messages.

On the day of that unforgettable visit, in September 1941, Churchill also inspected the Hollerith machine installation in Hut 7. As one breathless eyewitness account stated:

> The visitor was presented with a scene of intense activity. There were 45 machine operators in action at as many machines. Then all the machines were halted at the same instant, and in the complete silence that followed, Mr Freeborn [the man in charge of the Hollerith section] gave an introductory explanation . . . At the conclusion of the demonstrations, all machines were brought back into action as the visitor was conducted to the exit, but all brought to rest as Churchill paused on the threshold to make his farewells.[2]

Churchill's tour also took him into Hut 8, to meet Alan Turing; according to his biographer Andrew Hodges, Turing was 'very nervous'.

The Prime Minister then gave a short address outside Hut 6 to a group of gathered codebreakers, in which he said: 'You all look very innocent – one would not think you knew anything secret.' It was here that, famously, he went on to describe his audience as 'the geese that lay the golden eggs – and never cackle'.

John Herivel, in a lecture given to Sidney Sussex College in 2005, seemed a little less romantic and slightly more clear-eyed about this manifestation than Gordon Welchman had been. Nevertheless, his account still conveys something about the aura of true leadership:

> Word suddenly reached us in Hut 6 that he was coming and those in the Machine Room . . . were told to stand up facing their machines. People were much more biddable in those days, so we did what we were told and for what seemed an eternity waited patiently.
>
> Then the sound of many voices was heard in the distance,

gradually becoming louder and louder and reaching a crescendo immediately behind me before subsiding when Welchman's voice was heard saying, 'Sir, I would like to present John Herivel, who was responsible for breaking the German Enigma last year.'

On hearing my name spoken by Welchman in this totally unexpected manner, I turned automatically to the right to find myself gazing straight into the eyes of the Prime Minister! We looked silently at each other for a moment or two before he moved on . . . If I had the necessary presence of mind – which I did not – I would have reminded him that the day the Military Enigma was broken was soon after that on which he himself had become Prime Minister.[3]

Once again, the justifiable pride radiates through, finding as its focus the sudden connection with this near-mythic leader made flesh. On the subject of the address given outside Hut 6, however, Herivel went on to give a more soberingly realistic portrait of the man in whom Britain's destiny had been entrusted:

Soon he came and scrambled on to the mound where he stood rather uneasily for a moment – for it was a miserably dark day with a cold wind. We saw before us a rather frail, oldish looking man, a trifle bowed, with wispy hair, in a black pin-striped suit with a faint red line, no bravado, no large black hat, no cigar. Then he spoke very briefly, but with deep emotion . . . That was *our* finest hour at Bletchley Park.[4]

According to one history, when Churchill was at last about to be driven off, he lowered his car window and said to Alistair Denniston: 'About that recruitment – I know I told you not to leave a stone unturned, but I did not mean you to take me seriously.'

Just one month later, perhaps emboldened by the great honour of that visit, Welchman, together with Alan Turing, Hugh Alexander and Stuart Milner-Barry, wrote directly to the Prime Minister to make a special plea for more staff. In the first couple of years of the war, Welchman, by his own cheerful admission, had had no problems of any sort with recruitment. He had 'shamelessly' (to use his own word) gone around hiring his peers and valued colleagues from the smarter colleges, and with them coteries of their brightest undergraduates. However, as he was later to note:

> This kind of piracy was to be curtailed in 1941. The government decided that the use of the best young brains in the country should be regulated. C.P. Snow, of Christ's College Cambridge, whom I had known before the war . . . was put in charge of allocation of all scientists and mathematicians, and from then on I had to recruit my male staff through him.[5]

Turing and Welchman were careful to state that thanks to the efforts of Commander Travis, Bletchley was well supplied in terms of technology, and specifically in terms of bombes (though by this stage there were still not that many); they were after more codebreakers, and more Wrens. One might also see that the codebreakers were subconsciously asserting their own significance and importance in the face of dumb Whitehall silence:

> Dear Prime Minister,
>
> Some weeks ago you paid us the honour of a visit, and we believe that you regard our work as important. You will have seen that, thanks largely to the energy and foresight of Commander Travis, we have been well supplied with the 'bombes' for the breaking of the German Enigma codes. We think, however, that you ought to know that this work is being held up, and in some cases is not being done at all, principally because we cannot get sufficient staff to deal with it.
>
> Our reason for writing to you direct is that for months we have done everything that we possibly can through the

normal channels, and that we despair of any early improvement without your intervention. No doubt in the long run these particular requirements will be met, but meanwhile still more precious months will have been wasted, and as our needs are continually expanding we see little hope of ever being adequately staffed.

Turing went on to specify exactly what each hut needed in terms of clerks, typists, Wrens, etc. And he concluded thus:

We have felt that we should be failing in our duty if we did not draw your attention to the facts and to the effects they are having and must continue to have on our work, unless immediate action is taken.

The rank-breaking letter was signed by Turing, Welchman, Stuart Milner-Barry and Hugh Alexander, while the man deputed to deliver it was Milner-Barry. According to one history, he arrived at 10 Downing Street and had to spend a little time gaining entrance. The trouble was that he had forgotten to bring any official identification along with him. Eventually, however, he was allowed in and directed to see Churchill's Private Secretary, Brigadier Harvie Walker.

The brigadier was apparently extremely suspicious of this disorganised-seeming man without any of his official papers. His suspicions were not allayed by Milner-Barry's stubborn refusal to tell the brigadier the contents of the letter he had with him. However, Harvie Walker was eventually persuaded to place the letter before Churchill; and upon reading its requests, Churchill instantly responded, telling his Chief of Staff: 'Make sure they have all they want on extreme priority and report to me that this has been done.' This written instruction came with a sticker at the top of the letter, with the simple phrase: 'Action This Day.'

*

The fact that Churchill's one visit in 1941 made such an impression on the entire establishment is a vivid illustration of how starved it was of morale-boosting feedback. The codebreakers knew that they were not, like the RAF, 'Glamour Boys'. There was no Battle of Britain for them to reminisce over, merely days and weeks and months of calculation, of thought, of trial and error, carried out in circumstances of such intense secrecy that there were very few to bestow praise in the first place.

Also, unlike the operatives of MI5, MI6 and the Special Operations Executive, all trained to the highest degree and imbued with the accompanying hardness, a good proportion of the personnel of Bletchley Park were academics by profession and by temperament – meaning that they would have been used to the approbation of colleagues. The secrecy of their work must – just occasionally – have been maddening, no matter how vehemently so many veterans deny it.

Churchill continued to hold the work of Bletchley Park in the very highest regard as the war progressed; later, though, we shall find how some of his decisions concerning its post-war status are held by some to have held Britain back in fighting for its place in the new world order.

17 Military or Civilian?

'There was an awful lot of nonsense involving codebreakers having to join the Home Guard,' says one veteran, recalling that it was the only time in the war that he was required to put on a military uniform. For some of the more cerebral, bespectacled young men, the very notion of taking part in all-night exercises – with cork-blackened faces, or hooting like owls, or shimmying over security fences, or simply running around with rifles and attempting to hit targets – was a cause for irritation, especially when such exercises got in the way of valuable thinking time.

Others, however – including Alan Turing – found such duties and manoeuvres amusing and diverting. But the notion that it was compulsory goes to the heart of one of Bletchley Park's most beguiling, ambiguous and disorientating qualities.

As we have seen, the establishment was neither wholly military nor wholly civilian. Although in its earliest days, the directorate included a couple of senior military figures, such as John Tiltman, Bletchley Park was under the ultimate control of Sir Stewart Menzies, head of MI6, which itself answered to the Foreign Office and directly to the Prime Minister. The recruitment drive, moreover, was angled almost completely towards civilians. And unlike any military establishment, there were no drills, no parades, no training sessions – and crucially, no orders.

When one thinks now of the war, one's natural assumption is that practically the whole of society was in some sense militarised. Certainly, if individuals received orders from the government that they were to join up, or join another service, there was rarely any question of disobedience. How was it then that a set-up of the nature of Bletchley Park – handling crucial, top secret information – lacked what one might think would be essential military discipline? From the very beginning, who would these young code-breakers and linguists answer to? And what of the army of Wrens who were to descend on the place? Were they to answer to civilian or military orders?

'This place was very strange,' says former Wren Jean Valentine. 'There were the men's services, the women's adjoining services, and civilians. How could you impose any kind of discipline? It wouldn't have been fair, whatever you had done. If you had set the civilians above or below the rest of us, it wouldn't have been right. So I think the only way was just to run it was just . . . everyone was equal.'

Fellow Wren Ruth Bourne also recalls the seemingly casual air, in contrast to her later work at Eastcote, the Bletchley Park outstation in Middlesex: 'In BP there was everybody: civilians, ATS, Wrens, WAAFs walking around. No saluting. Everybody was the same. There was no hierarchy. Eastcote was much more structured to the naval module. You saluted your officers. Whereas at Bletchley Park it was all mixed.'

Oliver Lawn found from the start that he had an extraordinary amount of freedom: 'As far as I was concerned [the job] was absolutely self-regulating.' Indeed, adds Mr Lawn, the work of code-breaking could not have been further from the military ethos if it had tried. He recalls: 'Our chain of command was just the head of Hut 6. First of all, that was Gordon Welchman. Then he moved – went partly transatlantic and took a rather wider remit so we saw rather less of him.

'Stuart Milner-Barry succeeded Welchman as the head of Hut 6. And a very good head he was. He wasn't really a cryptographer, but he had a very good brain and a very good management and manner to look after us. And then at around the same time,' Mr Lawn adds, 'they had a chap called Fletcher who was a pure lay manager, and he was concerned with getting our equipment. He was concerned with the mechanics of making the bombes on time. And orders and that sort of thing. Supplies officer, in effect.

'But Milner-Barry was the father figure that we took instructions from. Now and again we had meetings and so on and discussed with him – but it was a very loose sort of management structure, as suited academe. It was a Common Room situation. It wasn't a service thing at all.'

In his Bletchley memoir, Peter Calvocoressi also recalls this occasionally bewildering ambiguity concerning who to report to, and in what manner:

Bletchley Park was a very unmilitary place. It paid scant attention to the hierarchies of either military rank or the civil service. Its chiefs were civilians on the payroll of the Foreign Office and there were also the pre-war veterans, most cryptographers. But these were vastly outnumbered by the wartime intake which proved to be very much greater in numbers than anyone had ever imagined. If unconsciously, Bletchley Park took its tone from them.

He continued with a fascinating insight into the minds and aspirations of those young people who *were* serving, and of what, in the early days, they had expected from the war:

Those of us who were commissioned officers wore uniform only when we felt like it – or when some top brass was expected on a visit. Bletchley Park was not a place where people went around saluting one another. Rank might be coveted for the extra pay or, in the latter part of the war, as a mark of recognition, but it did not affect personal relations. It never seemed quite real, partly because the war itself never seemed to be anything but an interlude.

Looking back, I remember no talk about how long the war was likely to last but I do not think that anybody felt that it was going to last long enough seriously to divert the course of our lives . . . This was subconsciously important. It meant there was very little jockeying for position among us. Our futures and our war work were unrelated.[1]

Keith Batey recalls that the arrangement, and the general mix-up of civilian and military, did not appear to cause any difficulty: 'As far as Hut 6 and Dilly Knox's outfit were concerned, there weren't any service people at all. Service people were in the Intelligence section, Hut 3 and Hut 4, the Naval Section. But of course the best cryptographer – certainly – was Tiltman, who was a regular officer. His sidekick Morgan was also an army man.'

A naval officer seconded to the Park, Edward Thomas, also recalled this curious atmosphere:

We naval newcomers were at once impressed by the easy relations and lack of friction between those in, and out, of uniform. Despite the high tension of much of the work, a spirit of relaxation prevailed. Anyone of whatever rank or degree could approach anyone else, however venerable, with any idea or suggestion, however crazy.

This was partly because those in uniform had mostly been selected from the same walks of life as the civilians – scholarship, journalism, publishing, linguistics and so forth – and partly because these were the people who saw most clearly what stood to be lost by a Hitler victory . . . Service officers served gladly under civilians, and vice versa. Dons from Oxford and Cambridge worked smoothly together.[2]

As regards the general question of hierarchy, it is worth remembering that the British had a very long tradition of looking to the 'intellectual amateur' when it came to matters of intelligence. In some ways, Dilly Knox and his fellow individualists in Room 40 were the perfectly logical culmination of a historically long-standing British approach.

If one reaches back to the sixteenth century, for instance – Elizabeth I's court, and the frightening proto police-state activities of Sir Francis Walsingham's 'Star Chamber' – one already sees the trope of clever young men being hired from Oxford or Cambridge for intelligence activity. The prime example is playwright Christopher Marlowe. He was recruited to travel through Europe, reporting back on suspected papist plots against the Protestant Queen.

As the years and centuries wear on, we continue to see that British intelligence is partly a military affair, but remains mostly one involving talented civilians. Historian Rebecca Ratcliff cites Lord Baden Powell, founder of the Scout movement, drawing pictures of butterfly wings that concealed diagrams of Turkish fortresses. And in popular fiction of the late Victorian/early Edwardian era, the heroes of William Le Queux's astonishingly successful spy thrillers were all gifted amateurs; smart, well-connected, well-educated men who would be called upon by friendly faces in the Foreign Office to investigate the diabolical schemes of enemy powers. Perhaps even more pertinently, there is the archetype of the gifted eccentric: what figure in English culture better fits this description than Sherlock Holmes?

And so, as we have seen through the amiable ramshackleness of the Admiralty's Room 40 throughout the First World War, it was clearly felt in the late 1930s to be important that the 'boffins' had space and freedom to think their brilliant thoughts. This meant that they were to be unencumbered by the restrictions and discipline imposed on everyone else.

In terms of taking charge of one's day-to-day work, there was the matter of who would be in charge of the various codebreaking and translating activities. The huts would have their 'heads'; but the sense of hierarchy was a great deal looser than that, as Mavis Batey recalls. She also remembers how, when a group of American soldiers came to visit the Park prior to a team of them working there, they were rather taken aback by what seemed to be an almost stereotypical British attitude: 'There was no one really to consult. You could ask Dilly – but he wasn't very good at explaining. And in any case, a newcomer with a bright idea could be just as good as anyone.

'And that is the beauty of the whole ethics and background of the Park and its work . . . it just so happened that I was in charge the day one of the Americans came round,' Mrs Batey adds. 'He couldn't believe that he was being told how to break codes by a nineteen-year-old – but I had got a corner into the work and I knew what I was doing.'

According to Rebecca Ratcliff's scholarly account, there was something of the commune about the way everyone worked at the Park:

> Co-operation began within each hut. The Watch, responsible for translation and forwarding of decrypts, encouraged collaboration. Members translated their decrypts around a table and frequently consulted each other on challenging difficulties. This encouragement of exchange included the clerical staff. One secretary described the 'Soviet' meetings, 'where any grievance was aired and any suggestion was examined,' whoever the speaker. This collaborative attitude 'did away with any underground feeling of dissent'.[3]

Perhaps there were outbreaks of resentment, as opposed to dissent – some service personnel regarded the civilians as being rather spoiled and pampered, with their games of tennis and their picnics, and suspected them of having somehow dodged their duty.

Later in the war, there were those, such as Captain Jerry Roberts, who although in the Service, were deemed more valuable working (as he did) on the 'Tunny' codes. But did Captain Roberts never feel a pang of frustration that his orders were to remain in the Park?

'I suppose I should have been unhappy that I wasn't fighting the true fight but this never bothered me,' Captain Roberts now says. 'One knew that this was immensely more important than any other single contribution that you could make as a soldier, or as an officer.'

But by 1942, the understandable harrying of the cryptographers by the services – with inevitable conflict about whether the navy or the military should be accorded more time for their respective codes to be run through the bombe machines – was never-ending. Some kind of a solution was eventually reached. 'A sudden demand by Hut 8 for a large number of machines would seriously disrupt the programme and the question of how many bombes for Naval, and how quickly, was often a difficult one to answer satisfactorily,' recalled one veteran. 'Moreover, only the technicians could answer it; the intelligence sections could lay down orders of priority in general terms, but the detailed decisions depended upon technical considerations. A body of five bombe controllers was therefore formed and a rota arranged, so that one of us was always on duty and available to act as bombe controller.'

Those men in civvies at Bletchley Park had their chance to fulfil a certain kind of service obligation, chiefly in the form of the Home Guard. For some, this proved to be an onerous distraction. Keith Batey recalls: 'I'd be engaged on breaking a cipher or something, and then had to put it down and pretend to go and be a . . . it was bloody silly, especially in 1944 when there was no danger of invasion. It was organised, we all had to do it, and we all had these stupid uniforms too. It really was fatuous.'

Conversely, Oliver Lawn found this dash of military experience provided some welcome light relief away from the serious business

Bletchley Park in 1926, long before its codebreaking days, when its then owners, the Leon family, would often give 'grand house parties'. *Getty Images*

Bletchley railway station, at which most of the recruits caught their first view of their wartime destination, some in the dead of night when the station was unlit and there was 'not a soul about'. *Lens of Sutton Collection*

Mavis Batey (nee Lever), a key member of Dilly Knox's codebreaking team; her highly-skilled work played a vital role in the 1941 Battle of Cape Matapan.

Courtesy of The Bletchley Park Trust

Oliver Lawn, who joined the Park as a young undergraduate mathematician from Cambridge and oversaw the building of the bombe machines.

Courtesy of Sheila and Oliver Lawn

Linguist and codebreaker Sheila Lawn (nee MacKenzie), recruited from university in Scotland, and who met husband-to-be Oliver (above) at the Park's recreational dancing sessions. *Courtesy of Sheila and Oliver Lawn*

Codebreaker and novelist-to-be Angus Wilson (second from right) at Bletchley Park; noted for his frayed nerves, he is reputed to have thrown a bottle of ink at a Wren.

Captain Jerry Roberts, who worked on the pioneering Tunny codebreaking operation later in the war and deciphered a message from Hitler himself. *Courtesy of Jerry Roberts*

Wren Jean Valentine; after a stint of bombe operation, she was posted right the way across the world to Ceylon to work on Japanese codes.

Crown Copyright, used with kind permission, Director GCHQ

The revolutionary bombe machine, as devised by Alan Turing and refined by Gordon Welchman; this technology was a vital key to Bletchley's success and its impact on the course of the war is almost immeasurable; its operation was a painstaking, physically arduous affair for the Wrens concerned. *Getty Images*

Brainchild of Dr Thomas Flowers, the Colussus codebreaking machine, used later in the war, was the forerunner of the modern computer. *Getty Images*

An early 1936 three-rotor Enigma machine; this was the elegant, portable enciphering technology considered by the Germans to be unbeatable. *Getty Images*

Dilly Knox

Alan Turing

Peter Twinn

Gordon Welchman

Frank Birch

Hugh Alexander

The masterminds: Bletchley Park's foremost cryptographical geniuses, each with their own rich and often surprising hinterlands. Knox and Birch were of the older generation; WWI codebreaking pioneers. *Photograph by James Veysey, CAMERA PRESS LONDON*

For codebreakers and translators alike, the need for total accuracy at all times in the handling of intercepts made the work at Bletchley uniquely intense and wearing.

Crown Copyright, used with kind permission, Director GCHQ

The Huts and blocks at the Park were very strictly demarcated for security reasons. There were operational rooms that the vast majority who worked there would never see.

Crown Copyright, used with kind permission, Director GCHQ

Hut 3 - felt by many, along with Hut 6, to be the real hub of the Bletchley operation, where the codebreakers would endure gruelling, incredibly focused eight-hour shifts.

Getty Images

Felt by some to be 'perfectly monstrous', the main house looks rather pretty in the severe winter of 1940.

Courtesy of The Bletchley Park Trust

The lake in front of the house froze over in the winter of 1940; the young codebreakers are clearly keen to get their skates on. In the background are some of the huts.

Courtesy of The Bletchley Park Trust

The cast of the revue *Combined OPS*; it has been suggested that all the amateur dramatics, opera singing and dancing that took place at the Park were a vital mental pressure valve for the codebreakers. *Courtesy of The Bletchley Park Trust*

Jean Valentine, who now gives talks at Bletchley Park, demonstrates a detailed recreation of a bombe machine. *Courtesy of The Bletchley Park Trust*

HRH Duke of Kent presides over the 2009 commemorative badge ceremony; with him are, from left, Kathleen Warren (far left), Oliver and Sheila Lawn, Jean Valentine, and on his right, former Wren Ruth Bourne, Captain Jerry Roberts, former Director of GCHQ Arthur Bonsall, and, far right, Baroness Trumpington. *Courtesy of The Bletchley*

of cracking ciphers. 'We all joined the Home Guard, where we had fun and games. And we went out on to the fields beyond Bletchley and watched to see if any German parachutes came in overnight.

'Academics in the Home Guard were great fun,' he adds. 'You can imagine, Dad's Army, some of them, the most brilliant, were the most extreme . . . Though one or two had army backgrounds. There was one chap called Michael Bannister, whose father was in the army. Bannister was very much the army type, and he tried to bring in all the army stuff, but without success. So he was the exception. We were very lame.'

Alan Turing was initially rather taken with the idea of Home Guard duty, as it was an opportunity to learn how to shoot; and his shot, as it turned out, was much more accurate than a lot of people's. However, Turing's interest in this activity waned sharply once his shot had been perfected, and around 1942, when after several years of anxiety, the prospect of a Nazi invasion of Britain had receded, he began to absent himself from parades.

The authorities were irritated by Turing's apparently casual approach, insisting that since he had signed up for Home Guard duties, he was under military law. Turing calmly pointed out to the furious officers in question that he was no such thing, and that he had stated as much on the form that he had signed. One of the questions on the form was: 'Do you understand that by enrolling in the Home Guard, you place yourself liable to military law?' Turing had written his answer: 'No'. Naturally, no one had noticed.

Despite the fact that the women, including the Wrens, at the Park greatly outnumbered the men, there was still the fact that the men were of course very firmly in charge. In the case of the Wrens, there would always be a male officer somewhere. For the civilian women, it was a matter of answering to the heads of huts, be they Gordon Welchman or blond, blue-eyed 'knockout' Hugh Alexander.

In matters of uniform too, there were the views of the ladies to consider. The Hon. Sarah Baring says that the presence of a military man always perked things up a little in the section in which she worked: 'There were very few service people, mostly civilian. But there were a few uniforms, which we thought was terribly exciting. If you saw a naval uniform, or an air force uniform, it was lovely. For instance, word would get round that someone from the navy had dropped in. And that was very exciting because it was quite rare.'

In terms of hierarchy, Sarah Baring gives a vivid account of that very lack of structure – a tale that contrives to combine military, civilian and class sensibilities into one imbroglio. 'One morning, I was working as usual in the Index Room when I heard many footsteps outside. The door opened and in walked my godfather. At that time, he was Vice Admiral, Lord Louis Mountbatten, Chief of Combined Operations and naturally privy to Ultra. He was accompanied by a lot of top brass and harassed looking Bletchley staff.

'I managed to splutter in my astonishment: "Uncle Dickie, what are you doing here?" "Oh," he said, "I knew you were here and thought I would see how you're getting on; show me the system of your cross reference index." Pink with embarrassment, I showed him, conscious of the waves of anger behind from the learned code-breakers . . .

'I was awfully pleased to see Uncle Dickie and, as the Index was considered fairly lowly work, all of us on watch were thrilled,' she adds. 'Doom descended the next morning with a peremptory demand to see Commander Travis forthwith. He asked me how I had dared to ask the Chief of Combined Ops to visit the Index. I assured him, eyes full of tears, that I knew nothing about the visit and that he was my godfather. He believed that I spoke the truth and, bless him, lent me a hankie to blow my nose.'

For Mimi Gallilee, promoted from messenger girl to clerical duties within the house itself, it was immediately clear that it was the figures in the house who held sway. Her sixteen-year-old self was a little in awe of these men, with their smart secretaries: 'I went to work directly under Nigel de Grey's secretary,' she says. 'And she taught me all sorts of little things. Everything from that point of view was more interesting, because it was in codes, or about things that I didn't understand.'

Mrs Gallilee also recalls that for all the apparent lack of military structure, this was still an age in which one did not speak out of turn. Especially not if one was very young: 'Sometimes I used to do Mr de Grey's bits of typing, and anything that he wanted. Take tea and coffee into him. He was a very silent man. Grim. Forbidding. I was afraid of him. I wouldn't have dared to put a foot wrong. One was terribly respectful of him.

'Others, like Harry Hinsley – well, he was one of us. He was lovely and we called him Harry and I believe he was the only boss there that we called by his Christian name. Certainly not Commander Travis or Captain Hastings or the rest of them. Colonel Tiltman was always Colonel Tiltman. We would never have thought to call them by their first names.'

Mimi Gallilee had authority issues of her own, and they concerned her own immediate boss, Miss Reed. For the senior women in administration had a reputation for ferocity very much more intimidating than the men. Mimi recalls: 'Miss Reed used to train me and coach me in the right way to present myself to the world. She said to me once: "I must have a talk with your mother some day, she really ought to know about some of these things that you've been doing." What she meant was the way that I was behaving in the office.

'And at the end of the day, I'd get home and I'd say to my mother: "Please let me leave. I hate her, I hate her!" Poor Miss Reed. It was only after the war that I realised what a gem she was.'

18 1942: Grave Setbacks and Internal Strife

'You mustn't think that it was all harmony at BP,' says one veteran. 'There were some pretty ferocious internal squabbles too.' As 1942 dawned, some of these internal pressures were finally to erupt.

While it enjoyed the untrammelled and deep admiration of Churchill, the quasi-academic atmosphere of Bletchley Park was not otherwise viewed outside with universal approbation. Particularly, it appears, within certain corners of Whitehall, there was disquiet concerning the way that information was parcelled out. And after the difficulties and frustrations of the previous year, with the immensely long struggle to finally break the naval Enigma, the Park was coming under fresh pressure from various directions.

Thanks to Dilly Knox, Bletchley Park had at the end of 1941 scored another tremendous, almost priceless success in the cracking of the Abwehr code – that is, the codes used by the German military intelligence service. The Abwehr used a subtly different Enigma machine, and the breaking of the Abwehr code was something of a personal triumph for Knox – now so ill with cancer that he was working from home.

Back at Bletchley, Oliver Strachey was specifically assigned to monitor messages between Abwehr HQ and its agents. And the decrypted messages were to prove to the security services the success of an audacious operation known as the 'Double-Cross' system.

The idea was that captured Abwehr agents should be left in their positions and simply turned by the British – in other words, made to work as 'double agents'. That way, not only could all German espionage within Britain be monitored but also, the information that these agents sought from the British for their German paymasters would tell MI5 exactly what German intelligence did and did not know about such things as defences and planned manoeuvres.

There was another terrific advantage: the reports that the German agents made, in code, would be followed through the Abwehr networks, helping to break the keys for their particular Enigma cipher.

Such a plan now sounds almost too preposterous to work; and yet it did, handsomely. Captured German agents were given a stark choice: either face a firing squad or obey the orders of an MI5 officer. Once turned, the agents were given information to feed back to their German masters. Most of this was accurate, though inconsequential; some, crucially, was completely false. In other words, these agents were used for strategic deception. As the war went on, one such agent, Wulf Schmidt, known as 'Harry Tate', was so spectacularly successful that not only did the British secret service consider him 'a pearl', the Germans were even more pleased with him and awarded him the Iron Cross.

As Kim Philby (himself turned down for a job at the Park, as we shall find later) noted in his otherwise not wholly reliable memoirs, the breaking of the Abwehr code also gave Bletchley Park a weird glimpse of 'the intimate life of German intelligence officers':

There was the case ... of Axel the police dog. He had been posted from Berlin to Algeciras, presumably to guard the Abwehr out-station there from British agents sneaking across the bay from Gibraltar. On the last stage of [the dog's] journey, Madrid sent a warning telegram to Albert Carbe, alias Cesar, the head of the Abwehr post at Algeciras: 'Be careful of Axel. He bites.' Sure enough, a few days later, Algeciras came up with the laconic report: 'Cesar is in hospital. Axel bit him.'[1]

But the beginning of 1942 was a time of crisis for the British forces. Although it seemed that the campaign to eject the Germans and Italians from North Africa had been going well in the Western Desert – the capture of Benghazi on Christmas Day had proved a national tonic – General Rommel suddenly turned and struck back with force. The British were back almost where they had begun.

February 1942 brought disaster on another front: the fall of Singapore. General Percival was forced to surrender to the Japanese on 15 February, and to lead a staggering 62,000 men into captivity as prisoners of war. Many of these soldiers were subsequently pushed into slave labour in conditions of horrific brutality, facing systematic beatings and beheadings as well as malnutrition, dehydration and diseases such as beri-beri.

There had been a clutch of cryptographers based in Singapore in the weeks before the surrender, intercepting and decoding messages; among them was Arthur Cooper, brother of Josh. The decoders and Y Service operatives escaped and were evacuated to Colombo in the nick of time. Once again, we see how fragile the Bletchley secret was; if these men had instead been captured and tortured, could they have withstood and refused to say a word?

In addition to the military setbacks, there was, for Bletchley Park, a disaster that the general public knew nothing of at that time – one that threatened to wipe out a large swathe of the codebreaking operation. For a suspicious Admiral Dönitz, concerned that somehow his codes were being read, decreed that from 1 February 1942, the German U-boat command should bring in an updated version of the naval Enigma machine.

From that point on, an extra, fourth rotor was fitted to U-boat Enigma machines. The immediate result was a total U-boat code blackout at Bletchley. Suddenly, without warning, the messages the cryptographers received could no longer be decrypted. In turn the Atlantic convoys were rendered horribly vulnerable once more.

After the great satisfaction of Hut 8's earlier successes, this was a stomach-punch of disappointment. It also caused a great deal of unrest and unease in Whitehall. One historian has noted that the only thing that ever truly frightened Churchill throughout the course of the war was the prospect of the U-boats gaining the advantage and wiping out the best part of the convoys.

There was a further complicating factor. After an accident in September 1941, when HMS *Clyde* was damaged in a collision with U-67, Admiral Dönitz had decided that the submarine codes should be set to a different key from that of the surface naval vessels. As well as decoding 'Dolphin', as the naval Enigma key was known, everyone in Hut 8 had now had to turn their attentions to what they termed 'Shark', the submarine key. With the upgraded Enigma machines, 'Shark' now had sharper teeth. Once more, Admiralty was faced with the nightmare prospect of all those vital supply ships and their crews effectively sailing without protection.

It could not have come at a worse possible time: the U-boats were cruising up and down the Atlantic coast of the United States, lying in wait to encircle, or even sail among the convoys; to wait, generally, until night – and then to start firing their torpedoes, so that when one ship went up in bright flame, the others would have to watch. Crews would perish in the stormy waters; vital supplies would be sent to the ocean bed.

All this coincided almost exactly with the climax of a prolonged power struggle within Bletchley Park itself. For some months, there were voices within the Park, throughout Whitehall and in other corners of the Intelligence community that the Park needed a new directorate; that it was inefficient, not doing its job properly. The Intelligence branches of the Services were becoming increasingly uneasy about the fact that Bletchley Park was producing so much intelligence autonomously (and possibly doubly uneasy about the fact that Bletchley appeared to have the wholehearted support of

Churchill). In other words, it was not only decrypting, but also analysing the information.

According to Harry Hinsley's account, Whitehall was growing restive about what was perceived as the poor organisation of the institution: 'GC and CS had increased in size four-fold in the first sixteen months of the war. At the beginning of 1941 it was, by Whitehall's standards, poorly organised. This was partly because the growth in its size and in the complexity of its activities had outstripped the experience of those who administered it . . .' Military chiefs also had very little taste for what they saw as 'the condition of creative anarchy, within and between the sections, that distinguished GC and CS's everyday work and brought to the front the best among its unorthodox and 'undisciplined' war-time staff . . .'[2]

Churchill himself was made aware of these furious wranglings, which included a suggestion that the director Alistair Denniston got on very badly with the head of MI6, Sir Stewart Menzies. The atmosphere grew fervid. As P.W. Filby recalled it:

Edward Travis was deputy to Denniston and a crony of [Nigel] de Grey. They had endless talks in the crucial days and although they were held next door, the walls were wooden and since we were almost always working in complete silence, I couldn't help hearing the conversation sometimes. De Grey's voice was that of an actor and I knew ages before it happened that they didn't feel Denniston could cope with the enormous increase demanded of Ultra . . .[3]

It was true that from the beginning of the war, Denniston had found himself swamped in administrative quicksand. The running of the Park, the efforts to ensure that there were enough personnel when demand from other departments and services was so strong, the constant battle for more machines, even enough building contractors to work on the huts . . . As Bletchley expanded, its practical needs were growing exponentially. All this quashed any hopes that

Denniston once had of contributing further to the Enigma code-breaking himself.

On 1 February 1942, Denniston was removed as Director of Bletchley Park. He was instead bumped sideways to oversee the Diplomatic and Commercial side of the codebreaking operation, in Berkeley Street, back in London. He never received the knighthood that might otherwise have been automatically his due. But this was not a time in which anyone could afford to be remotely sentimental.

In his place came deputy Travis – although according to Mimi Gallilee, who was working in the house at the time, Travis maintained the title 'Deputy' for a while after these events. Perhaps out of a residual sense of loyalty and propriety?

A fascinating gloss on this ugly struggle was later offered by one Robert Cecil, who subsequently worked with Denniston in Intelligence in Berkeley Street. Cecil told Denniston's son Robin that 'the huts rose up rapidly at Bletchley; but there were less scrupulous and more ambitious men on hand to skim off much of the credit. Denniston left Bletchley and came back to London to escape the backbiting and get on with the job; he disliked the in-fighting more than he feared the Luftwaffe.'

Cecil added of Denniston and his time in Berkeley Street: 'He always kept his ship on an even keel and his staff, who included a number of brilliant eccentrics, liked and respected him. One of them, whom I remember, had come down from Oxford with a First in Egyptology and had then become an astrologer; when his eccentricities began to affect his colleagues, Denniston just sent him on sick-leave and welcomed him back when he was restored.'[4]

We are invited to infer from this that Denniston's reign at Bletchley Park was composed of similarly enlightened touches. And Robin Denniston adds a salty personal view – which must have been shared by his father – of Sir Stewart Menzies: 'Menzies was a WWI hero and conducted most of his secret MI6 business at White's Club in St James's and BP's intellectual feats were simply beyond him.

Also, as a manager of difficult and clever men, he [Menzies] was almost useless.'[5]

This image of the Intelligence man as club-haunting dilettante was very much part of a generalised impression of the secret services, certainly in the years following the First World War. But in the case of Stewart Menzies, the idea of a cocktail-glugging club-dweller was an unfair slur. It seems that he was initially distrusted at Bletchley on being appointed head of MI6 in November 1939; his predecessor, Admiral Sinclair, who had of course bought the house, was much liked. Not least because he was a naval man – the background of Bletchley's senior personnel echoed back to Room 40, which was a naval concern. Menzies by contrast was an army man. The old service rivalries died hard.

According to Nigel de Grey, commenting more diplomatically later, these and other internal Bletchley Park conflicts were 'an imbroglio of conflicting jealousies, intrigue and differing opinions'. Yet those furious threats of resignation from Dilly Knox – perhaps exacerbated by ill-health or simple short temper – interestingly also accused Denniston of not being up to the job.

Even the 'Third Man', Kim Philby, had a view on these intrigues, as he related in his memoirs: 'Much of their work was brilliantly successful. I must leave it to learned opinion to decide how much more could have been achieved if the wrangling inside GC and CS had been reduced to manageable proportions.'[6]

One can easily see how difficult everyone's position at Bletchley must have been; for the more successful the huts and the codebreakers became at their work, the greater the demands that were as a result placed upon them. And these demands had to be met with finite resources. While a number of bombe machines were now in operation, there was continuing conflict about how much time was dedicated to the decrypts relating to each branch of the Services. Obviously there were only so many hours in every day, so which would receive priority? And who ultimately had the power to parcel out these chunks of time?

Of course the leaders of the different huts were going to fight each other for use of the bombe machines – it was hardly professional rivalry, it was an understanding that the lives of countless others depended upon the work that they were doing. For all the jibes about 'ambition' and some being 'less scrupulous' than others, the conflicts at Bletchley were rather more than outbreaks of office politics. For all parties concerned, the stakes could not have been higher. Many who worked there had relatives who were out in Europe, in North Africa, in the Far East, fighting. Naturally they would stop at nothing to provide all the assistance and intelligence that they possibly could.

In any case, there were a great many at Bletchley Park who saw the advent of Edward Travis as Director as unquestionably a good thing. He was a man much better able than Denniston to deal with the myriad administrative difficulties – from bombe time to security to the absurdity of tea rations – that the place regularly threw up.

Gordon Welchman clearly had a lot of time for Commander Travis, as he revealed in his memoir:

> As a wartime leader, Travis had some of Winston Churchill's qualities. He was definitely of the bulldog breed, and he liked to have things done his way, but he also had a great feeling for what it took to create happy working conditions . . . He would get around to all our activities, making contact with staff at all levels, and he had the gift of the human touch. Once he personally organised a picnic for Hut 6 staff, which was a tremendous success. In spite of his heavy workload after he became Director, he still showed his personal interest in our activities, including those at the bombe sites.[7]

It might also have been the case that the era of the gifted amateur was over, and that a new, more systematic and disciplined approach to the work was needed. With the sheer volume of traffic that was now being dealt with, day by day, hour by hour, the Park had to ensure that all this invaluable information was given to the right people. Moreover, with the coming of the machines, and the increase in personnel that this brought, there was a sense in which the functions of Bletchley were becoming industrialised.

A new class of what might be termed 'technocrats' were coming forward, of which cocksure young Gordon Welchman seemed the prime exemplar. The old ways of Alistair Denniston, and of Room 40, with its volatile and unpredictable individualists, had been extremely effective in their time. But how could they be expected to cope with these new and extraordinary demands? How could they match the most implacable enemy that Britain had ever seen?

Codebreaker Ralph Bennett – who had been sent to Egypt to co-ordinate the work of Hut 6 – came back to Bletchley Park in 1942. 'I had left as one of a group of enthusiastic amateurs,' he wrote. 'I returned to a professional organisation with standards and an acknowledged reputation to maintain. Success was no longer an occasional prize, but the natural reward of relentless attention to detail.'[8]

There were extra recruits coming in; the brilliant young mathematician Shaun Wylie, for instance, arrived in 1941. His recruitment had in part to do with Alan Turing; for the two men had met in the late 1930s at Princeton University. A formidable intellect, Wylie was also an excellent hockey player. He joined Turing's hut, Hut 8, and the effort to smash naval Enigma. He was to become head of crib subsection, making a special study of phrases and subjects likely to form a part of encrypted texts, such as weather conditions and the locations of Allied attacks.

And the debutantes in their pearls were proving their worth in the cross-referencing card index, which had been steadily growing and growing. Thanks to their painstaking and unimaginably tedious labours, the index was so minutely detailed that the codebreakers could now tell, for example, when Admiral Dönitz was communicating with a captain who was a personal friend, because of the appearance of the name of that captain's wife.

The card index was equally formidable for Bletchley's Air Section. 'My recollection,' said veteran Hugh Skillen, 'is of many thousands of cards in shoe-boxes along both sides of a long hut. When a new word came up in the message you were translating – a neologism, new type of jet fuel, or machine part – you looked for it and if it was not there, the indexer put it in with a reference time and a date stamp.'[9]

After the Japanese attack on Pearl Harbor in 1941 – the event that finally brought America into the war – Colonel Tiltman was determined that Bletchley's codebreakers should be trying everything to master the Japanese codes. Immediately, however, he faced twin hurdles: in 1942, there were very few people in Britain familiar with Japanese; and nor is it an easy language to learn.

Tiltman himself was a partial exception. By this stage, he had already taught himself some Japanese to get a feel for it, and to gauge the possibilities of new young recruits being able to master it sufficiently in order to handle encrypted messages. The colonel was an optimist. The call went out to Cambridge and Oxford, for classics scholars who would by now be in some other part of the military structure. Sixth-forms with pupils about to sit for Oxbridge were also contacted.

'I realised that this is EXACTLY what I wanted to do,' wrote veteran Hugh Denham. Invited for interview with Colonel Tiltman and others, he was asked: 'Do you have any religious scruples about reading other people's correspondence?'[10] What followed was an exhausting and intensive six-month course in Japanese, taught at the Gas Company in Bedford, and defying the conventional assumption that it took at least two years to grasp a working knowledge of the language. There wasn't the scope, wrote Michael Loewe with nice understatement, 'for much attention to the niceties of Japanese history or culture.'[11]

A short introduction to codebreaking followed. But in the early days, there was, understandably, a lot of frustration; the intercepts they were working on were old. Moreover, 'none of the thousand or so characters that we had learned were there on the [message] page before us', commented Maurice Wiles, another Classics scholar.[12] Michael Loewe talked of the 'long weary hours' that would be spent simply indexing the code-groups that they had managed to identify.

And there were not many people in the section – either code-breakers or clerical staff – to help with what must have been unbelievably complex filing needs. 'At Bletchley Park, we were over-awed by the presence of those whom we saw as experienced professionals,' wrote Michael Loewe. 'The tall and lanky figure of Hugh Foss seemed to look down from a great height on the raw recruits assembled in his office.'[13]

None the less, 'we got there in the end', said Maurice Wiles. 'Fortunately it was not the most difficult of codes, but it took time for us to figure out what was going on and how to tackle the problems it posed.' In other words, a magnificently insouciant response to a problem that most of us would not begin to know how to solve.

Work on the Japanese codes also threw up an interesting rivalry with Bletchley's Washington counterparts, who were thought to out-number the British staff by ten to one. Those at Bletchley found that the prospect of stealing of a march on the Americans, who were studying the same messages, offered a powerful incentive for get-ting codes cracked as quickly as possible. If a transmission came through from the USA with the solution to one such problem, the mood within the Bletchley section deflated accordingly. This rivalry with Washington carries echoes of America's anger and frustration with the British – at least at the political and diplomatic level – for not sharing the Enigma secret in the early years of the war.

Even more irksome were the occasions when they found that they had spent many of those 'long weary hours' simply duplicating work that the Americans had been studying simultaneously. Michael Loewe said of the Japanese section of Bletchley that it was 'the Cinderella' of BP, 'where the main effort was understandably directed to German and Italian problems', and in the midst of which its own efforts were not accorded anything like the same sense of paramount urgency.

For some, like Hugh Denham and Wren Jean Valentine, the Japanese work would take them all the way out to Colombo, in what was then Ceylon, an extraordinarily exotic contrast to Bletchley, with its 'woven palm-leaf cabins', the 'phosphorescent sea' and the 'snakes in the filing cabinet', as Denham recalled. The work of this small, concentrated team would mostly track Japanese activity in the Indian Ocean.

'One thing to record,' Denham wrote, 'is the priceless sense of community that formed. We were in our teens or twenties, thrown together, Wrens, civilians and officers, working to a common purpose, sharing unusual experiences.'[14]

Jean Valentine's spell as a Wren based at Adstock and working at Bletchley came to a startling end in 1944. One day, as she says: 'A notice went up on the wall saying, "The following are required to go overseas."' Her name was among the 'following'. For a nineteen-year-old girl who had never before left Britain, the notion of travelling right the way across the world – U-boats or no U-boats – was extraordinarily daunting.

'We went out into the Atlantic, down, and then through the Straits of Gibraltar, and eventually dashed across the Red Sea, and then across to Bombay,' says Jean. 'We were in Bombay for a week, then got a dirty old tramp steamer – which had been condemned before the war – and that took us from Bombay to Colombo.'

Upon arrival in her little concrete hut in Colombo, Jean found that the work was rather more congenial than simply tweezering the inner workings of a giant bombe. 'We were breaking the Japanese meteorological code,' she says. 'So I didn't need to speak Japanese. It was all figures.' After the privations of Britain – the constant shortages, the rationing – this exotic new billet proved surprisingly pleasant. The ease with which this girl from Perthshire adapted to her new life tells us something about the last years of the British Empire, when even the remotest corners of the world had a sort of instant familiarity and comfort – as long as one made the correct introductions and got to know the right sort of people.

'I was there fifteen months,' says Jean. 'I left Britain in the middle of the blackout, with all that severe rationing. I got to Colombo and there was no blackout.' And, by pleasing coincidence, a family connection enabled Jean to settle in a little further. Her cousin's fiancée, who had visited Ceylon as a member of a ladies' golfing team, had told her, 'If you should find yourself anywhere near Ceylon, I've got a business card for this tea-planter, do use it . . .'

Jean contacted the man, 'And subsequently he invited us up to his beautiful tea-planter's house, four thousand feet up. It was a different life. Here was a man sitting in his beautiful bungalow with bluegrass that he'd imported from Kentucky before the war. A bell at the end of the table. When anybody laid down their knife, he quietly rang and servants would come.'

Back in Britain, despite the dreadful setback of the even more complex naval Enigma, the Battle of the Atlantic was by no means over. However intractable the new 'Shark' U-boat key, Hut 8 began after a while to make headway with 'Dolphin', the codes that related to German ships. This was illustrated vividly in March 1942, when the formidable German battleship *Tirpitz* was stalking an Arctic convoy bound for Russia. '*Tirpitz* was the big bad wolf of the war in home waters,' wrote naval historian John Winton. 'All by herself she constituted a "fleet in being" and, while she still floated, she remained a potential threat . . . the mere knowledge of her presence lying up in some northern fastness cast a long shadow over the convoys.'[15] Thanks to the almost instantaneous decrypts that Bletchley provided – the translated messages instantly being transmitted to the Admiralty – the convoy was able to take evasive action from both the *Tirpitz* and the U-boat wolf packs.

However, an attack on the *Tirpitz* itself came to nothing. A few months later, and that 'long shadow' was hanging over convoy PQ17, which consisted of thirty ships, sailing through the wind and the ice of the northern seas. The *Tirpitz*, and other enemy ships, started hunting them down; again, the codebreakers at Bletchley worked at terrific speed, and the decrypted messages were passed to Admiralty. This time however the messages were misunderstood.

The Admiralty gave the order for the convoy to be dispersed; back at the Park, Hut 4 liaison officer Harry Hinsley tried to persuade the Admiralty that the convoy should not disperse and should instead sail back towards the home fleet. The Admiralty would not listen.

Twenty-four Allied ships were sunk – some from the air and some by U-boats. This was no failure of Bletchley; rather, it was a failure of those who gave orders on the basis of the intelligence that they received.

Yet in spite of such catastrophes, and the anguish of the 1942 code blackout, Bletchley could still console itself in one small sense, according to cryptographer Edward Thomas. 'The evasive routeing of convoys made possible by Hut 8's [original] breaking of the Naval Enigma in the spring of 1941,' he wrote, 'had, according to some historians, spared some 300 merchant ships and so provided a cushion against the heavy losses to come.'[16] Despite the blackout, he noted, this earlier work of Bletchley Park meant that Dönitz's new offensive came to very little, and that losses were in decline.

And in the spring of 1942 Hut 3 made significant inroads into the Luftwaffe codes. As a result, better defensive measures could be taken as 1,000 bomber raids were carried out, meaning that the RAF could carry out more daring raids while keeping the loss of aircraft to a minimum. Although many of these raids were ineffective and inaccurate when it came to hitting serious industrial targets, they nevertheless had a powerful propaganda effect, especially among the British. The German raid on Coventry had hardened British public attitudes towards retaliation. After the destruction of the London Blitz – and horrific assaults such as that on Coventry – the RAF were at last seen to be giving it back.

Despite its disastrous start, 1942 eventually proved to be the year that Churchill was able to describe as 'the end of the beginning'. There was the key triumph of El-Alamein, possibly the most important British battle in the war: after months of morale-corroding setbacks in North Africa, General Montgomery's armies at last pushed behind German lines, forcing Rommel's Axis forces into a long retreat. 'By the summer of 1942,' recalled Y Service signals intelligence operative Aileen Clayton, who by that stage was based in Malta, 'there can have been little Enigma traffic between the German forces in Africa and their masters back in Berlin and Italy that we did not intercept, and now that the cryptographers at Bletchley were so quickly decoding the messages, it was almost like being a member of Rommel's staff.'[17]

The results were spectacular. Thanks to Bletchley, Montgomery had access to an unprecedented amount of information about his enemy's army; about numbers, about armaments, about the supply situations. 'Alamein was marvellous,' recalled one veteran, 'because you had these desperate messages from Rommel saying, "Panzer Army is exhausted, we've only enough petrol for 50 kilometres, ammunition is contemptible", and so on.'

We do see here some of the ambiguity felt by the British military towards the intelligence that Bletchley Park was providing – there is a suggestion that General Montgomery did not wholly trust what he was being told. 'We told Monty over and over again how few tanks Rommel had got,' recalled Bletchley Park veteran and historian Ralph Bennett. 'So Monty could have wiped Rommel off the face of the earth. Why he didn't, I simply do not know.'[18] Nevertheless, throughout General Montgomery's attack on the Axis forces on 23 October 1942, and the subsequent twelve-day battle, he was given a stream of decrypt information concerning German troop and weapon positions. And as Montgomery launched his second attack, it was Enigma decrypts that gave him crucial insight into the crumbling state of the German and Italian forces.

Meanwhile, on the eastern front, the Russians were engaged in the extraordinarily bitter and prolonged struggle of which

Stalingrad became both the focus and the symbol. The turning point arrived after many gruelling months in which the Germans had been convinced that the Russians would simply collapse under the weight of the German attack. Stalin himself was receiving information from Churchill 'based on intelligence sources' concerning the state of the German forces and their possible next moves. As the Germans eventually began their retreat, Churchill provided more small gobbets of such information, while keeping the true source carefully concealed.

The codebreakers still had little idea of how their work was being utilised. As Oliver Lawn recalls: 'I was concerned with the code-breaking and that was it. When the code had been broken, the decoded message was passed through to the Intelligence people who used the information – or decided whether to use it. The content of messages was of no concern to me at all. I knew enough German to get an idea of what it was all about. But I had no idea of the context. And it wasn't my business. I could read the messages but they were so much in telegraphese, jargon, that they would mean nothing.'

Nevertheless, it was perfectly obvious that the work was important. And the success of Bletchley was also being reflected, late in 1942, to the extent that it appeared to be expanding physically. There had come a point when all those wooden huts, with their attendant discomforts, were no longer sufficient for the task. And so the Blocks – plain constructions of brick and steel, some two storeys high, and explosive-resistant – started to appear. In Block A, Josh Cooper's Air Section got the first floor, while Frank Birch's Naval Section was moved into the ground floor.

There were more Blocks to follow, up to D. Block A was equipped – in one of those nice little touches that always seemed to bring an element of the quotidian into the Bletchley effort – with a pneumatic tube system previously used in John Lewis stores and employed at Bletchley for zipping messages on paper between rooms. It was a step up from the hatchway/tray/pulley arrangement that had previously been a feature of inter-hut communication. The pneumatic system was brought in by Hugh Alexander, who before the war had been Chief Scientist to the John Lewis chain.

Despite such innovation, working conditions were still far from luxurious. For example, the conveniences, or lack of them, were sometimes a talking point. In February 1943, an agitated Frank Birch wrote a letter to the works manager, Mr MacGregor:

> Sorry to bother you again, but I should be very grateful to know the latest developments as regards the plan for extending the congested portion of Block A, as the problem is getting more and more acute.
>
> I went over Hut 7 this morning to see how my chaps fitted in. It all seemed very comfortable and the light was very good indeed, but they really are in a bad way about lavatories – I think there is only one for men and one for all the women, which is not enough for the 200 authorised.

Notwithstanding the delicacy of the subject, Birch continued:

> Mack told me some time ago that you were going to build a lavatory between the main building and the hut. If this could be incorporated in a passage, it would remove also the remaining disadvantage, namely having to go through the open air in the hot or the cold or the dark to reach another part of the section.[19]

But even with these and a great many other physical discomforts, the institution was running with great efficiency. Hugh Alexander, who succeeded Alan Turing as Head of Hut 8 in 1941, was a formidable and rather frightening intellect. He was also something of a heart-throb with the ladies. Diana Plowman described him thus: 'Alexander was my boss, and we all thought he was crazy. Tall, blond, huge blue eyes, never stopped talking, a terrible energy . . .'

It was this man, with his huge blue eyes, who had, with the greatest gentleness, eased Turing out as head of Hut 8. There was no malice involved – simply a recognition that the job had to be done by someone with more of a sense of everyday practicality. As a brilliant mathematician, Turing was a rather vague and disorganised administrator. Moreover, the Bletchley authorities understood that he would work a great deal more effectively if he took a step back from the daily duties of hut work.

In fact, Alexander had slowly been doing more and more of the job in any case. And his admiration for Turing, as he later testified, was utterly untrammelled:

> There should be no question in anyone's mind that Turing's work was the biggest factor in Hut 8's success. In the early days, he was the only cryptographer who thought the problem worth tackling and not only was he primarily responsible for the main theoretical work within the Hut (particularly the developing of a satisfactory scoring technique for dealing with Banburismus) but he also shared with Welchman and Keen the chief credit for the invention of the Bombe . . . the pioneer work always tends to be forgotten when experience and routine later make everything seem easy and many of us in Hut 8 felt that the magnitude of Turing's contribution was never fully realised by the outside world.[20]

The intransigence of the 'Shark' U-boat key was by November 1942 the source of acute anxiety in the War Office. The OIC sent a message to the Bletchley authorities. The Battle of the Atlantic, it said, was 'the one campaign which BP are not at present influencing to any marked extent – and it is the only one in which the war can be lost unless BP do help.'

Help was to come very soon afterwards. Spotted sailing off the coast of Palestine, U-559 was depth-charged by HMS *Petard*; and thanks to the terrific bravery of the two British crew members who swam the sixty yards to the stricken vessel, a vital discovery was made.

The U-boat's crew had abandoned ship – the vessel was sinking. By the time Lieutenant Anthony Fasson and Able Seaman Colin Grazier swam to it, followed by sixteen-year-old Tommy Brown, only its conning tower was visible above the waves.

Despite the fact that the U-boat was about to be submerged, Fasson and Grazier boarded the vessel. Some lights were still on inside. And what they found was the four-rotor Enigma machine that had defeated Bletchley, along with a book of the current Shark keys.

With astounding presence of mind, the pair ensured that both the Enigma machine and the keys and the bigram tables were wound securely in waterproof material. They passed the machine and the books to Tommy Brown, who was outside. He in turn passed them to fellow crew members in a whale boat. But it was too late for Fasson and Grazier. U-559 sank, taking them with it into the depths. They had given their lives so that this information could be passed back. Both men were posthumously awarded the Victoria Cross, while Tommy Brown received the George Cross.

When the machine and the documents reached Bletchley Park a few weeks later, it at last became possible for the codebreakers to crack the 'Shark' key. And very shortly afterwards, they did. After the dark months of code blackout, the naval Enigma operation was back in business.

The relief at Bletchley, and throughout Whitehall, was immense. The task ahead was still formidable: ensuring Britain's survival was not the same thing as winning the war, and the Wehrmacht, embedded throughout much of Europe, right to the edges of the continent, was ferociously resilient. Nevertheless, even if no precise details were known by most individuals at Bletchley Park, it was now possible for those who worked there to sense the impact that their work was starting to have; to have an inkling of how the German war machine, which two years before had seemed utterly indestructible, was now being harried on various sides.

The rise in personnel numbers demanded by the work also led, with a certain warm inevitability, to the formation of more and more romantic relationships. It is an aspect of Bletchley life that one might have expected the authorities – for the reason of 'careless talk' – to patrol with the greatest of care. But actually, for many, the course of love ran remarkably smooth.

19 The Rules of Attraction

It is perhaps a generational thing; but when one thinks now of what might loosely be termed 'wartime romance', one is struck by two stereotypical images. The first is that of young English roses being swept off their feet by sharp-talking American soldiers with bribes of fancy cigarettes and bubblegum; the second, the agonies suffered by Celia Johnson and Trevor Howard in black and white at Carnforth railway station in *Brief Encounter*. In general, the Americans are depicted as forthright sexual vulgarians, whereas the British are every bit as repressed as their stiff upper lips would imply.

Such clichés, of course, have no value whatsoever, but it is interesting to contemplate the chasm that has opened up between that wartime generation and our own. The *Brief Encounter* repression may have been overdoing it a bit – according to many contemporaneous accounts, it assuredly was – but a great many stories from within Bletchley Park tell us that wartime romance was in some senses quite different from today's version.

It is perhaps the most sweetly inevitable part of the Bletchley Park story: a well-educated community of young people – the women greatly outnumbering the men – and a great number of those young people pairing off romantically.

Park veteran S. Gorley Putt put it slightly differently, referring to the 'hot-house confinement' of the Park, and how it created a fervid atmosphere in which 'sexual infatuations . . . became obsessional . . . nerves tautened to breaking point by round-the-clock speedy exactitude would fumble, in off-hours, for emotional nourishment.'[1]

Doubtless so; and given the claustrophobia of the community, added to the tension of the work, perhaps the occasional outbreak of sexual hysteria was inevitable. However, alongside this rather Bloomsbury-esque vision of the Park are the more subtle, though none the less pleasing stories of the many relationships formed that did actually continue. What surprises now, though, as one hears various accounts of the beginnings of long, happy marriages, is how remarkably relaxed the Park authorities seemed in matters of the heart.

Mathematician Keith Batey recalls how one of his very first memories of Bletchley Park was the sight of 'nubile young ladies' wandering to and fro. But it was not long before he and Mavis Lever met. He was in Hut 3; she was working with Dilly Knox in the Cottage. One night, she had an operational message to convey to Hut 3. Their eyes met, as both now laughingly recall: 'Late one evening, I was in the hut, on the evening shift, and that's how I met her,' says Keith. 'This little girl arrived from Dilly's outfit with this message or problem – she didn't know how to solve it.

'I didn't see her again for another year,' says Keith, laughing. 'And she never admitted it, but it was true.'

Mr Batey is not exaggerating greatly about the amount of time it took them to meet again. Those who worked in different huts and different parts of the Park seldom met or crossed over, because the workings of each department were kept closely sealed. If they did meet, any conversation concerning work was forbidden.

Given this level of concern, one might have thought that the Bletchley Park authorities would look with concern upon the blossoming of any inter-hut relationship. However, as Mavis Batey recalls, things seemed easier than that once she and Keith became an item: 'There were no rules against "courting". We thought we had been very secretive – but when we announced our engagement, we were told that there were bets on when we would. The person who handled booking for the lunch sittings had noticed that we always made sure we had the same allocation.'

In other words, despite their efforts to remain unnoticed, Keith and Mavis were fully clocked, but in an apparently wholly benevolent way. Mavis recalls that Dilly Knox jokingly tried to warn her that 'mathematicians are very unimaginative'. She assured him that hers was just fine. The engagement went ahead and marriage followed not too long after. Mavis Batey continues: 'It was only when we were married that we were required by the regulations to work in different rooms. But that was plain civil service rules and nothing to do with the Secret Service.'

Sheila and Oliver Lawn not only found a similarly promising and benign atmosphere, but also realised, long before they met, just how conducive to romance the Bletchley Park set-up was. On top of this, they had observed the growing tenderness between Keith Batey and Mavis Lever. Says Oliver Lawn: 'There was quite a bit of romance. There were several in Hut 6 who married while they were at Bletchley. There were the Bateys, of course. Sheila and I married later, because Sheila had to go off and finish off her qualifications.'

'Oliver and I met at the Scottish Reels club,' says Sheila. 'I had just joined it. I noticed that when Hugh Foss [the Bletchley Park king of reels] was absent, Oliver used to take the class. And I remember this rather nice dancing lad. I suppose we danced together and Oliver thought that I was an adequate partner for him. We also did ballroom dancing, and Latin American.'

It is a treasurable image: the sound, echoing out of the big house, of a gramophone record playing Latin American dances, and the continual rumble of feet on the dance floor. Like the Bateys, Sheila Lawn cannot recall that the authorities had much to say when it became clear that she and Oliver were stepping out: 'I don't think the powers that be could take much control over the issue of relationships because you would meet your people when you were off duty.'

Besides which, adds Mr Lawn, there was simply so much of it about: 'The other couple I recollect was Bob Roseveare and Ione Jay. He was a mathematician, straight from school. He hadn't even gone to university. Very brilliant chap from Marlborough. He married Ione Jay, who was one of the girls in Hut 6.

'Then there was Dennis Babbage, who was a don similar to [Gordon] Welchman. Same sort of age. Babbage married while he was there.'

It was obviously not always a case of automatic marriage. 'Some of our old Bletchley Park flames have come out of the woodwork,' Mr Lawn adds, laughing. 'I had one and Sheila had one. Mine was a lady who I saw for quite a short time. This was long before I met Sheila. We did quite a lot of dancing, I think ballroom dancing rather than Scottish dancing. And this lady and I got quite friendly, over the period of a few months. And then she was moved abroad and spent the rest of the war in Singapore, I think it was.'

Love crossed many barriers at Bletchley. Codebreaker Jon Cohen recalled: 'I took up with a girl who I was quite surprised to find was a countess's daughter. Because with my middle-class Jewish background, that wasn't the sort of person I would normally mix with. But it was a place where all sorts met and there were dances and parties and we enjoyed ourselves to a certain extent.'[2]

Another prominent romance – and indeed subsequent marriage – was that of Shaun Wylie and Wren Odette Murray, both of whom worked in the Newmanry. In 1943, their eyes met across a chuntering Heath Robinson machine; in 1944, they married. Given the not especially romantic backdrop of this vast, noisy machinery, it is a heroically sweet tale. And Shaun and Odette had their moments away from the technology. 'Most of our courting was in Woburn Park,' Odette Murray said. 'The Abbey is a huge imposing building and the central part has a large podium on top of it, very high up. I used to go casual climbing so that I could sit on top of this to watch Shaun on his bicycle coming up the drive.'

It seemed also that love could make a leap across the huts. Thinking back to his days in Hut 8, Rolf Noskwith recalled that one of his colleagues, Hilary Brett-Smith, gave him a précis of the sinking of the *Bismarck* and how the crucial signal had been spotted at the Park by a certain Harry Hinsley. Hilary and Hinsley were later to be married.

One Anglo-American pairing came with officer Robert M. Slusser and WAAF lieutenant Elizabeth Burberry. She was attached to Hut 3 and, just prior to Slusser's arrival, had applied for a transfer. They met, romance blossomed, and the application was withdrawn. Nor did the happy Bletchley couple waste much time. They were married on 27 June 1944, just a few days after D-Day. On 10 April 1945, their daughter Elizabeth was born – a child of Bletchley Park.

On the artier side of things, codebreaker and poet F.T. Prince met his wife-to-be Elizabeth Bush at the Park; and poet Henry Reed met Michael Ramsbotham. Meanwhile, historian Roland Oliver fell headlong for Caroline Linehan.

But perhaps the most poignant relationship at Bletchley Park – not to say the most unexpected – involved Alan Turing. In the summer of 1940, a mathematician called Joan Clarke (later Murray), who had been studying at Cambridge, was recruited to Hut 8. By the spring of 1941, the system of Turing's bombes, and the punch cards, and the mechanical regularity of the shifts needed to operate the whole procedure, was at the centre of Bletchley Park's work. It was also in the spring of 1941 that Turing and his Hut 8 colleagues made the vital break into naval Enigma. And against this extraordinarily intense backdrop, Turing and Joan Clarke's friendship started to develop.

They went to the cinema. They spent days on leave together. During that period, such behaviour could only lead to one conclusion. And despite his sexual orientation, Turing clearly felt that he had to fit in with this overwhelming social norm. With surprising swiftness, he proposed marriage to Joan – although with characteristic honesty, he was careful to tell her that it might not be an ideal marriage because he had what he termed 'homosexual tendencies'.

Perhaps such things were not understood quite as they are now, for Joan was apparently not deterred by this confession, and the engagement went ahead. He met her parents, she met his. There was an engagement ring. Andrew Hodges suggests that Turing's use of the word 'tendency' masked the altogether more sexually active truth, and that if Joan had known this, she would have been shocked.

But again, this was an age in which such things were never discussed, certainly not in public, or in novels, films and stage plays. The terms 'nancy' and 'pansy' were well known, but such stereotypes as could be found within public discourse were feline mincing characters, extravagantly effeminate and knowingly, insidiously deviant. Clearly Turing did not fit in with these depictions.

The other essential point about their relationship was that, unlike many of the other non-mathematician girls who came to work at Bletchley, Turing never had to talk down to Joan; her mathematical training was sharp and their exchanges were relaxed. They played chess, they played tennis, they had lengthy discussions concerning the Fibonacci series of numbers and their recurrence in nature, such as in the folds of pine cones.

But deep down, he knew that it was not going to be. In the summer (since everyone at Bletchley was allowed four weeks' leave a year), Turing and Joan went off for a holiday in Wales, with bicycles and ration cards. When they came back, Turing told Joan that the engagement was off.

They did, however, contrive to remain friends, and later, when Turing had returned from a spell in the US in 1942–3, he brought her back a present of an expensive fountain pen, and dropped vague hints that perhaps they should try the relationship again. Joan, wisely, gave no response to his suggestion.

*

Elsewhere – and talking of the many other romances to be found within the 'Whipsnade Zoo wire fences' as one lady put it – many Park veterans point out that in terms of matters like premarital sex, this was a different era, as innocent as many presume. It wasn't simply that the Pill didn't exist. It was because matters of sex were so rarely, if ever, discussed, that for many young people – or more particularly, young middle-class people – the whole business remained shrouded in mystery. On top of this, there was the real threat of family disgrace. 'If, heaven forfend, you were to come home pregnant,' says one Wren now, 'your mother would have banished you from the house. It would have been unthinkable.'

Perhaps, like many aspects of British life, this might have more to do with class and background than anything else. It is not a great exaggeration to suggest that in the countryside, sex tended – and probably still does tend – to happen sooner than in the overcrowded cities, for the very simple reason that there is the freedom to take off and find privacy. It is also easy to suspect that reticence about sex was much more prevalent among the middle classes; women who knew just how precious one's reputation was, and how easily it was lost. One might say that for upper classes and working classes alike, there was less to be lost in this way, and as such things were a little more relaxed; whereas for the young middle class, one's good name was crucial when it came to maintaining one's hard-won social standing. In some ways, the middle years of the twentieth century were more censorious than the famously repressed Victorian era.

There were always rumours, including stories of unwanted pregnancies and illegitimate births; it was said that one Wren at RAF Chicksands gave birth but the baby died soon after. She attempted in her distress to hide the little body but the authorities found it. The girl was then taken away, and no one knew what became of her. Yet when it came to sex, one former Wren interviewed by Marion Hill responded with a curious blend of worldliness and innocence: 'There were a lot of romances going on. Of course you couldn't actually share a room with a man in a hotel. They asked to see your marriage certificate first. But where you will, you find a way. There was plenty of opportunity for walks in the countryside, bike rides. I can remember drinking Champagne on hilltops with young men.'[3]

They must have been very wealthy young men. Champagne in wartime north Buckinghamshire cannot have been very abundant. And the mention of hotel rooms illustrated perfectly what young suitors were up against; nevertheless, for many, the very idea of trying to get such a room in the first place wouldn't have been countenanced.

Another Park veteran recalled: 'BP contained a network of long-standing relationships ... The Section would ensure that arrangements for shift-working took due account of them ... for it was difficult to do much "carrying on" with someone on a different shift.' Equally, if a romance was starting to wither, 'it might have been advisable to reshuffle the shifts. On the whole, the system worked pretty well.'

Young Mimi Gallilee too could see romance all over the Park, but she succinctly expresses the innocence that was very much a keyword at the time: 'There were lots of marriages. Other liaisons,' she adds, 'you didn't know about.'

20 1943: A Very Special Relationship

The idea that a close partnership between Britain and the United States was forged during the Second World War has become one of the abiding assumptions of our political landscape. They gave us the tools, and we finished the job. What we lacked in material resources, we more than made up for with bulldog pluck; a pluck that earned the admiration of Uncle Sam, and created a bond between the two mighty nations that has remained strong until today. It is a stubbornly enduring image. The war, it is believed, shifted the relationship between the two countries irrevocably from one of mutual suspicion to one of mutual respect.

Yet it is obviously not that simple, and indeed seemed very far from being the case throughout the war itself, according to several historians who have written recent studies on the subject. Walter Reed believes that while the rapport between Churchill and Roosevelt was very strong, the opposite was the case for the military advisers and ministers beneath them; as Reed sees it, Congress and the US Treasury viewed Britain with immense suspicion during the war.

According to historian Michael Howard:

Roosevelt's personal bonhomie was based on a shrewd appreciation that Britain must not be allowed to lose the war, and then – once the Americans had been precipitated out of a neutrality they would far rather have preserved – that she must be humoured until the United States was strong enough to take over the direction of the war and wage it as she thought fit. He needed Churchill's help to overcome the visceral dislike of the British that penetrated deep into his military and political elites. Ironically, Churchill was to do this so successfully that today he is far more of an iconic figure in the United States than Roosevelt.[1]

Some of these tensions were reflected in miniature by the workings of Bletchley Park, both before December 1941, when the USA entered the war, and after. Suspicion in some corners persists to this day that Bletchley Park learned from decrypts in early December 1941 about the forthcoming Japanese attack on Pearl Harbor, and that Churchill suppressed the passing of intelligence in order to ensure that the bombing would go ahead, thus ensuring that the Americans would join the war. But even in 1940, over a year before America entered the war, both countries were, at best, tentative with regard to the sharing of information and intelligence. Although it was clearly understood that Britain and America should co-operate in terms of ciphers, the extent of this co-operation soon became a cause of ill-will. According to the Bletchley official history: 'In the British archives there is no intelligence of any importance that was not available to the Americans.' Nevertheless, the mere fact that such a suspicion could arise is telling. And from the start, the relationship between Bletchley and American Intelligence was far from easy.

In December 1940, a full year before America entered the war, an agreement was signed in Washington between Britain and the USA which would mean both countries having a full exchange of technical information concerning German, Italian and Japanese codes.

A month later, a small party of four American cryptographers – two army and two navy – sailed over to England to see the Bletchley operation for themselves.

Having been greeted at the docks by the then Deputy Director Edward Travis and Colonel John Tiltman, they were driven to Bletchley, where they met Alistair Denniston at midnight. Denniston's personal assistant, Barbara Abernethy, recalled:

> I'd never seen Americans before, except in the films. I just plied them with sherry. I hadn't the faintest idea what they were doing there; I wasn't told. But it was very exciting and hushed voices. I couldn't hear anything of what was said but I was told not to tell anybody about it. I guess it wasn't general knowledge that the Americans had got any liaison with Bletchley. It was before Pearl Harbor, you see, and presumably Roosevelt was not telling everybody there was going to be any liaison at that stage.[2]

Throughout the several weeks the American party spent in England, they were put up in the nearby manor house of Shenley Park, and as well as Bletchley Park, were shown U-boat tracking stations and radar stations. One of the key elements of their visit was their mutual interest in cracking the Japanese codes. The elegant Scotsman Hugh Foss, together with Oliver Strachey, had penetrated the Japanese diplomatic code machine in 1934. Moreover, Colonel Tiltman had cracked Japanese military codes as far back as 1933, and the new army ciphers in 1938. Such expertise was naturally going to be of interest to the Americans, who had been monitoring the Japanese closely.

Meanwhile, the Americans had succeeded by 1940 in getting their own decryption machine, devoted to Japanese codes, working. The machine was called 'Purple'. The American cryptographers brought one such machine over with them to England, where they presented it to Bletchley Park. By all accounts, British and US codebreakers got on tremendously well in an atmosphere of mutual respect and excitement.

Only in the weeks after the visit did this cordial relationship start to grow bumpy and sour. For there were some on the American side who considered that the British had not reciprocated the invaluable gift of the Purple machine. No matter that Bletchley Park had sent the Americans detailed documents about Enigma and the cracking thereof, and even parts of Alan Turing's notes on the same; what the Americans wanted was a bombe machine. And British Intelligence, as well as Alistair Denniston, was determined that the US should not have one.

On the face of it, this seems a puzzling denial; why shouldn't an ally have full access to any technology that could help in the wider conflict? Was it simply – as American cryptographers suspected – a jealous possessiveness on the part of Bletchley Park? Was it a symptom of Bletchley Park's neurotic insistence on maintaining control?

Or could there have been fear on the British side? Some have suggested that Bletchley Park was deeply reluctant to let the Americans anywhere near the bombes because thus far, American security had been relatively lax. If the Americans latched on to the British technology, the reasoning went, there was always the grim possibility than an enemy agent in the USA would find it very easy to fathom what they were doing, and pass the information back to Germany.

There was also the fact that in 1940, there were just six bombes in operation, and these were working at full stretch. Bletchley Park could not afford to lose even one of these machines. MI6 told Bletchley that they should not cite this reason, however, in case the Americans suggested that the bombe blueprint should be sent instead so that they could build their own.

The American reaction was – perhaps not unreasonably – an angry one. Crucially, though, this diplomatic frostiness did not affect the personal relationships between the senior cryptographers themselves. Alistair Denniston struck up a warm and enduringly useful friendship with senior American cryptographer William Friedman; in turn, it has been written, Friedman greatly admired and respected Denniston.

Though Bletchley refused to give up its bombes, it tried to help the Americans in various other ways. In November 1942, for instance, it sent the United States Alan Turing in person. He crossed the Atlantic on the *Queen Elizabeth* at a time when all such shipping was intensely vulnerable to the all-pervasive menace of the U-boats. Turing had been in America before, in the 1930s, and had friends there; this visit was with the purpose of creating new ones. In essence, Bletchley was lending out his intellectual expertise to their formidably wealthy ally, in the hope that his genius combined with their technological knowhow and unlimited resources would create further breakthroughs.

Having arrived at Communications Supplementary Activities (Washington), known as CSAW, Turing moved from department to department of the American cryptography operation, with an understanding that he was there by permission not of the army or navy, but of the White House itself. He was allowed complete access to all the new systems that the US cryptographers were working on, and his skills began to pay dividends. The positions of the Atlantic U-boats were at last trackable once more.

He next set to work in Bell Laboratories in New York where a top secret new idea was being developed. It was concerned with speech encipherment and call scrambling, using devices such as the Vocoder, which was being developed in Dollis Hill back in London. Known within this community as England's top cryptographer, he based himself in Greenwich Village for work on this and other military security systems which involved twelve-hour days.

Still there was an ungovernable streak though. His biographer Andrew Hodges writes that colleagues there:

complained of Alan giving no sign of recognition or greeting when he passed them in the halls; instead, he seemed to look straight through them. [Colleague] Alex Fowler, who was an older man of just over forty, was able to take Alan to task.

He was abject, but made an explanation hinting at why he found so many aspects of life difficult. 'You know at Cambridge,' he said, 'you come out in the morning and it's redundant to keep saying hallo, hallo, hallo.' He was too conscious of what he was doing, to slip into conventions without thinking. But he promised to do better.[3]

Turing even claimed aloud to have been approached sexually by another man in a hotel – the sort of boast that was assuredly not a conventional topic around the water-cooler in the US in 1943.

Later in 1942, Commander Travis went out to Washington himself but received what Gordon Welchman described as 'a frosty reception'. On the US side, there was still intense resentment at Bletchley's refusal to share the bombe machines.

Despite this difficulty, an agreement between Britain and the USA was signed concerning the pooling of cryptographical knowledge. Part of this agreement involved, finally, Bletchley relinquishing its knowledge in return for information and precious resources. The USA would develop bombe machines based upon Turing's designs.

Construction got under way in Dayton, Ohio. The first two of the machines, the design of which was inspected by Turing, were called Adam and Eve. From that point in 1942, Bletchley continued to take the lead on German naval decrypts, but would also send raw decrypts over to Washington. This was an extraordinary arrangement – the first time ever that two sides, regardless of their ally status, had so readily and widely pooled their codebreaking intelligence expertise.

And while the Americans got Turing and new bombes, Bletchley Park got some Americans – soldiers who also happened to be expert cryptographers. Codebreaker Oliver Lawn recalls their arrival: 'The American army sent over a batch of cryptographers to work with us in Hut 6. They were led by a chap called William Bundy, who was then a captain in the American Army. Latterly after the war he became very prominent in American politics.

'We got on very well with him. He brought half a dozen people with him and they mucked in with us on our shifts. Did the normal work with us and just became part of our team.'

According to his account of Bletchley Park, Peter Calvocoressi was equally impressed at the ease with which the Americans slid into day-to-day operations. He wrote:

One day in April 1943, a Colonel Telford Taylor was introduced into Hut 3, the first of our American colleagues. He already knew a great deal about Ultra and it seemed to take him no more than a week to master what we were up to. Others of similar calibre followed. They too were temporarily mobilised civilians and their backgrounds were roughly comparable with our own except that there were rather more lawyers among them than among us.

They were slotted into our various sections and in next to no time they were regular members of those sections.

When American army and air headquarters were set up in England and later moved to the continent, they had their own American Ultra intelligence officers and their own special communications with Bletchley Park, but at Bletchley Park itself British and Americans were integrated.

In 3A for example, some of the Air Advisers were American, but all the Advisers served all American and British commands without discrimination. The addition of the American contingent was so smooth that we hardly noticed it. Presumably this was in part due to the sense of common purpose but it must also have owed more than we realised at the time to the personalities and skills of the first Americans to arrive . . .[4]

This warmth was very much returned by Colonel Telford Taylor, who later wrote:

I cannot adequately portray the warmth and patience of the Hut 3 denizens (and to a lesser degree those of Hut 6 and other huts as well) in steering me around and explaining the many aspects of the work. At first I had no office, but Jim Rose and Peter Calvocoressi gave me a seat in their office ·. . . 'C', Travis and de Grey were entirely civil, and Travis really friendly . . .

I take pride at the ease, goodwill, and success with which the merging was accomplished by Britons and Americans alike.[5]

Colonel Taylor was also at the centre of something of a scandal; he embarked upon an affair with English cryptographer Christine Brooke-Rose. She later confessed to Michael Smith that her husband reacted in a way that seems inordinately of a piece with the times: 'He was very very British and he and Telford talked together. Telford was terribly amused afterwards, because he thought my husband was so British, shaking hands and saying everything was all right – which of course it wasn't, because our marriage broke up.[6]

Elsewhere, Mimi Gallilee also has a particular memory of these socially adept American newcomers: 'I had a friend, in the Wrens, and I don't even know which Hut she was working in, but at the end of the war, whiling away time before she was posted to the Admiralty to finish out her service, before she could be released . . . she was going out with an American army man there, Bob Carroll. I believe they got engaged before he went back to America. It took well over a year for her to be able to join him and marry out there.'

The notion of American soldiers coming to Britain and making free with the available women is one of those comical tropes as deeply embedded as the idea of the special relationship itself. It even featured in a recent episode of *The Simpsons*, where Grandpa feels impelled to revisit his English love. As we have seen, Bletchley Park lent itself to romances of all sorts.

Contemporary caricatures – good-natured ones, all the same – abounded in popular culture. One of the characters in the wildly popular BBC Radio comedy *It's That Man Again* was an American sergeant called Sam Scram; elsewhere, in Powell and Pressburger's *A Canterbury Tale* (1944) one of the three leads was a young American sergeant who finds his 'pilgrimage' to Canterbury diverted temporarily by a quirky foray into Kentish village life. Powell and Pressburger were to return to this theme of Anglo-American melding in *A Matter of Life and Death* (1945); here, airman David Niven falls for American wireless operator Kim Hunter.

One Bletchley Park veteran, Harry Fensom, recalled with great good humour the 'remark of an amazed American lieutenant' who had been visiting codebreaking sites. This American observed that 'the buildings contained marvellous machines and many attractive ladies. The machines were made by the British Tabulating Company and the ladies by God.'[7]

The American contingent at Bletchley Park clearly found life in the Buckinghamshire countryside congenial and stimulating in a variety of ways. Consider this account from an American soldier, collected by Marion Hill. He spoke wistfully of the lively social life he and his compatriots enjoyed among the Wrens:

'We were 100 American men, at least half of whom worked side by side with the natives, many of them female. In the community at large, there was a shortage of men, many of the local lads being away in the service. Consequently, Americans were always invited to dances. At least half of us were married, but there is little evidence we forgot it. A few of the single men did marry British girls.'[8]

Similarly, some of the women who worked at the Park had starry-eyed (and curiously innocent) recollections of these American dreamboats. One said: 'We used to go to dances with the American airmen ... because they had beautiful food and ice cream.' Another, equally artless, had this to say: 'Bill, a Captain in the American signals, drove a jeep. I was looking at it with great envy – I'd never ridden in a jeep.'

Obviously, there was going to be the odd moment when the two cultures gazed upon one another with mutual incomprehension.

There was the matter, for instance, of culinary tastes. One American serviceman at Bletchley noted that one could always do swaps in the canteen: 'The Britons were always hungry for protein and it was a delight to see the English girls attack my kipper with vigour while I ate my toast.' Conversely, Lord (then plain Asa) Briggs found himself saucer-eyed at the prospect of American food – and indeed American further education. At Bletchley Park, he recalled, 'I first heard of tomato juice, American bacon, American coffee, and, not least for me, American universities.'[9]

And an American officer after the war summarised what he considered the great charms of Bletchley Park: 'If you had to be in the Army, it was nice to be in a place where you wouldn't be shot at. If you had to have a desk job, it was satisfying to have one you believed was extremely important to the war effort as well as offering a heavy mental challenge. We could be smug in the knowledge that we had been in an important place at a crucial time.'

In 1944, it was Gordon Welchman's turn to travel to the States, and his account of the voyage illustrates the frustrations and satisfactions that this secret life at Bletchley brought to a proud man:

> I went to America on the *Queen Mary* in February 1944 and found myself sitting at the Captain's table with several well-known people, including a minister in the British cabinet, the head of the National Physical Laboratory, and film producer Alexander Korda.
>
> During the voyage it became apparent that the cabinet minister resented the presence at the Captain's table of this Gordon Welchman, who didn't seem to be doing anything important. However, when we reached New York, and the passengers were awaiting instructions, we heard a broadcast announcement: 'Will Mr Alexander Korda and Mr Gordon Welchman please disembark?' I happened to be standing near the cabinet minister and saw the look of amazement on his face![10]

Welchman does not record the pleasure that he doubtless felt upon seeing this expression.

He was in the USA as an invitee of Sir William Stephenson, a senior Intelligence man who, at the behest of Churchill, had set up a shadow 'British Secret Service' in the USA, in the event that the Germans invaded and overran Britain. But the focus of Welchman's admiration was on America and its people. He so enjoyed all he saw and experienced there that in 1948, he emigrated for good. This was his account of his first encounter with his US counterparts:

The Americans, I found, are particularly good at putting people at their ease by preliminary talk about this and that before serious matters come up for discussion. When I first arrived in Washington, before I was allowed to make contact with the cryptanalysts, I had to be introduced to some of the top brass, whose approval was needed.

No doubt they would have made things easy for me by a period of general conversation, but in my case no such ice-breaking was necessary. I had only just arrived from England, where our wartime diet was simple, and was suffering from my first exposure to American food. As soon as we reached the building, I had to ask: 'Where is it?' . . . when I finally arrived [to meet the dignitaries], everyone was grinning and there was no ice to be broken.

In other words, even as the two countries' senior military personnel found themselves in continual dispute, among the codebreakers there was an unusual camaraderie, warmth and mutual respect. For America, the relationship was vital – Britain had made so many of the giant, and sometimes devious, intellectual leaps that made such an operation possible. Conversely, much in the way that America was helping Britain out with military resources, it was also proving invaluable in terms of supplying Bletchley.

*

What then, from 1941 onwards, of Britain's other allies? When it came to the existence of Bletchley Park, the French turned out on many occasions to be the source of tremendous anxiety in Whitehall.

It was of course alongside Gustave Bertrand, with his 'Scarlet Pimpernel' pinches, that – before the start of the war – Alistair Denniston and Dilly Knox had been fed information by the Poles. After the Germans invaded France in the spring of 1940, the Polish mathematicians, having already left Poland, now had to be evacuated again. They pitched up in England, though they were felt to be too much of a security risk to allow near Bletchley Park. If this seems unjust, it has to be balanced against a thoroughly practical sense of paranoia. And as it happened, Rejewski and his fellow mathematicians were allowed to set up a separate unit in Middlesex analysing Russian intercepts. Meanwhile, the gallant General Bertrand remained in France, under the Vichy government.

This in turn caused the administration at Bletchley Park great anxiety; for what if the Germans were to find Bertrand and his French cryptography experts and force them to reveal Enigma secrets? As it happened, by some extraordinary oversight, they never did. But there was an incident concerning General de Gaulle's Free French forces. In 1943, General Henri Giraud announced to a crowd that he had seen an intercepted message from a senior ranking German. This in turn was reported in London in *The Times*. An incandescent Churchill demanded an immediate investigation at Bletchley Park. The administration could not find any message or decrypt that matched the one that General Giraud claimed to have seen. Once again, it was a claim that appeared to set off no alarm bells within German intelligence; nevertheless, Bletchley Park ensured that the Free French were never passed any identifiable decrypts.

Another dramatic naval battle in 1943 was to hammer home both the Park's tremendous power and its peculiar vulnerability. In

September of that year, Ultra decrypts were revealing, in close detail, the movements of the powerful German battleship *Scharnhorst*. This vast vessel, responsible for the sinkings of many Allied merchant ships, had become a near obsessive target for the British navy. It was based in Altenfjord, Norway. And by Christmas 1943, thanks to Enigma decrypts, enough was known of the ship's movements and intentions for the navy to strike.

After an extraordinary chase through the black northern waters involving many warships – *Sheffield, Norfolk, Belfast, Duke of York* – while the *Scharnhorst* took repeated evasive action, changing course desperately, it was finally run down. *Duke of York* scored a palpable hit, and shortly, torpedoes from the other ships were searing through its hull. Thanks to the continuous stream of communications being decrypted at Bletchley – and instantly passed on to the Admiralty – the mighty *Scharnhorst* sank beneath the waves on 26 December 1943.

In the spring of the following year came a renewed Allied attack on the last of the great German marauders, *Tirpitz*, after other attempts had ended in failure. The ship was harboured, once again, at Altenfjord. Guided by Enigma decrypts concerning the time it intended to set sail, an Allied bomber raid was unleashed one dawn in March. While extensive damage was done – and a great many sailors were killed – it wasn't quite enough. And this, it seemed, was also a very near miss for Bletchley.

'It was as well,' noted John Winton, 'that the Germans remained absolutely confident that the Enigma was inviolate. Even the least suspicious . . . might just have wondered why, after *Tirpitz* had been so many months under repair, a powerful and clearly well-briefed and trained force of enemy aircraft should just happen to arrive overhead, not only on the day but at the hour, even at the very minute, when *Tirpitz* was putting out to sea.'[11]

Nevertheless, information from Enigma decrypts meant that *Tirpitz* was dogged as closely as if she had been bugged. Her final battle came a few months later, once more off the coast of Norway.

This time she sank, taking over 1,000 of her sailors with her.

But the secret of Bletchley could so easily have been deduced by the Germans. Indeed, it still remains a matter of some wonder that it was not; manoeuvres and battles of this sort would always carry that inevitable risk. But the authorities at Bletchley – with thousands now working at the Park – faced an equally pressing and constant anxiety. Regardless of the Official Secrets Act, and the need for utter secrecy being impressed hard upon all those who came into contact with the place, what could the Park do in the event that the secret was accidentally blurted out? Or worse, deliberately revealed by means of espionage?

21 1943: The Hazards of Careless Talk

In Robert Harris's best-selling 1995 novel *Enigma*, the core of the story concerns a spy at work at Bletchley. The tension mounts inexorably because the consequences are so utterly unimaginable. For if the Germans gain one whisper or one inkling that the British have cracked their encoding system, then they will make that system infinitely more complex – and with that, they will be almost impossible to defeat. It is one of those rare thrillers where the publisher might say with some justification that the fate of the world depends upon the novel's heroes.

Some Bletchley veterans are fans of the novel; they admire the way that Harris skilfully evoked life at the Park while adding a thriller element. But that very element, they say, while entertaining, is in fact extremely implausible. Secrecy and security, according to some, was woven into the texture of life at Bletchley to an extent that it became almost pathological. Some veterans were to recall that security at the Park was heavy and unremitting. There are stories of women who worked there who refused even to have medical operations carried out for fear of blurting indiscretions out under anaesthetic. There was a story concerning a lady academic at Cambridge attending parties in London, getting drunk and boasting about her work . . . and she was never heard of again. Intriguingly, there were other slips – accidental, unintentional – that were to demonstrate just how vulnerable the Park was to careless talk.

When western Europe shockingly fell to the Germans with such speed in 1940, the popular belief in Britain that the country would suffer a similar fate had been extremely strong. As Mimi Gallilee recalls, everything possible was done to confuse potential invaders: 'everyone had to stay quiet about everything then – for instance, all railway station names were removed from platforms.

'And all directions were deliberately muddled – so that if we were invaded, or if there were people who shouldn't be in this country – they couldn't find their way easily by signposts.'

But this was not just a matter of marauding soldiers or cunning foreign spies; it was a matter of the butcher, the baker, the candlestick maker, any one of whom might be plotting away with secret wireless sets. It was around this point that the notion of the 'fifth columnist' – the outwardly normal citizen secretly working with the enemy to undermine society – seized the national imagination. German propagandists played upon this anxiety in broadcasts to Britain, in which they would, for instance, announce that the church clock in Banstead, Surrey, was running five minutes slow. How, people wondered, could they acquire such information unless such places were crawling with fifth columnists? But the Germans might not have had to work all that hard to create conditions of paranoia. In every city and every town, any transgressive or unusual behaviour was noted and reported.

What Bletchley Park veterans tend not to refer to now are the episodes when the Park was itself caught up in espionage dramas – not merely the cunning British transmissions of false information and black propaganda from the riding stables of nearby Woburn Abbey (by means of a fake German radio station called Gustav Siegfried Eins, which specialised in smears about Nazi officials), but murkier episodes that across the years have provoked allegation and counter-allegation. As we shall see, there were instances where care-less talk *was* talked – by Wrens, by lieutenants, by mechanically minded clever-dicks – and on these occasions, the Bletchley author-ities were swiftly on the case. There was no shortage of voluntary surveillance in Britain at that time.

But while the necessity of keeping the secret was obviously vital above all else, it seems that the Park hierarchy was largely remark-ably trusting of its young recruits. For the ordinary young men and women, the very notion of espionage or indeed of spies moving among them rarely even occurred.

Teenage runaround Mimi Gallilee – just fourteen when she was taken on as a messenger in this top-secret establishment – recalls her induction very well. 'There was the Official Secrets Act to sign. There wasn't a lecture – I can't even remember if they said "This is the Official Secrets Act." I didn't know what kind of a place I was going to work in. I didn't know what my mother did there. And there was no reason for me to have ever asked. I just know that I had signed the Act. And of course we were told that we mustn't breathe a word to anybody of where we were working.'

The nature of her job meant that she could at least attach names to certain huts, which is a good deal more than any of the cryp-tographers or linguists could do. But, she says, this was a period in which all natural curiosity was numbed. 'You just accepted every-thing you saw and you didn't ask. If there was a need to know, you were told. Because of the job, I used to walk around all day. The Park used to get deliveries of messages, communications – a mini-mum of four deliveries a day each, which I then had to make to the huts.

'And that entailed knowing where everything and everybody was – including who was in charge of the huts – but you weren't allowed to roam around the house.

'And some huts you weren't allowed to go into at all. For instance, there was Hut 11 – where you had to ring the bell outside. Then one of the Wrens or someone – who were locked in – opened up and you just handed across the doorway what you were carrying.'

The odd technological glitch could result in alarms being triggered. In May 1943, H. Fletcher of Hut 6 sent this warning memo to his superiors: 'I think it should be seriously considered whether the fitting of scramblers is necessary. A Wren, using a public call box in Newport Pagnell, and conversing with her mother in a trunk call, was able to overhear a menu being telephoned to [the Bletchley Park outstation at] Gayhurst. Her mother also heard this conversation and remarked on its curious nature.'[1]

What seems rather striking now to the Hon. Sarah Baring is the fact that she cannot remember what the penalty would have been for any slip of the tongue. 'The people I worked with in Hut 4, we could talk between each other,' she says. 'We were doing the same thing. I'd be translating, another friend would be doing something else. So we could talk. But only within your hut. You never talked outside your hut.

'But the awful thing was they couldn't give you the sack. Because you knew too much. So God knows what they would have done if anyone did talk. And nobody ever did.'

Oliver Lawn recalls: 'There was certainly absolute secrecy in that sense, that you didn't talk about your work to anyone outside your section. Some people have criticised that, saying that it was unnecessarily blinkered. We should have been able to be a little freer in knowing what was going on. It would have helped our work.'

Even though recruits might maintain secrecy within the establishment, however, the question arises: how could Bletchley Park security be expected to police those who were on leave? When these codebreakers and linguists and clerks went home for time off, what did they tell their families, their friends, their neighbours, their local communities, about the nature of the work they were doing?

This was a particularly germane issue for the young men, for it would be natural for many people to think of them: 'Why is he not in uniform?' Gordon Welchman recalled in his memoir that the issue became a source of acute discomfort for some:

> Some of the young men who were sent to Hut 6 because of their brains found themselves trapped there by the demands of security. They longed for active service in the air force, the navy, or the army, but they knew too much about our success with the Enigma for their capture by the enemy to be risked.
>
> They were doing an exhausting job, and it was obviously helping the war effort, but many of them longed to play an active part in the fighting. There was, too, the inevitable feeling that not being at the front was somehow dishonourable; one young man received a scathing letter from his old headmaster accusing him of being a disgrace to his school.[2]

Conversely, some of the codebreakers appeared to live in communities that either valued discretion, or had a sense of what it was that the homecoming lad was really doing. This seemed to be the case for Keith Batey whenever he got leave: 'As to going home, and lack of uniform: no one found it odd. People knew that everything was pretty strict. This business about call-up, reserved occupations and what you were doing. Everyone was directed to what they were doing. No question about that. And no one asked me what I was doing.

'Though there was my brother . . . he wasn't in Bletchley,' Mr Batey continues. 'He was younger than I and was still at Oxford in the middle of the war. Then he went to the RAE, then after the war he became a parson. Many years later – quite recently in fact – he said to me: "It was pretty obvious what you were doing. There were you, a mathematician, and Mavis speaking German. There was never a doubt." So you can see that lots of people put two and two together and sometimes got the right answer.'

From the moment one left the Park and embarked upon a train journey, one was under an infinitely intensified version of the phrase: 'Careless Talk Costs Lives'. But for some, there seemed to be little in the form of stern lectures or admonitions. Nor were there any restrictions on leave, or where that leave might be spent. It was understood from the start by the Park's administrative authorities that after the exhausting focus of the work, after all the concentration and the unremitting shift system, these young people would need their breaks simply to maintain their sanity.

But for the others, it was all a matter of self-discipline. A prevailing sense of anxiety that Germany might after all win the war helped enormously. One veteran recalls how she hated to drink even the smallest amount off-duty, because she was terrified that if she got drunk, she would blurt out confidential information that could be overheard by anyone. Another veteran developed a fear that she might talk in her sleep.

Sheila Lawn recalls her own regular journeys home to the far north of Scotland, and how, as soon as she walked through the gates of Bletchley Park to the railway station, she was under her own jurisdiction. She also recalls what for many of us would be a trying journey, even now.

'Of course, the trains were more reliable then,' she says smiling. 'We used to get a week's holiday four times a year. They paid your fare, third class, which for me was a great matter because I went up to Inverness to see my parents to have a nice few days there. You'd go down to the station, you'd try to make it a suitable shift, you'd walk down with your case to the station, and usually the trains were absolutely crowded in that area, and so often I was shovelled in with a great lot of Forces chaps, and hopefully find a seat, though sometimes it was a case of sitting on your case in the corridor.

'And then sometimes the trains would be rerouted. Whether it was because of difficulties on the line because of bombing, I do not know . . . so sometimes, you would be pretty late in getting up to Inverness. But they got there. In those days, once you got to the lowlands of Scotland, they changed the engines, they put a double engine on, to draw you up over the Highlands.

'I always used to be a bit dirty with the flakes from the engine. They would fly into the carriage through the window. So first thing on getting home, I used to have a shower, or a bath, I can't remember which, and mother would have a hot drink for me, and she always asked me what I wanted for lunch, so I'd tell her, and it would be all ready for me. This would be luxury.'

And luxury, indeed, with no one asking her anything about the nature of the work that she was engaged upon down in Buckinghamshire.

The Hon. Sarah Baring – that cheery habituée of Claridges and other smart London spots – remembers the strategies she would employ to bat off unwelcome queries about what she was doing so far outside the capital, and why she was spending so much time doing it: 'When you were on leave, people would say to me: "What are *you* doing?" It was difficult. I used to say: "Oh, nothing much, frightfully boring job." "Oh. Well, what is it?", they'd say. And I'd say: "I'm a typist, would you believe it?" I would then add: "I could tell you more if you want . . ." Then they would back away and say: "Oh no thank you, we don't want to hear about typing."

'And that was it. Quite easy after that. You could see them thinking: "Don't ask Sarah what she does, she's so boring about it." If you're boring enough, they stop asking you.'

Even at home, in the bosom of one's family, Sarah Baring says that somehow it became second nature not to pry: 'My family didn't ask me. My father just used to say – my mother had died, unfortunately: 'You all right, darling?' And I would say: 'Yes, poppa, I'm fine, don't worry.' My brother was fighting in Anzio at the time – he wouldn't have talked either. The information somehow becomes so precious. It's the lives of your comrades, isn't it.'

There were lapses of discretion, however. Some came about for the most touching and innocent and human of reasons. Take this incident, reported by a J.B. Perrott to Bletchley Park's administrator, Nigel de Grey. Perrott, in Signals, had this formal complaint to make, still to be found in the archives today:

On 18 Feb 1943, I met [Wren] Gwen Knight at a Harpenden Gramophone Society recital. Afterwards, on Harpenden station, she stated that she knew what work was being done by this unit, and mentioned types of discriminant, such as 'shark', 'cockroach', 'chaffinch', as well as the expression 'BP' ... I ascertained that she was in some way connected with deciphering ... to the best of my knowledge, Wren Knight is satisfactory on security grounds – her parents would seem to have no knowledge of the nature of her work, she is ostensibly training as a 'writer'. I consider that the unnecessary remarks made on February 18th were solely to impress me.[3]

Wise Nigel de Grey was inclined to take this view of the matter too. He wrote back to a Colonel Wallace with these remarks:

I have personally interviewed the Wren in question and I do not think she will transgress again. I gave her the name of the officer who reported her and I think that alone may cause the friendship to cool off a bit. She made the fatal mistake of thinking that anyone connected with our services was entitled to the same information as she has herself ...

It is always extremely useful to me to know where people have gone wrong.[4]

Sometimes, worryingly, it seemed that word had seeped out even wider than Wrens and Signals men. There was this anxious report to de Grey from a Mr Fletcher of Block D:

Mr Chicks, one of the British Tabulating Machine employees, engaged upon the final assembly of the bombes, was recently at home in Chelmsford where his father is a works manager. His father told him he'd met a man, an Air Ministry inspector, who, on hearing that his son worked at BTM Letchworth, said: 'Oh I know what they do there. They make decoding machines.'

Chicks neither confirmed nor denied this to his father but told him it would be as well if he didn't talk about it.

This case presented de Grey with a little difficulty, as he revealed in his reply: 'the matter is one which I think will have to be followed up, though Travis wishes me particularly to emphasise the delicacy of allowing even MI5 into the bombe secret . . .'[5]

A little later on, and a small number of American officers also apparently found it difficult not to hint at what they were doing. One Lieutenant Skalak seemed alarmingly garrulous when among British officers, or at dances with Wrens. Indeed, such was the fright he caused that Bletchley Park prevailed upon the FBI to investigate his background thoroughly. Skalak's loyalty was beyond doubt. He had simply been behaving rather overenthusiastically. This also seemed true of a young Letchworth machine operator who had been dropping hints in social situations about the importance of his work. 'He seems a decent young fellow,' wrote one colonel after a full investigation. 'All the same, a little salutary fear won't do him any harm.'[6]

One Park veteran recalled the day when one of the lower-scale administrative staff was apprehended: 'I remember John Harrington, because he disappeared. When I went into the Accounts Office, I had the shock of my life. There were two burly MI5 men either side of him. He was such a clever man and I had asked Miss Molesworth why someone so clever was doing this sort of job. But he seemed to know a lot about everything, so I told Miss Molesworth and that's how he was picked up – he was a spy.'

But in general, it appears that if indiscretion was suspected, action was swift and low-key. One gets the sense that the Bletchley method of securing silence was mostly a visit from an Intelligence operative to put the frighteners on the offender. 'The trouble about taking any drastic action,' wrote Colonel Vivian to Nigel de Grey, 'is that it is often likely to draw attention rather than to conceal.'

Despite the intense seriousness and constant tension surrounding all questions of security, isolated cases were in their own odd way slightly amusing. There were accidental indiscretions in the most startling places: in school and parish magazines. Occasionally, famous Old Boys or parish notables would be written up, together with the news that they were working at Bletchley Park.

And the case of one billetor near Bletchley, a Reverend Harry L. Clothier, was brought to the attention of Nigel de Grey. The reason? Unlike most other people in Bletchley, he was constantly trying to catch his younger billetees out for information about what they were up to. At first sight, this looked rather sinister, but it became clear that the reverend gentleman thought he was playing some sort of game. 'As a host, Reverend Clothier is very kind,' wrote Colonel Vivian to de Grey. 'I think the time has now come when he will have to be officially warned to keep his mouth shut. In fact I think he wants a thorough frightening . . . he is not a bad man, but a foolish one.'

Intriguingly, MI5 became concerned about the possibility of hypnosis being used to extract information about Bletchley's activities. This was specifically because of one officer who had suffered a nervous breakdown. The officer's doctor, based on the Isle of Man, came under Intelligence scrutiny when it became apparent that he was using hypnotism as a means of helping the officer to recovery. There was no evidence of anything more sinister than that. But the very idea of this sort of treatment was regarded by some within MI5 as black magic, and the notion of its potential use in espionage undeniably grabs the imagination.

In the directorate, there was a constant concern about the inherent danger of drunkenness. There were flurries of disquiet if, for instance, people were heard to be speaking too loudly at smart drinks parties about subjects which they should not know that much about. Another source of anxiety was what they termed 'superior persons' – for example, senior university dons who felt that the stringent confidentiality 'didn't apply to them'. Added to this, personal letters were scrutinised and censored as a matter of course. Wrote one intelligence officer: 'I enclose six letters which I think require looking into.'

There were also discussions about the potential trouble that could be caused by marriage. Nigel de Grey stated that the 'best plan is to warn young women. Very specially against talking to her future husband on the subject of her work.'[7] This precaution proved, across the decades, to be phenomenally successful. Wives said nothing to husbands, and it worked the other way around too. Meanwhile, vulnerable young Wrens were to be warned against 'confidence tricksters' – plausible-seeming American soldiers, for instance – who would dupe them into talking with such lines as 'I know all about your show.'

In 1942, a striking communiqué was sent around all GC&CS employees, appealing to their sense of personal, rather than institutional, responsibility. It read:

> Secrecy. This may seem a simple matter. It should be. But repeated experience has proved that it is not, even for the cleverest of us; even for the least important. Month after month instances have occurred where workers at BP have been heard casually saying things outside BP that are dangerous. It is not enough to know that you must not hint at these things outside. It must be uppermost in your mind every hour that you talk to outsiders.
>
> Even the most trivial-seeming things matter. The enemy does not get his intelligence by great scoops, but from a whisper here, a tiny detail there . . .

It went on in a manner calculated to bring a blush to the cheeks:

> There is nothing to be gained by chatter but the satisfaction of idle vanity, or idle curiosity: there is everything to be lost – the

very existence of our work here, the lives of others, even the
War itself.

Some of these breaches were rather sad. Particularly poignant
was the incident in which a shop girl in Knightsbridge sparked a
security alert at Bletchley Park when a couple of Wrens went into
the shop, bought some clothes, and gave the address for them to be
sent on to. The shop girl, seeing their address, immediately became
very chatty about Bletchley and asked the Wrens if they were working on bombes.

The reason the shop girl knew so much about it was that she herself had worked at Bletchley, and in an extremely rare case had
been discharged owing to 'ill-health and incompatibility'. After this
incident, she was 'duly cautioned' by MI5.[8]

In his account, Peter Calvocoressi was fascinating on that crucial
point of secrecy: that, in the vast majority of cases, once a recruit
was in on the purpose of Bletchley Park, there would be no way
for them to back out and go elsewhere.

The Ultra community at BP saw itself as – perhaps was – an elite
within an elite. Many of the things which made it successful
made it also intense: the narrow catchment area, the small-
ness . . . of its cryptographic and intelligence sections, the edgy
pressures of relentless work around the clock, the sense of
responsibility and achievement, and the fact that there was no
escape.

The rule, dictated by security, was: once in, never out. And
this rule was rarely broken. There was a board or committee to
which an inmate of BP might address a plea for a posting elsewhere. An application to this board would be followed by an
interview and, almost invariably, the rejection of the plea.

A girl who had broken her heart and wanted to get away to
give it a chance to mend might find sympathy, but she would
not get release. The only transients on the Ultra side were

officers who came to BP to be indoctrinated and trained before going to intelligence staffs in the field where they would handle Ultra material.[9]

Against this careful security, however, there were always fears among the administrative hierarchy. They were perfectly justified, it would seem. For instance, some now suggest that an unidentified spy, with the codename of 'Baron', operated within the Park in the early years of the war – a spy, crucially, feeding information not to the Germans but to Britain's Russian allies. One name put forward is Leo Long, who worked in the War Office. In May 1941, he leaked a raw decrypt from Bletchley Park concerning the Germans' forthcoming Barbarossa campaign against Russia.

Conversely, those who chose to help Russia on their own account were more alarmingly slapdash about the methods that they employed.

22 Bletchley and the Russians

Accidental babbling and careless drunken boasts were one threat to security, but the Park was also vulnerable to more calculating figures. And a more full-time and notorious spy at Bletchley Park, it emerged in the late 1990s, was John Cairncross – known to some, in tabloid terms, as 'the Fifth Man'.

Bletchley had already experienced an extraordinary near-miss. In 1940, a *Times* correspondent called Kim Philby – later to become notorious as 'the Third Man' – was kicking his heels, looking for war work. In his 1968 memoir, *My Silent War*, written five years after his defection to the Soviet Union, Philby recalled:

I had one promising interview, arranged by a mutual friend, with Frank Birch (before and after the war, a don at King's College, Cambridge), a leading light in the Government Code and Cypher School, a cryptanalytical establishment which cracked enemy (and friendly) codes. He finally turned me down, on the infuriating ground that he could not offer me enough money to make it worth my while.[1]

We now see how much credit Frank Birch deserves for this decision, regardless of the reasons for it. Philby, along with Guy Burgess,
Donald MacLean and Anthony Blunt, was of course one of the so-
called 'Cambridge Spies', who had been engaged in passing
information to the Russians since the 1930s. There is little question
that, had he been hired, Philby would have tried to pass Bletchley
decrypts to his Soviet controllers. As it happened, Philby was taken
on by MI6. But the Bletchley authorities very wisely limited knowledge of its activities, to the extent that even a number of SIS
operatives had no clear knowledge of what was being achieved
there.

John Cairncross, meanwhile, had been at Cambridge, studying
Modern Languages at Trinity College having gained a scholarship
after attending Glasgow University. An intelligent, spikey man, a bit
of a loner, he came to know Kim Philby and Anthony Blunt.
According to one account, he very much disliked them.

Blunt was interested in sounding Cairncross out in terms of
doing some work for the Russians, but the antipathy between
Cairncross and Blunt was too strong. But then Cairncross met the
Marxist James Klugman. It was Klugman who persuaded him – by
rather underhand means, according to Cairncross himself – to provide help for the Soviet cause.

Cairncross joined the Foreign Office in 1936. Around that time,
Klugman arranged to meet him in Regent's Park in London, seemingly for purely social reasons. But as soon as Cairncross arrived at
the rendezvous, he wrote in a memoir, a round, moon-faced man
appeared from behind a tree and introduced himself as 'Otto'. He
was KGB. Klugman made his excuses and left 'Otto' and Cairncross
to it. 'Otto' wanted Cairncross to work for the Russians.

In his memoir, Cairncross professed to have been acting out of
a burning zeal to see Nazism defeated; the best means for this to
be achieved was by co-operation with Soviet Russia. But in this
account, he also suggests extra motivations, including blackmail
(fear of losing his Foreign Office position) and money (the need

to live at a smarter address and not in a dowdy west London suburb). The Molotov/Ribbentrop pact of 1939 made his life distinctly uncomfortable.

During the war, Cairncross became private secretary to Lord Hankey, who had a general supervisory role over the intelligence services. In this capacity, between 1940 and 1942, Cairncross would have had direct access to the decrypts coming from Bletchley Park. After a brief spell of army training, Cairncross came to Bletchley itself in 1942, as a captain, and joined Hut 3. A Bletchley Park cryptographer called Henry Dryden recalled Cairncross in a postscript he wrote of an account of his own time at the Park:

John Cairncross and I went up to Trinity College, Cambridge in October 1934, he as a Major Scholar and I as an Exhibitioner in Modern Languages. Whilst we were not close friends, I saw something of him at lectures and supervisions, and once at a cocktail party for the Trinity Cell of the Communist Party of Great Britain, which I had just joined.

This was a surprise, because he had never given me the impression of being politically inclined. I handed back my CPGB card in January 1935, my brief flirtation having ended in disillusionment.

After graduating, we went our separate ways. It was probably in December 1942, whilst on a liaison visit from Cairo to BP, that I bumped into him in the passage of Hut 3, having not seen or heard of him since 1936. He was dressed as an Army Staff Captain . . . he stayed at BP until the summer of 1943, when he transferred to a post in MI6.

Our next and last contact was when he invited me to lunch at the Travellers Club in February 1949, when he was back in the Treasury. In the middle of the meal he disconcertingly asked: 'Are we still reading Russian ciphers?' I had no first-hand knowledge of any current work on Russian, though I did know that on 22 June 1941 what work there was had been dropped, and the only off-putting response I could think of, on the spur of the moment, was to shake my head and mutter 'One time'. He did not pursue this.[2]

It was in 1942 that Cairncross began regularly taking decrypts out of the Park in order to pass on to his controller Anatoli Gorsky at the Russian Embassy in London. His moral justification was, apparently, that he was unhappy at the way that Britain had been withholding vital military information from its Russian ally. In fact, from 1941, Churchill had for tactical reasons personally been feeding Stalin information gleaned from Bletchley Park; the more difficulties that Hitler encountered on the Eastern Front, the better for the Allies. However, the consequences of Cairncross's actions could have been utterly catastrophic.

For while the Russians knew of the existence of Bletchley Park, they would not have known the exact provenance of the decoded messages issuing from there. And Russian internal security was defective and leaky – so there was the danger that *their* intelligence would alert the Germans to the fact that their traffic was being systematically decoded. In other words, Cairncross jeopardised the entire Bletchley Park operation – and with it, potentially, countless lives – for the sake of his ideological beliefs.

Actually, Cairncross managed to pass so much raw material over to his Soviet friends that alarms were sounded in the Lubianka; the Russians simply could not believe that it would be possible for one man to steal such intensely secret and sensitive material, carry it down to London and hand it over. A trap was initially suspected. No security system could conceivably be so permeable. But the Russians overcame these initial doubts and suspicions, shook their heads, acted upon the information – and found it all to be perfectly accurate. Thanks to Cairncross and his decrypts, for instance, they were given advance warning to develop tanks with stronger shells in the light of German armament reports.

Curiously, in the BBC drama *Cambridge Spies*, it was suggested that

Cairncross felt terrific unease about sharing information with the Russians. According to the drama, Anthony Blunt started threatening him should he decide to hold back. And there are those who might even now take a more favourable view of Cairncross's actions: that his information from Bletchley enabled the Soviets to win the Battle of Kursk, an obscure yet bloody engagement that took place near Kiev in 1943 – indeed, Cairncross himself was happy to claim almost full credit for it – and that such a victory helped towards the eventual defeat of Germany; that even though Cairncross's actions were dangerous, with potentially horrifying consequences, they did, however obliquely, help towards the ending of the war.

Possibly it will be many years before we hear the whole truth. But the question arises, was MI6 really so blithely unaware of Cairncross? It was alarmingly unaware for some time of the activities of Philby, Burgess, MacLean and Blunt, it is true. But even though they were at the apex of Intelligence, those four didn't work at the most sensitive establishment in the country, one near-miss aside. Might it have suited the British authorities for the Russians to be fed morsels of information at certain key times, to aid their fight against Germany?

The Germans invaded Russia in June 1941 in the action known as Operation Barbarossa, smashing the Molotov/Ribbentrop non-aggression pact of 1939. It has been suggested by some that Churchill believed that Hitler would take this course as long ago as November 1940; the Prime Minister's suspicions had been pricked both from diplomatic channels and from Bletchley Park decrypts. And without any cynicism, a German offensive on Russia would inevitably be good news for Britain; while all those divisions were tied up in the East, an invasion of the United Kingdom would be extremely unlikely, if not impossible. But it seems that Churchill was at odds with some Whitehall and Intelligence figures, who persisted in taking the more pessimistic line that Hitler's priority was the subjugation of Britain. Indeed, Hitler himself continued to give signs that this was his foremost intention.

As 1941 wore on, it became increasingly obvious thanks to the messages being deciphered by Bletchley that the Germans would indeed be launching an assault on Russia. It was the belief of many in Intelligence that if this was the case, then the Russians would capitulate very fast, possibly within weeks, which would then leave Hitler free to turn his attentions back to Britain.

So how could Russia be warned without the source of British information being compromised? In April, the British ambassador in Moscow, Sir Stafford Cripps, was deputed to send a warning to Stalin that such an attack was looming. Stalin's initial reaction was that Hitler was bluffing. However, Russian defence was stepped up. And from the day of the German invasion onwards, Churchill, though anti-Bolshevik to his core, ordered that Russia be helped in various ways.

At the end of June 1941, when Hungary declared war on the Soviet Union, with the result that Russia was fighting on multiple fronts (as well as Germany, it was also in conflict with Finland, Romania and Albania), Bletchley Park managed to break the 'Vulture' Enigma key; this was the key that concerned German military orders being given on the Eastern Front. The very next day, Churchill ordered that Stalin should be vouchsafed this intelligence, as long as its source was obfuscated. The job of passing it on was given to Cecil Barclay, who worked in British Military Intelligence and was based in the British Embassy in Moscow.

The Russians were extremely slow to show any gratitude for the nuggets of intelligence passed their way through such tortuous routes. Indeed, they greeted with disbelief and suspicion the news, deduced from Bletchley Park, that the Germans had penetrated the Russian cipher system: they took that to mean that their ciphers had been broken by the British.

So how much information did Churchill spoon-feed to the Soviets? There has been recent speculation about the Russian 'Lucy' spy network in Switzerland, which passed back extremely high-quality intelligence to Moscow; so good, in fact, that it was believed to have emanated within German High Command. The speculation has been that much of 'Lucy's' top information was gleaned from Bletchley Park, and that Churchill covertly chose to use the 'Lucy' route in order to pass vital knowledge to Stalin. But Bletchley's official history states baldly that there was no truth in this.

Later, in 1943, the Bletchley decoders broke a German key which they called 'Porcupine'. For a few weeks, they were able to intercept all German air force messages, particularly those relating to movements and operations in southern Russia. The passing of information was carried out with the greatest of care – sometimes, as before through the British Embassy in Moscow – in order to jealously protect the source of the information.

And how much did the Russians really know or understand about Britain's system of codebreaking? One would immediately think that the Cairncross handover of decrypts must have provided a fairly strong indication. As the war progressed, the Russians certainly learned of the existence of Bletchley Park, which they referred to as 'Krurort'. According to Miranda Carter's biography of Anthony Blunt, he also handed over Bletchley decrypts to his Soviet controller. If this is the case, then it does seem remarkable that the Russians never worked it out. However, according to Peter Calvocoressi, Russian intelligence never grasped the scale, or indeed the method, of what had been achieved at the Park.

What makes the Cairncross story doubly astonishing, though, is the apparent ease with which such raw messages could be spirited out of Bletchley Park in the first place. When his flat was raided by the security services in 1951, they found thousands of incriminating documents; in a ten-year period he passed on some 6,000 documents to the Kremlin. In the Robert Harris novel a stolen scrap of encrypted text is hunted down and proves difficult to hide. Yet here, it seemed, one man could walk out of the Park with wodges of such material with impunity.

Almost paradoxically, it does not appear that Bletchley – the most secret operation in the country – was officially policed in any heavy-handed sense. For instance, those leaving the Park did not seem to be subject to routine searches. Nor was any sort of track kept upon movements – or, at least, none that was noticed, even by spies. Nevertheless, Cairncross's own account of this information-smuggling strains credibility now. He wrote:

> . . . there was no problem about obtaining the German decrypts for they were left around on the floor after having been processed. I also added to these the collections of my transla-tions into English, since they expanded the coverage. I concealed the documents in my trousers in order to pass them out of the grounds, where I was never subjected to a check. I then transferred them into my bag at the nearby railway station.
>
> After that, they were handed to Henry [his codenamed Soviet handler] in an envelope at some spot in the suburbs of west London. I would meet him at the entrance to the tube sta-tion, follow him to the platform and get out of the train when he got off. I would then trail him to a quiet spot, where the envelope was handed over.[3]

One wonders if security could really have been that relaxed. Is it not more reasonable to suspect that the Park authorities and MI5 knew exactly what this man was up to and simply fed him scraps of information that might have minimised damage? Given, for instance, all the tiny accidental leaks which were so efficiently cracked down upon, it is practically impossible to imagine that anyone could walk out of such an establishment, having found exactly the decrypts he needed handily scattered about – among all those fractions of messages and weather reports and other miscel-lany – and then jammed them into his trousers.

As mentioned, in his memoir, Cairncross appears vaingloriously to claim the entire credit for the Soviet victory at the Battle of Kursk. According to historian Martin Gilbert: 'An Enigma message at the end of April . . . confirmed that the German intention on the eastern front was to cut off the Soviet forces in the Kursk salient by means of a pincer movement . . . These facts were passed from London to Moscow on April 30.' Several hours before the German attack was to begin, the Russians attacked first, hitting the artillery lines: they had had prior warning.

As codebreaker Captain Jerry Roberts now recalls, however: 'We were able to warn the Russians that the Germans were planning this – how the attack was going to be launched, and the fact that it was going to be a pincer movement. We were able to warn them what army groups were going to be used. And most important, what tank units were going to be used.

'Now I can remember myself, strangely enough, breaking messages about Kursk. You know, the name sticks in your mind. We had to wrap it all up and say it was from spies, that we had wonderful teams of spies, and other sources of information.' If any credit at all is to be claimed, is it not then more reasonable to surmise that the Bletchley Park command was one step ahead of Cairncross, who was clearly a strange, bitter man?

But what of those who sought to aid the Soviets without the British authorities learning of it? Recently, the British Library published, some twenty-five years after his death, a 30,000 word memoir written by Anthony Blunt; in it, far from expressing remorse, he seems more agitated by the sense of social disgrace that was brought down upon him by his 1979 exposure as a Soviet mole. Many will argue ferociously that his treachery led to the deaths of many valued British agents. And the notion that in the 1930s, when he was swayed by Communism, little or nothing was known of the pathologically murderous nature of Stalin's regime, seems thin.

Yet, despite the earlier Molotov/Ribbentrop pact, the fact remains that from 1941 to the end of the war, the Russians were, for coldheartedly pragmatic reasons, Britain's allies. Was it therefore the blackest treachery to pass information to them that would help them in their fight against the Germans?

Authors such as Chapman Pincher and Christopher Andrew would emphatically – indeed, furiously – say yes. They argue that the actions of the Cambridge Spies resulted in the brutal deaths of a great many British agents whose identities had been betrayed. Added to this, the leaking of information throughout the war to Stalin gave him an unfair advantage in bargaining terms at the Yalta Conference. And of course, there was the gravest betrayal of all. In his later years, Cairncross denied that after the war he had passed on nuclear secrets to enable the Soviets to start their own atomic weapons programme. Yet such secrets were passed; and such secrets kept the Cold War in frost for decades and eastern Europe unwillingly under the thumb of an oppressive regime.

Despite the evidence of the Cairncross case, there was a huge amount of vigilance around the country. The general wartime assumption was that unusual or furtive behaviour would be immediately spotted by colleagues, and reported. During the war years, civilians would regularly report the suspicious behaviour of others to the authorities concerned.

Not only that, but they were highly effective in doing so. As a vivid example, in 1940, three German agents – two men and one woman – disembarked from a submarine off the coast of Scotland. They sailed by dinghy to the tiny fishing harbour of Port Gordon. There, having concealed the dinghy, and obviously dressed in civvies, they made their way through the village up to the railway station at the top of the hill.

At the station, one of the agents tried to buy train tickets for the three of them; he gave the station master a fifty-pound note. Never having seen such a thing in his entire life, the station master excused himself, went into his office and made a quiet telephone call about the three people 'who didna' seem right'. Minutes later, they were arrested. The outcome was that the two male spies were hanged.

As it happens, this was the village that my father was born and brought up in, and the story was repeated proudly throughout his childhood. The woman, my father says, 'went on to marry someone in the village'. An exceedingly fine joke – but the point still stands that not only were ordinary people constantly on the alert for spies, they were perfectly right to be so.

The John Cairncross/Bletchley story also highlights something else that is rather striking; the fact that such major breaches of security – if indeed that is what it really was – did not happen more often.

There is a fascinating story in Andrew Sinclair's study of the Cambridge Spies, *The Red and the Blue*, in which the motives and philosophy of such treachery was debated by Kim Philby and Malcolm Muggeridge at the villa of Victor Rothschild in Paris 1944 after the liberation. According to Sinclair, Rothschild 'vehemently opposed Churchill's decision to withhold from Stalin the Bletchley information about German battle plans on the eastern front'. He was not aware that John Cairncross had been smuggling some of that very information. Muggeridge told Rothschild that 'caution over the Bletchley material was legitimate because the Russians had passed on to the Germans all they knew about the British during the Nazi-Soviet pact'.[4] At this point, according to Sinclair, an outraged Philby declared that everything should be done to support the Red Army, even if it meant compromising the Bletchley material.

As Sinclair points out, neither Kim Philby nor Guy Burgess had any access to Bletchley documentation; nevertheless, that even such a conversation could be held is a stark illustration of how fortunate it was that the Bletchley secret was never disclosed.

For reasons still unknown, John Cairncross was never prosecuted. Instead, he went to live abroad, and eventually joined a United Nations food agency. To this day, there are allegations of cover-ups; that Cairncross was the alleged 'Fifth Man', after Burgess, Philby, MacLean and Blunt, who had betrayed the whole of the British intelligence service to the Soviet Union. It also seems inconceivable that a man of his sympathies, openly expressed, could have passed the vetting to have worked in an establishment like Bletchley Park (without, that is, the authorities deciding for their own purposes to place him there).

But in general terms, what vetting was there? Certainly some veterans were aware that before they started work at the Park, discreet enquiries about their characters and lives had been made with headmasters and the like. They were left in no doubt that their lives had been thoroughly scrutinised.

To this day, Sheila Lawn is never entirely certain what process led her to the Park. 'I simply came in because there was quite a tranche of people from the Scottish universities,' she says. 'And I suppose the fact that I had taken my name out of signing up to be a teacher, and into this – they may have thought, "Well she's keen enough to do that." I don't know.'

This prompts her husband Oliver to recall: 'When Sheila came – with this tranche from the Scottish universities – this other girl-friend that I had at the Park before Sheila was *also* one of them. There were quite a few from the Scottish universities. They were scouting quite carefully.'

Mrs Lawn herself recalls one unusual day at university before the summons for Bletchley came: 'I was invited to my amazement by the principal and his wife to Sunday afternoon tea, and the other people there were a lot of senior, older students. I had a very pleasant tea, and chatted with people and so on – but it struck me as being very odd because I hadn't heard of any of my own age group on my French/German course being invited.

So I thought, "I wonder what the reason for that tea was? Whether they just stick a pin in and say, 'We'll take this one, we'll take that one'?" Though I didn't feel in any way that I was being conscripted.'

As the Hon. Sarah Baring has mentioned, some of the debs were scrutinised only so far as to ensure that they were not madly in love with Hitler. And as for the codebreakers themselves? It wasn't a question of old school tie so much as the old university gown. Also, given the youth of so many of the original intake of codebreakers and linguists, they would not have needed more than the usual check – there is a limit to the amount of seditious activity that an eighteen- or nineteen-year-old in pre-war Britain could have engaged in, give or take the odd Cambridge Apostle or two.

The same James Klugman who apparently recruited Cairncross to the Soviet cause was also implicated in another suspected security breach involving Bletchley a little later in the war. This involved Yugoslavia, and the apparent need to ensure that Churchill gave his backing to the partisan leader Josef Tito and not the Royalist leader Mihailovic.

Klugman was suspected by some of having secretly influenced the government decision to back the partisans, despite the fact that Tito and his supporters were Communist sympathisers, and almost certain to take post-war Yugoslavia down a Communist road. It was felt that the governance of the country would be best left to its people; but in the meantime, the government would support the side that appeared best placed to fight Hitler's armies.

Documents uncovered in the 1990s appeared to show that information sent from Bletchley Park to Downing Street and the relevant Whitehall departments concerning the complex layers of the Yugoslav situation was somehow not reaching the people that it should. An anonymous Bletchley operative came forward and said:

> I was at Bletchley Park with the job of preparing a weekly summary of the Yugoslav situation for Churchill. At the time I wasn't particularly suspicious that our information didn't seem to be acted upon, but have become so since. I now wonder if many of our reports were sent to the section where people like Philby were working. Certainly Klugman seems to have played a more important role than was thought. Two former communist wartime agents assured me that he did, but they didn't elaborate.[5]

Of course, Britain had its own agents out in the field, and its own elaborate plans for counter-espionage coups. One came in 1940, when Alan Turing and Peter Twinn had still to crack the impossibly complicated naval Enigma. A young lieutenant-commander from Naval Intelligence came to Bletchley Park to discuss possible means of tricking Germans out of their key settings.

That young commander was Ian Fleming, and the man he conferred with was Dilly Knox. Fleming's eventual plan had the working name 'Operation Ruthless'. It involved the use of an 'airworthy German bomber' to be obtained from the Air Ministry; a 'tough crew of five, including a pilot, WT operator and word-perfect German speaker. Dress them in German Air Force uniforms, add blood and bandages to suit'. The plan was to 'crash the plane in the Channel after making SOS to rescue service' and, justifying the operation name, 'once aboard rescue boat, shoot German crew, dump overboard, bring rescue boat back to English port.'

The idea, of course, was to snaffle the ship's Enigma key settings. Fleming himself volunteered for the mission, although there was no chance that he would be accepted for it; anyone with any knowledge of the Enigma operation, and of the work being done at Bletchley Park, would never be allowed out into the field for fear of capture by the enemy and subsequent torture, leading to top secret information being revealed.

Unfortunately, the weather conditions and other circumstances were never quite right for 'Operation Ruthless', it seemed, and eventually it was shelved. Alan Turing and Peter Twinn apparently looked like 'undertakers cheated of a nice corpse' at the news.[6]

This scheme aside, Fleming would be a regular sight at the Park, liaising between the codebreakers and Naval Intelligence. 'About once a fortnight I visited Bletchley Park,' he said. It has been wrily noted by Mavis Batey in her monograph on the subject that his creation James Bond would have enjoyed no such privilege, and indeed would not have made it past the sentry post – access to the secret of Ultra and Enigma was granted, outside the Bletchley Park staff, to very few.

On top of this, it might also be noted that two of Fleming's Bond novels – *From Russia with Love* (published in 1957) and *You Only Live Twice* (1964) – are more explicit than any of the other 007 adventures when it comes to codes and codebreaking. In *From Russia with Love*, the complex plot revolves around a Soviet enciphering machine called LEKTOR. In *You Only Live Twice* it is a Japanese deciphering system called 'MAGIC 44'. There is no mention of Bletchley; after all, Fleming had signed the same Official Secrets Act as everyone else. But, as he once said of his own work: 'Everything I write has a precedent in truth.'

Perhaps the reason we have heard so little about security breaches at the Park is because such information remains sensitive today. There was one dramatic episode in 1942 which showed, however, that Britain's code encipherments had in fact been penetrated by the Nazis.

Given the amount that the British knew about Enigma right from the start of the war, it was obvious that they should develop a different, more advanced system: this was Typex (Or 'Type X'). Thanks to Bletchley, rigorous orders on the use of this system were given out: for instance, that no proper names should be used within the coded message itself (such inclusions, as had been discovered with Enigma, made cribs easier to find).

Nevertheless, for a while during the North African campaign in 1941, Rommel appeared to have an almost supernatural sense of Montgomery's every move, and was outmanoeuvring the British with seeming ease. Frustration and anxiety mounted. British Intelligence knew that it simply had to be a security breach. And they were right.

Bletchley Park decrypted an Italian message stating that Rommel owed all his good fortune to the fact that an American cipher sent from Cairo was being read regularly. Churchill was informed, and the Americans were swiftly on to the case. The unfortunate leaker was one Colonel Fellers, who had simply been sending news of British positions back to his superiors in Washington. An enquiry found that he was innocent of treachery; the problem was that the code he had used was too easy to crack.

The men and women of Bletchley would have to live with the effects of this intense and obsessive secrecy for decades to come. But at the time, with the tremendous pressures that they were all facing, what sort of pressure valves were there? One extraordinarily fruitful one was the Park's artistic life: what had started in the early days with little clubs and societies forming was, by 1943, a wide-ranging mix of classical music, opera, dancing and amateur dramatics. Hard as Bletchley's people worked, they knew on some level that it would be necessary to play hard too, in order to keep their minds fully refreshed. And the nature of the cultural activities that they engaged in tells us much about the aspirations of a smart young generation.

23 The Cultural Life of Bletchley Park

When one listens now to wartime songs and entertainers, one is generally listening to the material that was performed to the troops, and played into the dance halls and the factories: Flanagan and Allen; George Formby; Tommy Trinder; Arthur Askey; the Andrews Sisters; Anne Shelton; Billy Cotton and his Band; Jack Buchanan; Vera Lynn. The tone was ceaselessly uplifting and ceaselessly uncomplicated, from George Formby's risqué suggestions of knowing what to do with his gas-mask to Vera Lynn and her white cliffs. This is not to say that such entertainments were naive, or even simple; merely that they were pitched at a certain emotional level that could be enjoyed by all – popular culture at its best.

Tellingly, though, the sort of culture that the denizens of Bletchley Park went in for was, from the start, markedly more high-brow. One senses that this was not in any way deliberate; it was simply that many of the young codebreakers and linguists had been pulled away from their university lives (and in an age when fewer than five per cent of young people in any one year would attend university), and part of their education had been to inculcate an interest in the arts.

Indeed, outside the Park, even for those who had had relatively rudimentary primary educations – such as the philosopher Bryan Magee, who recalls, as he became a teenager during the war, how he would be suffused with a desire not only to hear the finest classical music, but also to see the best theatre – the arts were becoming seen as something that all should aspire to appreciate and enjoy, as opposed to being the preserve of a wealthy metropolitan elite. Inside the Park, they managed to enjoy an extraordinary range of cultural – and indeed, entertainment – pursuits.

Oliver and Sheila Lawn have especially fond memories of the way that Bletchley-ites contrived to use their leisure time: 'There was music,' says Mr Lawn, 'Play readings. And play actings. Quite a bit of amateur dramatics. And concerts of all kinds.'

'Some very gifted people were there,' adds Mrs Lawn. 'Some concerts were given by people who were already there.'

Specially invited artistes would make the journey up to Buckinghamshire as well. Says Oliver Lawn: 'I remember Myra Hess coming. And one or two – at that time, well-known – quartets came.' One wonders quite how much – if anything – these artistes were told about the nature of the audience they would be facing. Some musicians were told nothing at all. They would travel up in vans, clamber out with their instruments, perform to great acclaim, and then be driven back to London without having the faintest clue from whom they had received this acclaim.

Sheila Lawn adds, 'A little later the authorities built an assembly hall outside the Park, where we could have dances, meetings, all sorts of things, so that other people from Bletchley could enjoy some of that too.'

Both Oliver and Sheila had an abiding passion for the pursuit of Highland dancing. Unlikely though it may seem, the Park had its own home-grown expert in this pursuit, in the shape of Japanese codebreaking genius Hugh Foss. As well as being renowned for his good-humoured, easy manner, he was also apparently a fantastically elegant figure on the dance floor. 'Highland Reels was one of the very active social clubs,' says Mr Lawn.

'He was tall, elegant, danced beautifully,' adds Sheila. 'But of course we had no idea what he did.'

Oliver Lawn goes on to evoke an amusing and rather lovely image of those evenings when the dancing took place: 'We did our Scottish reels first of all in the hall of the mansion. It was a long hall, which was ideal for Scottish reel dances. And when they built the assembly hall outside the Park, we moved there. And then in the summer, when the weather was good, we danced by the lake, on the croquet lawn.'

Another veteran recalls how Hugh Foss would practise during lunch hours and hold 'more elaborate dances every three to six months with a full dress dance on St Andrew's nights. We wore out his record of Circassian Circle and had a collection to buy him a new one.'

Dancing seemed to be one of the great overriding passions at Bletchley. One codebreaker recalled being so keen to get to a dance that he managed, by dint of getting the date wrong, to turn up an entire week early. It also broke out in amusingly informal ways. One Wren recalled: 'The kitchen at BP House was so large that one could dance. During supper break I taught one of the men to waltz. We only had one record – "Sleepy Lagoon" [now better known as the theme tune of Radio Four's *Desert Island Discs*].'

Even Bletchley's fiercest figures could not resist the call of the hop. Mimi Gallilee recalls that her boss Miss Reed – so severe and so unyielding – was nevertheless transformed completely when it came to her leisure hours: 'Doris Reed used to go to the dancing. The Highland reels. And she would always go during her lunch hour.'

Lucienne Edmonston-Lowe, who worked in Hut 6's Registration Room from 1942 to 1945, also had extremely warm memories of these entertainments. 'If one was involved in a play or a concert, there were rehearsals and so the shift-list was very much referred to if one was on night or evening shift,' she recalled. 'I remember a song from the first Christmas revue I ever went to – sung by three smart girls. It went something like this.

"Six days out of seven we do penance,
In this awful God-forsaken place,
Six days out of seven we do penance,
For a single day of grace,
Cast aside what our mothers knit us,
Put on clothes that really fit us,
Sophisticated black is de rigueur,
And a smart hat a woman's cri de coeur.'"[1]

Even the Soviet spy/fellow traveller John Cairncross expressed an admiration for the creative side of Bletchley life. In his memoir, he wrote:

The . . . high spots I recall on our limited social life were a concert of German Lieder sung by a colleague, and the Christmas pantomime where we were regaled with such items as a Russian partisan in a fur cap singing about his life, and revue items with cracks such as 'working and partly working' – courtesy of T.S. Eliot – and saving water by having baths à deux.[2]

For young Mimi Gallilee, whose age would have precluded some of the straightforward socialising opportunities, this array of activities was extremely beguiling to behold. 'There were lots of different clubs,' she says. 'There was country dancing, morris dancing, different kinds of music, and you'd sit and listen to gramophone records in those days. One of the rooms at the front of the house became like a lounge really. There was a library. And the people within the huts – they formed their real groups of friends, in their own huts. And so you knew these people and there were plenty of people for you to know, within your own realm.

'They started to form these clubs within about a couple of years. That was how I went to some of the music recitals. They were with records in the big main lounge, the club lounge. Once they had built the cafeteria, I believe then they built a concert/dance hall at the end of the road.

'The revues were usually put on once a year and I went to a number of those. They were marvellous, fantastic – the people were so mad.'

Another great admirer of the seasonal revues was Hut 4 veteran Diana Plowman, who recalled: 'At Christmas time, all these great beings put on a revue. I've never seen anything like them before or since – wit, colour, eloquence, beauty, breathtaking . . .'

Bletchley Park's revues were also noted for their professionalism. Other veterans recall the care that went into the writing and performance of shows such as *The Naming of Parts* And in this, we hear an echo of what might have been for these young people; in a university career uninterrupted by war, they might well have been performing in the Cambridge Footlights and similar undergraduate shows. Certainly these variety shows were pitched at a higher brow than those entertaining the troops in ENSA.

But it wasn't just revues, and Dorothy Hyson and Frank 'Widow Twankey' Birch were not the only theatrical talent; according to Mimi Gallilee, 'There were many acting professionals at Bletchley.' Despite the 24-hour shift system and the constant grind of work, the Bletchley Park inmates – prominent among them gifted mathematician Shaun Wylie, who became head of the Bletchley Park Dramatic Club – also contrived to stage theatrical productions such as *French Without Tears*, *Much Ado About Nothing*, *Candida*, *Gaslight* and J.B. Priestley's *They Came to a City*.

This last play, almost never seen now, seems to have been one of the most popular and fashionable works of the war years. In essence, it is a Utopian fantasy: nine people arrive from nowhere into a city where poverty and hardship and prejudice are unknown; these people are from different walks of life and all respond to this dream city in different ways, with five of them eventually finding themselves quite unable to stay there. It is a sort of quasi-socialist middle-class vision of a type that was to prove extremely popular in the post-war period, examples being the productions of Ealing Studios and the richer imaginings of Michael Powell and Emeric Pressburger.

It is equally beguiling to see these serious young codebreakers and linguists throwing themselves with the same gravity into amateur dramatics. Some suggested that it was simply a valve for releasing all the tension of work, a means of forgetting the nature of their working lives. But it was not simply escape on stage. The amateur dramatic companies also produced professional-looking programmes for their performances; and in the photographs that survive, one can see the astonishing ingenuity that went into both the costumes and the stage design. In a production of *By Candlelight*, a young John de Grey is clearly portraying a footman of some sort – but where the Dickens did he get hold of that elaborate eighteenth century-style coat? And the set behind the two elegant ladies in simulation of an elegant drawing room has been styled and painted with bewildering attention to detail.

Not everyone joined in with the amateur dramatics. Indeed, Captain Jerry Roberts, busy trying to crack the 'Tunny' decrypts in the later years of the war, felt distinctly out of it. He recalls: 'I didn't get much of a sense of culture. But other people I knew did. Perhaps the reason was that I had a long walk home to the billet. I used to go to cinema meetings in the town, and the Wrens who worked in the Newmanry used to have dances occasionally out at Woburn Sands. They would invite us to a dance and we would have a coach to take us out there and bring us back. But it was difficult otherwise to be too social.

'There were plenty of clubs: chess club, drama club,' he continues. 'And people who lived nearby, or had bicycles, tended to go to that sort of thing. If you lived half an hour's walk away, you weren't going to walk all the way back again from the drama things.'

This was a memory echoed by Irene Young, although she did recall managing to get to the 1942 Christmas revue, despite being wholly dependent on local buses: 'Enjoying this recreation, I could not banish the occasional thought that although work at BP was undeniably of vital importance, we were living a comparatively sheltered life.'[3] The show clearly did not succeed in lifting her out of herself. Clearly, however, a walk of half a day would not have deterred a lot of the young codebreakers, and perhaps the more senior ones too.

There was also an enthusiasm for keeping fit and outdoor pursuits. In 1942, one L.P. Wilkinson, chairman of the Bletchley Park Recreational Club, sent this wheedling memo to Commander Bradshaw: 'It would be a great convenience if the Summer House beside the tennis courts could be used as a changing room for tennis players. It would require little or no alteration. May we have your permission for this?' The gracious answer was a yes.

There were other clouds on the tennis players' horizons: not only a shortage of balls (a wonderfully polite surviving letter in the National Archive from manufacturer Dunlop regrets the inevitability of this), but indeed a struggle to keep the court itself smooth and even. A specialist firm – En Tout Cas – 'The largest makers of hard lawn tennis courts in the world' – was consulted by Commander Bradshaw over the matter of the cost of putting these faults right.[4]

Emboldened, the Bletchley Park Recreation Club also put in a request for 'a radiogram' and Commander Bradshaw investigated the cost of getting a good one. The model favoured cost £45 – at the time an extraordinary sum of money. But a further technological innovation had caught the eye of the Recreation Club: 'a combined television radiogram' which would have cost an eye-watering 65 guineas. Sadly the records do not disclose if this item was ever purchased.

Of course there was live music too. Bletchley had tremendous choral societies; Gordon Welchman's fond memories of codebreakers singing madrigals on a summer evening by the side of the Grand Union Canal were but a single example.

Again, some of the Bletchley staff had a specialised interest in

their civilian lives. One was a director of music with the BBC, while
by 1942, one team was led by opera singer Jean Alington, and various categories and files in Bletchley Park huts came to be named
after composers and conductors. These more musical Bletchley-ites
would give recitals of Brahms, and of Purcell's *Dido and Aeneas*.
Added to this, they were able to draw specialised artistes to the Park
to give performances. Oliver Lawn is not the only veteran to recall
the occasion when world-famous pianist Myra Hess came to give an
evening performance. Opera singer Peter Pears also went to the
Park.

Equally impressive was the fact that Bletchley Park organised a
couple of ballet performances, again bringing professionals up
from London. When one looks at the opening scene of Powell and
Pressburger's 1948 film *The Red Shoes* – a jostling crowd of young
people desperate to get into the Covent Garden opera house to
see the premiere of a new, specially composed and choreographed
ballet – one thinks about a generation starved of this sort of artistic stimulation. One can easily envisage how the young of
Bletchley eagerly leapt on these highbrow diversions as a means of
forgetting their vital but otherwise often very repetitive and grinding work.

As the war went on, there also emerged a Cinema Club, again
presumably in stark competition with the two commercial cinemas
that graced Bletchley town centre. This was, of course, a period in
which cinema attendances in Britain were still enormously high;
most people would go once, if not twice a week. Oliver Lawn recalls
catching such epics as *Song of Bernadette* at the Bletchley Odeon.

One film from that period not only tells us much of the national
mood at the time, but also illustrates this thirst, manifested so
clearly at Bletchley Park, for something a little better. In 1944,
Laurence Olivier left the navy and went to great trouble to film
Shakespeare's *Henry V*. Commentators have long noted how the
political motivations of Henry were toned down for this film, so that
the audiences might not miss the patriotic echoes of what they saw

on screen: English soldiers preparing to fight on French soil, behind a charismatic leader.

But this *Henry V* is far beyond a simple tub-thumping exercise in morale-boosting fervour just months and weeks before the D-Day landings; its determination is to take Shakespeare's language – and by extension, the *heritage* of the audience, the culture for which they had been fighting – and make it live fully. With its score by William Walton, it was almost self-consciously a film designed to proclaim the indomitability and brilliance of English art and culture.

At Bletchley, the Park inmates were keen cineastes, though their tastes, it seems, did not run so much to Will Hay as to more specialised productions. The Bletchley Park Cinema Club was, as one veteran recalls, more likely to show productions like *Night Train* and even the odd vintage German film. Bear in mind that this was a good fifteen or twenty years before cinema even began to be regarded as an art form.

There were language classes too (quite apart from the more formal lessons held in Japanese at Bedford for those working on 'Purple'); these would include not only the usual modern languages, but also Latin.

Clubs were not just academic. There were more traditional forms of socialising too. 'In Newport Pagnell,' says Sheila Lawn, 'we formed a very informal club. It was more a walking club, serving coffee and tea. Anyone could come in and we met people from the same village, we were all billetees together.

'And then on your days off,' she continues, 'if one of your friends or companions had the same day off, you might agree to go away with them: be it a visit to London, if you could afford it, or into the country for a walk. When I met Oliver, I remember we went down to Stratford, by train, on one occasion and we went to a play.'

Towards the end of the war, the dancing craze was the unlikely source of a security panic at Bletchley Park. For the time and effort put by the Bletchley authorities into providing special dancing facilities had somehow reached the ears of a London journalist. He was called Harry Procter, and he worked for the *Daily Mail.* In fine investigative style, Procter was now hot on the trail of the story, inspiring a terse and rather desperate Bletchley memo:

> a) The telephone exchanges at BP to be warned to be on a look-out for a call from Harry Procter of the *Daily Mail.* Procter will probably ask for 'Bletchley' or 'for the country branch of the F.O.' and will wish to speak to the Club Secretary.
> b) Should such a call come through, the operator will reply after some delay that the Club Secretary is out and ask for Mr Procter's number to ring him back.
> c) The 'magnificent dance hall' will be laughed off and we will explain that the truth is that we have built a small temporary room in the office enclosure for recreation.[5]

It is nice to see, with this gambit, that the practice of 'spin' is a little older than many now assume.

But not all press coverage of Bletchley's out-of-hours pursuits was deemed so hostile. Among the townsfolk of Bletchley and the surrounding districts, the dramatic theatrical productions seem to have made a considerable impact. Indeed, right at the end of the war, the *Bletchley Gazette* reported with some regret that the Bletchley Park Drama Group was producing its last play, and looked back fondly over the last few years of productions. The newspaper's un-bylined reporter wrote:

> The Group in the early days were in great demand in the district, and they roamed about the countryside in BP transport, giving entertainments in conjunction with The Musical Society, in village halls . . . subsequently, the demands became so heavy that this could not be continued . . .
> The Group was indebted to the people and particularly to

the traders of Bletchley who have always given lots of support –
such as the loan of cutlery and furniture and, in one case, last
minute gargles!

One of the ways the Group was able to repay was in under-
taking the make-up for the Co-Operative Pageant, when
something like 600 faces were made-up . . .

This newspaper report pointed up the accusations raised by a few
local townspeople concerning the cushy nature of the Park's
recruits' lives – for such an apparently intensive programme of theatrical excellence must surely have taken up rather a lot of time.
The reporter sided with the Park, at the same time giving no hint
about what actually went on there:

A suggestion that the Park people had plenty of time for
rehearsal . . . was quickly killed. Life at the Park had not been
fun. Transport to and from their billets; awkward working
hours; the strangeness of communal life; and the Drama Group
had been the means of saving a lot of people from a mere
'work, sleep and eat' existence.[6]

But there was more to it than that. It was to do with the sponta-
neous creativity of young people who, despite the terrific
responsibility of their wartime roles, were equally earnest about the
importance of art and culture – things that would be vital when the
war had ended and the nation was to be rebuilt and remodelled.

24 1943–44: The Rise of the Colossus

By the start of 1943, Dilly Knox was succumbing to illness. The previous year, requiring an operation for a returning cancer, he had gone into hospital but was reluctant to have the operation carried out, on the grounds that a man should not be transformed 'into a piece of plumbing'. And so, for the past few months, he had been working from home, a house in the nearby Chilterns, in which he lived with his wife Olive (he and Olive Roddam had met back in the First World War in the corridors of the Admiralty; they married in 1920 and had two sons).

Now, nursed by his wife, he knew he was dying; but he wanted to hear no expressions of sympathy from relatives and friends. As he wrote:

A wanderer on the path
That leads through life to death
I was acquainted with
The tales they tell of both
But found in them no truth[1]

It was now, however, that he learned he had been awarded the Companionship of the Order of St Michael and St George. His son Oliver wrote of Knox at this time:

It was not in his nature to be daunted. By this time eighteen or nineteen years old, I was given compassionate leave to be at home during his last days. He had just been awarded the CMG. It has been explained to my mother that security considerations precluded his being given some more illustrious honour. Far too ill to travel to London, he deemed proper receipt of the honour to be a duty; he insisted on dressing and sat, shivering in front of the large log fire, as he awaited the arrival of the Palace emissary. His clothes were now far too big for him, his eyes were sunk in a grey face, but he managed the exercise all right. 'Nothing is impossible,' he said.

After the receipt of this honour, in January 1943, Knox wrote a letter to his colleagues in the Cottage. Heartfelt, and piercing to the root of the nature of Bletchley Park, it began:

Dear Margaret,
Mavis,
Peter,
Rachel etc
    Very many thanks for your and the whole section's very kind messages of congratulation. It is, of course, a fact that the congratulations are due the other way and that awards of this sort depend entirely on the support from colleagues and associates to the Head of the Section. May I, before proceeding, refer them back . . .

He then proceeded to make several rather salty points about Alistair Denniston's attitudes towards codebreaking and code-breakers, and about the way that, as he saw it, barely analysed messages were handed over to intelligence men. What this was really about, however, was the shift in Bletchley Park's underlying ethos from a brilliant amateur operation into a steely, professional one – something Knox found difficult to accept in intellectual as well as emotional terms:

> Latterly, we have recruited from ... the universities. And Academic tradition does not understand the idea that a half-fledged result should be removed from the scholar who obtains it and handed over to another. The discoverer loses all interest in further discovery and the recipient has no interest in the off-spring of another's brain. Until we know who will handle and circulate any result we get, the aurum irrepertum of our search will very probably be sic melius situm ...
>
> In bidding farewell and in closing down the continuity though not, I hope, the traditions of the Cottage, I thank once more the section for their unswerving loyalty. Affectionately, Dilly.[2]

The honour was sent over to Bletchley, since Knox felt that it was as much an acknowledgement of the department's works as it was for him. Increasingly at Bletchley, his had been a singular and some might say anachronistic approach to the breaking of codes. But it none the less evoked admiration.

'He had this feeling for looking for anomalies,' says his colleague Mavis Batey, 'and as ancient scribes did things wrong when they were copying out Greek texts, Dilly would always look for that sort of thing in the codes. He was the first one to extrapolate and really get down to the business of procedural errors made by operators.'

Mrs Batey remembers with terrific fondness how, even in the early days of the Cottage, Knox's eccentricities had come to the fore. He would contrive, absent-mindedly, to try to leave the room via the cupboard door. He would visit the punch-card operators in his dressing gown, even if it was the dead of winter. His enthusiasm for hot baths never waned. He was – an unusual privilege this, in straitened times – allowed real milk for his coffee, which came fresh from an obliging local cow.

And when all the changes came to Bletchley Park – not merely the gentlemanly removal of Alistair Denniston, but also the mechanised systems that were being employed to break into Enigma, Knox was extremely watchful, and also on occasion fiercely scornful. But he was no Luddite. According to Penelope Fitzgerald, Knox was fond of Alan Turing, whose Asperger tendencies were in no way reined in at Bletchley. The playwright Hugh Whitemore, in *Breaking the Code*, added a further, speculative layer, hinting that Knox, like Turing, had homosexual feelings and had had such relationships in the past.

Knox died in February 1943, and a certain style and approach died with him. The old cryptographic world of classicists versed in labyrinthine antiquities had given way to a new, mathematical, technologically driven machine age; the dawn of the computer era. Knox was remarkable in having straddled two such worlds, and with such success, right until the end.

Ingenious though the Enigma machines were, it was always inevitable that at some stage a more complex process of encoding would emerge. It was equally inevitable that, faced with such demands, the theoreticians and engineering geniuses who worked for Bletchley Park would make giant strides forward in terms of technology.

The one name that shines out in terms of engineering ingenuity was Tommy Flowers, familiarly known as the 'clever cockney'. There are some who argue that the name should be known in every household – for, they believe, he was the man who realised the dreams of Alan Turing and truly brought the computer age into being.

In 1943, Bletchley Park had seen the establishment of a new section known as 'The Newmanry'. It was set up under the aegis of mathematician Professor Max Newman from St John's College, Cambridge, and the idea of it was to find ways of applying more advanced machinery to codebreaking work.

It had been Professor Newman who in the 1930s, with his lectures on 'mechanical approaches' to solving mathematical problems, first led Alan Turing to start pondering on the idea of 'Turing Machines'. Indeed, Newman had lectured Turing directly. Newman, born in 1897, was a very popular figure at the Park; many veterans recall his openness, and his enthusiasm for everyone sharing their ideas. An American sergeant, George Vergine, had this to say about the Professor:

> Max Newman was a marvellous fellow and I always sort of felt grateful to have known him . . . we used to have tea parties . . . which were mathematical discussions of problems, developments, techniques . . . a topic would be written on the blackboard and all of the analysts, including Newman, would come, tea in hand, and chew it around, and see whether it would be useful for cracking codes.[3]

As well as Enigma, German High Command was now making use of Lorenz teleprinter machines to transmit encrypted messages. These used the Baudot Murray system, a series of holes (though not Morse) punched through tape, each series of five in different configurations representing a different letter of the alphabet. What made these communications – which became known around Bletchley Park as 'Fish' or 'Tunny' – particularly crucial was that many of them involved messages sent to and from German High Command. These were not merely communications between men out in the field; they were communications between generals and orders from the Führer himself.

The breakthrough on this complex system was made by a young chemist/mathematician called W.T. Tutte. In the meantime Alan Turing, having returned from several months in the USA, eagerly dived into discussions on the subject, having spent his voyage back reading up on the science of electronic circuits. Turing spent many weeks formulating methods through which the thing could be cracked; these were referred to as 'Turingismus'. Also present at Bletchley Park was one Dr Charles Wynn-Williams, a circuit expert brought in from radar research who had the wherewithal to build digital circuitry with electronic valves that could switch a thousand times faster than a relay.

It was at this point that the expertise of the Dollis Hill Post Office Research Station was called upon. Dollis Hill is a pleasant suburb of north-west London that overlooks Wembley and from which central London can be seen in the distance. The establishment in question – which also played host to an underground bunker for Churchill's use – was at the top of the hill. It was here that Tommy Flowers was based. Along with Wynn-Williams, Flowers began work on constructing a machine known – rather sweetly – as the 'Heath Robinson'.

Looking precisely like the sort of zany contraption that one of William Heath Robinson's illustrated inventors might contrive, this machine has been described by some veterans as being 'held together with elastic and bits of string'. However, no matter how comical it may have looked, it could run teleprinter tapes at high speed, like a super-fast bombe, at a rate of over 1,000 characters a second. It was this machine that was to pave the way for its successor, Colossus.

The Heath Robinson did its level best, especially given the exceptional nature of its speed. It demonstrated that it could be used to find the settings on one bank of the 'Tunny' code wheels. While it proved possible to break such codes manually, the velocity of the machine meant that more were ordered; soon, Bletchley had twelve improved models.

Despite the machine's assistance, however, the work was still laborious. 'They [the Hut] would put the message to be broken on the table and if you failed to break it, you'd put it on a pile and then somebody else could have a go at it,' says Captain Jerry Roberts. 'And if they broke it, well and good.

'But that pile of the non-broken messages, the dead ducks, was never big. I deduced from this that we were breaking certainly better than ninety per cent of what we were being given to break.

'It certainly did require patience but also don't forget if you're having a high success rate, even if it took you four, five, eight hours to break a day's traffic, the reward was very great because you could decipher a lot more messages using the information you'd discovered.'

And it could be a dispiriting business. A slightly reluctant codebreaker, in 1944 Roy (later Lord) Jenkins found himself pulled away from active duty to a job in the Newmanry. There were a few other distinguished figures on that 'Tunny' codebreaking crash course at Bedford too, it seems. Lord Jenkins wrote in his memoirs:

> I was greeted with news of instructions from the War Office that I was required for special intelligence work and that I was to proceed at the beginning of January to an unspecified 'course' at Bedford. I was destined for cryptography at Bletchley Park and work on the messages sent out by the German High Command in Berlin to the various commanders in the field, Rundstedt, Kesselring, Mannstein, Rommel and several others. A.D. Lindsay had been involved and had decided that the traditional role of Masters of Balliol . . . of placing Balliol men in what they regarded as appropriate jobs outweighed any irritation with my poor philosophy mark. Why he thought I would be a better cryptographer than a philosopher I do not know, but the fact that he did appeared to be decisive.
>
> Those on the Bedford course gave the impression of having been incongruously gathered in from the hedgerows. There was Charles Buckingham, erudite curator from the British Museum who wore a private's uniform . . . there was Francis Dashwood of West Wycombe Park, who was a civilian recruited straight from

school, there was a very unglossy university-educated North Midlands second lieutenant who shared a civilian billet with me, there was a sophisticated Etonian other rank who lived in Sloane Street, and about ten others I cannot remember distinctly.[4]

As Jenkins recalled in an interview: 'You could spend nights in which you got nowhere at all. You didn't get a single break, you just tried, played around through this long bleak night with total frustration and your brain was literally raw. I remember one night when I made thirteen breaks. But there were an awful lot of nights when I was lucky if I made just one, so it was exhausting.' Quite so, although another veteran recalled that Jenkins, although a first-class mind, was 'not the world's most talented codebreaker'.

But the work – when one hit a successful streak – had its own extraordinary rewards. The messages now being intercepted were invaluable. These were communications from Berlin to Italy, and to German divisions on the eastern front. Captain Jerry Roberts recalls one extraordinary day when he realised just how far into German High Command they had managed to penetrate: 'The people the messages were going to and coming from would be given at the beginning of the message. So you would have General so and so sending to Army HQ in Berlin. Most of them were signed by a general. Some were signed by Hitler. I can remember myself deciphering at least one message – he just called himself: "Adolf Hitler, Führer."'

For the brilliant minds who were making the Colossus possible, it was not so much knowledge as mechanical problems that they faced. It was very difficult to keep the teleprinter tapes synchronised. The machine also put a huge amount of strain on electronic valves, which repeatedly failed. But in the course of the many in-depth three-way discussions between Professor Newman, Alan Turing and Tommy Flowers that took place in order to improve the machines, what was debated was the feasibility of what was, in essence, the very first computer.

To be precise, they knew it as an 'electronic valve machine'; what made it a step up from the Heath Robinson was that instead of relying on two tapes that had to be run synchronously, it had just one. Flowers also made other modifications, such as replacing the sprocket drive with a set of friction wheels. As a triumph of engineering, and of bringing a theoretical design to life, it was unquestionably his; although the astonishing machine had much of Turing's logical reasoning at its core, there was also ingenuity in the way that Flowers improved upon the electronic valves, making sure that they were never switched off once they were in service, which hugely improved their reliability. Moreover, the contraption could read 5,000 characters a second, five times faster than the Heath Robinson. Flowers and his team at the Post Office research department developed and built it in a matter of ten months.

On 25 November 1943, the first Colossus machine was given a test run. By the beginning of 1944, this machine and its ilk were proving invaluable to Bletchley.

Among those who worked with the machines was Harry Fensom, who recalled:

The Colossi were of course very large, hence their name, and gave off a lot of heat, ducts above them taking some of this away. However, we appreciated this on the cold winter nights, especially about two or three in the morning. When I came in out of the rain, I used to hang my raincoat on the chair in front of the hundreds of valves forming the rotor wheels and it soon dried off.

Of course it was essential that the machines were never switched off, both to avoid damaging the valves and to ensure no loss of code-breaking time. So there was an emergency mains supply in the adjoining bay which took over automatically on mains failure.[5]

The machines had an element of the mad scientist's laboratory equipment to them – not merely because of the extraordinarily long message tape that had to be carefully threaded, but also the ever present hazard of electrical danger. In an echo of a previous incident with one of the 'bombe' machines, Fensom continued:

> One day I heard a shout from Gillie Sutton, one of the Wren operators . . . I rushed over; she had rested her vanity mirror on a convenient part of the control desk, there was a flash, and it melted away. She had placed it across two terminals, very big brass-looking knobs. Unfortunately this time she had used a metal mirror and the terminals were live.[6]

It was not fully appreciated at the time how much Tommy Flowers had invested in all this work. And Captain Jerry Roberts still feels that Flowers has never received an ounce of the recognition that he should have done. Although Flowers was discreetly awarded the MBE after the war (and also given an Award to Inventors in the sum of £1,000), Captain Roberts feels that a man of his talents and achievement deserved, and should have received, far more attention.

But there was another dimension to Flowers's work, and that was the scepticism and occasional hostility with which he was treated by Gordon Welchman.

Thomas Flowers was born in East Ham, the beating heart of London's East End, in 1905. He was the son of a bricklayer. His story is a powerful and surprising illustration of the power of education, in a period long before the term 'social mobility' became common currency.

As a boy, Flowers showed a precocious talent for mechanics and science. Thanks to this, he won a scholarship to a technical college. In the 1920s, this in turn led him to enter an open competition for a job as a trainee telephone engineer, a competition in which he came first. Early telephones came under the aegis of the government-run Post Office, and as it turned out, thanks to technological progress, it was an exciting time to be joining. The telephone network was becoming more automatic – with direct dialling, as opposed to going through an operator – and the Post Office's engineers would be expected to keep up with the latest innovations.

To do so, Flowers had to take evening courses, for the generosity of his new employers did not extend much beyond giving him a job. So he worked by day and studied theory by night. This industrious – and enthusiastic – approach meant that by 1930, he was seconded to the Post Office Research Establishment at the top of Dollis Hill.

The nature of his work was now advanced research, into such matters as how international telephone calls might be made by direct dialling. This led to work with electric circuits, and probing the various uses of electronics, a science very much in its infancy. Several years later, the matter of electronics would also come to fascinate Alan Turing at Trinity College, Cambridge.

The two men met for the first time at Bletchley Park in 1939. Flowers had been asked along by his boss Dr Gordon Radley, director of the Post Office Research Office. He and Flowers were the first of a very small number of engineers to be entrusted with the secret of Enigma.

In these first meetings, Flowers and Turing found that they had a certain affinity; certainly it appears that Turing found it easier to talk to Flowers than many others, possibly because of the other man's unaffected enthusiasm, as well as his expertise. Respect was mutual; in addition to Flowers's visits to Bletchley Park, Turing made trips down to Dollis Hill, to Flowers's workshop.

In these initial encounters, one idea was that Flowers should look into the idea of building a machine that could decrypt Enigma by means of electromagnetics. Such an idea was not to prove practical at that time – the technology was not ready. But the principle lodged in Flowers's head.

But however well he got on with Turing, Flowers found himself attracting the disdain of Gordon Welchman. This first became apparent towards the end of 1941 when circuit expert Charles Wynn-Williams was working on a new decoding machine called Mammoth, one of the forerunners of Colossus. It required electronic valve-sensing units, a task delegated to Flowers. Rather than work to the designs provided by Wynn-Williams, however, Flowers produced his own. These were deemed to be unsatisfactory. The result was friction. Welchman began to refer sarcastically to 'Mr Flowers of Dollis Hill'. He openly showed preference for Wynn-Williams's expertise over that of Flowers.

This unpleasantness – seemingly over the use of relays as opposed to the more innovative and untested electronic valves – went on for some months, with Welchman leaving Flowers and this Dollis Hill colleagues in the cold, as he instead sought the expertise of the British Tabulating Machine Company and Harold 'Doc' Keen, who had been so instrumental in building the first British bombes.

This, it seems, was too much for the pride of the Dollis Hill contingent. At a meeting, Flowers, according to Welchman's account, declared that Keen should not be 'allowed to get away with it'. What he appeared to be referring to was the fact that since those first bombes, BTM had failed to make any steps forward.

The more assertive Flowers grew, the more disdainful Welchman became. In a memo dated 4 June 1943, he wrote:

Dr Wynn-Williams has found it difficult to get on with the Dollis Hill people, and feels that Mr Flowers's idea of co-operation is to run things himself . . . It may be that Mr Flowers honestly thinks that he is better able than Mr Keen, Dr Wynn-Williams and myself to direct the policy of bombe production, but if so, I am quite sure that he is wrong. He is probably very good at his ordinary work, and also very good at designing apparatus for a definite problem that he can understand, but I have found him slow at grasping the complications of our work and his mind seems altogether too inflexible.[7]

Possibly so. Yet one can also hear a trace, possibly subconscious, of another sort of resistance going on; that of a Cambridge mathematics lecturer to the ideas of a partly self-educated, bumptious East Ender. Out of the senior figures in Bletchley Park, it was Welchman who always seemed most interested in tight control of both research and day-to-day operations; to have this Dollis Hill contingent come in and cast aspersions on Welchman's own home-grown talent was apparently almost too much for him to bear.

Indeed, Welchman's ill-will towards Flowers grew and grew – he wrote, 'the influence of Dr Radley and Mr Flowers must be completely removed' – to the extent that he approached the Admiralty supplies department and told them that Flowers was recklessly squandering good valves in the name of his research; and that he and the Dollis Hill team should be excluded altogether from such matters.

The Admiralty chose not to heed him. In due time, Welchman was promoted and set sail for the United States. This might have made things a little easier for the Dollis Hill team. But the remarkable thing, according to historian Paul Gannon, is that the decision to go ahead and develop Colossus properly was taken by the Post Office Research Establishment unilaterally, regardless of the feelings of Bletchley Park. The Park was all set to go with the Heath Robinsons – which worked, despite breakdowns – feeling that the war might be over before a more advanced machine could be put to use; the view of the Dollis Hill contingent was that the war would be going on a little longer than that.

The money, material and staff for the research into Colossus were therefore provided by the Post Office, though – thanks to wartime bureaucracy, and despite Churchill's continued bias in favour of the codebreaking work in financial terms – Flowers often made up the financial shortfall for various pieces of equipment himself. The Heath Robinson may have had something of a makeshift genius character about it, but the string and the elastic came from Tommy Flowers's pocket. Flowers himself said: 'It was a feat made possible by the absolute priority they were given to command materials and services and the prodigious efforts of the laboratory staff, many of whom did nothing but work, eat and sleep for weeks and months on end except for one half day a week ... the US also contributed valves and an electric typewriter under the lend-lease'.[8]

And so this monster, this Colossus, was delivered to Bletchley in January 1944; and with it, many argue, came the dawn of the computer age. For this was more than just a huge, elaborate counting machine; it worked to a program, via electronic valve pulses and delicate, complex circuits, at a rate hitherto unimagined, opening up the Lorenz messages at a terrific rate.

Tommy Flowers was vindicated; the work he did proved utterly invaluable. His nimble engineer's mind had overcome extraordinary problems. And of course, he would not be allowed to tell a single living soul.

Adjusting to peace after years of war was extremely difficult for a great many people. It seemed almost cruelly so to Tommy Flowers. It wasn't just that his boss Gordon Radley was knighted, whereas he simply received that discreet MBE and Award to Inventors. In those days, of course, £1,000 was a very substantial sum, almost enough to cover half the price of a house. But in a way, it was beside the point; for what would the money mean if Dr Flowers was not permitted to share his extraordinary and innovative electronic knowledge with peers and colleagues?

Worse than this, according to Paul Gannon, was that while a few of Bletchley Park's decoders could, after the war, decamp to the States and join up with computing projects there, Flowers was stuck in a department where no such transfers would be possible. The Post Office Research Office was extremely respectable and offered the now unimaginable security of a job for life. But it was also excruciatingly limited for a man of Flowers's talent. And his frustrations grew as the British government's post-war insistence of keeping every single one of Bletchley's operations secret further blocked off any advances that he might have made; advances in a budding computer industry to which he had claim to have a greater stake than most.

Not all accept the charge that secrecy held British technological advances back. Harry Fensom concluded a talk given to an Enigma symposium with this thought:

> I know some of the Colossi were broken up: we smashed thousands of valves and I believe some panels went with Max Newman to Manchester University. But the know-how remained with a few and the flexibility and modular innovations of Colossus led to the initiation of the British computer industry, such as the work at Manchester and NPL. And also of course to the beginning of electronic telephone exchanges. I therefore give my tribute to Dr Tom Flowers, without whom it would never have happened.

However, Captain Jerry Roberts articulates what he believes that Britain lost, thanks to that insistence on absolute post-war security. He is still furious on behalf of Tommy Flowers today: 'Dan Brown [author of *The Da Vinci Code*] wrote a book called *Digital Fortress*. And he says in that that the computer was invented at Harvard in 1944. That's the damage that has been done.

'Part of the trouble,' Captain Roberts continues, 'was that the Colossus machines were all destroyed, except two which got away. There were ten machines – eight were dismantled and destroyed, and two were kept at Cheltenham at the new GCHQ.

'It was at the orders of Churchill. He didn't want to reveal anything to the Russians. But this meant – crucially – that Britain couldn't develop this new computer industry. And I'm sure they could have found some form of cover for the technology – helping building supersonic aircraft or whatever you like to invent.'

When interviewed some years ago, Dr Flowers himself recalled with some sadness the moment in 1960 when the orders came through to destroy the last two remaining Colossus machines, which had been shipped to GCHQ. 'That was a terrible mistake,' said Flowers. 'I was instructed to destroy all the records, which I did. I took all the drawings and the plans and all the information about Colossus on paper and put it in the boiler fire. And saw it burn.'

As a postscript to his work, however, there is now, at the Bletchley Park museum, a fully working recreation of a Colossus machine. It stands, vast and unbelievably complicated, as an enduring testament to an outstandingly brilliant engineer.

25 1944–45: D-Day and the End of the War

The use of Enigma decryption was not confined to intercepted enemy messages; it also played an active role throughout the war in operations designed to deceive. And the most crucial of these was the Pas de Calais gambit of 1944, part of the preparations for D-Day. Indeed, it was reckoned by Bletchley Park veteran and renowned historian Harry Hinsley that, without Bletchley, the D-Day landings might well have been a catastrophic failure and the forces could have been 'thrown back into the sea'.

Here is how they did it. Over the space of several months, German intelligence operatives found themselves monitoring a gigantic new military formation which was apparently termed the First United States Army Group (FUSAG). German Intelligence was also receiving word of the Twelfth British Army, whose many divisions looked poised to move into Norway, into Sweden, into Turkey, Crete and Romania. The Allies, it seemed, were massing. German Intelligence gradually gained an impression that the Allies were planning a substantial cross-channel assault. And no area was more threatened than the Pas de Calais, the point at which the Americans – apparently – planned to enter and then swarm into France.

It was all, of course, a vast and elaborately planned deception, which had the effect of taking German attention off the real target of the Normandy beaches. And on top of this, noted Ralph Bennett, 'bombing and sabotage cut enough land-lines in northern France in the weeks before D-Day to force a proportion of useful intelligence on to the air'. Land-lines were a problem for Bletchley because communications made by telephone could not be intercepted. Now, thanks to the work of Bletchley, the Allied commanders were able to see that the lies had worked, receiving confirmation via broken messages from various corners of the German military machine.

With the coming of D-Day, the work of Bletchley was reaching its climax. As one veteran recalled, the approach of Operation Overlord changed the atmosphere of the Park quite dramatically, not least because there was a sudden travel ban: 'This was a miserable restriction, as most of us had nowhere to go for our weekend off. We were also forbidden to eat at the cafeteria and had to eat in a Nissen hut by ourselves and the food was much worse. Our work intensified under pressure.'[1]

One Wren kept staccato diary notes of this pressure, recording such memories as: 'Monday 12th June – Started the nightmare', 'Tuesday 13th – Gosh, what a day!' and 'Weds 14th – Hectic day!' Another recalled the unexpected results of being briefed:

We started at midnight and the Head of the Watch said, 'Before you young ladies sit down tonight, I want you to come and have a look at this map.' He showed how all round the south coast the Army, Navy and Air Force were grouped ready for invasion the next morning. He said, 'Because of that you will not be allowed to speak to anyone outside of the room tonight or go on your canteen break.'. . . how did they think three Wrens in the middle of Bletchley were going to warn Hitler we were about to invade?[2]

These quibbles aside, Bletchley played its part on 6 June 1944, even as the Allied armada was setting sail across the Channel. Various messages from the Germans, involving U-boats and reports of parachute landings, were decoded, translated and sent to the relevant authorities all within the space of half an hour. Although the precise details of the landings were secret, it was clear that something very significant was about to happen. Mavis Batey recalls of the build-up: 'I remember that we knew when D-Day was coming because I can see myself going up to London on a train from Bletchley and thinking "I suppose I am the only one on this train who knows D-Day is tomorrow."'

For codebreaker Harry Hinsley, D-Day involved him sitting firm behind his desk for over twenty-four hours. The climax was marked by an important telephone call from Downing Street. First a woman asked him to confirm that he was Mr Hinsley, then he heard Churchill's voice asking: 'Has the enemy heard that we are coming yet?' Hinsley assured the Prime Minister that the first Bletchley decrypts of German messages were coming on the teleprinter.

A couple of hours later, Churchill called Hinsley again: 'How's it going? Is anything adverse happening yet?' After forwarding more decrypts, Hinsley finally allowed himself to leave his desk, return to his billet and go to bed.

But in general terms, 1944 was by no means the end. Following D-Day, there was a lethal German technological weapons breakthrough, targeted on London. Indeed, later in the year, one of the last V-1 rockets to land came down very close to the Stanmore bombe outstation, although damage was kept to a minimum because of the blast wall that had been built to protect the machines.

Sarah Baring was by working at the Admiralty. Under the forty feet of reinforced concrete, known as The Citadel, that sat atop this maze of passages and offices, the prospect of lonely night-watches, although not entirely welcome, did offer one consolation. As she recalled: 'It was horrible sitting in my flat alone with these bloody rockets crashing down. And the short walk to the safety of the Citadel . . . was too tempting to resist . . . it may have looked like Lenin's tomb to some people. But I got to love the old dump and was amused to notice on bad nights the portly figure of the First Lord of the Treasury prowling the corridors in his bright red silk dragon-patterned dressing gown.'

Mavis Batey vividly recalls the V-1 rockets and the means by which the codebreakers at Bletchley Park sought to thwart them. 'We were working on double agents all the time, giving misinformation to their controllers. And because we could read the Enigma, we could see how they were receiving this misinformation. One of the things when the V-1s started was that the double agent was asked to give a report to the Germans on where the rockets were falling. Because of course they were wanting them to fall on central London.

'At that point, the bombs *were* falling in central London so intelligence here wanted them to cut out at a different point. So this double agent was instructed to tell his masters that they were falling north of London. The result of this was that the Germans cut the range back a little and as a result, the rockets started falling in south London. Just where my parents lived.'

In this case, it seemed that to Mrs Batey at least, ignorance was preferable to any other state; for security reasons, she knew nothing of this double-cross operation, or the messages that confirmed its success. 'I had no idea and it is just as well that I didn't. So when I saw the devastation at Norbury, I did not know that it had anything to do with anything I was doing. It really would have been a terrible shock to know that.'

The decisive turning of the war brought Bletchley into a new phase. Plans were being made for the allocation of encryption work after the conflict. Nevertheless, as the Allies took France and it appeared, finally, that the Germans were in retreat, the workrate intensified dramatically at the Park, for the very fact of turning fortunes meant that the volume of German encoded traffic had risen dramatically. On top of this, German intelligence had further tightened security around the encryptions. In fact this was one of the most tiring phases at the Park. By September 1944, Hut 8 was recording naval decrypts at a peak rate of about 2,200 a day.

Happily, as the weeks of the Allied assault wore on, the effect on German communications staff was deleterious; as a result, attention to security became more slapdash. By this time, the Colossus technology was firmly bedded in. A further six of the revolutionary machines were delivered to the 'Newmanry' and a new block, Block H, was built to house them. More were to follow as the year went on.

Indeed, for this final stage of the conflict, personnel numbers at Bletchley had almost doubled from what they had been just two years previously. As well as the codebreakers and the Wrens, there were large support teams (including 152 house staff – cleaners, handymen, etc.) and a transport section comprising 169 drivers, some fifty of whom were women. Transport didn't just deal with despatches – there was also, according to one who worked in the department, 'a Wolseley and a Hillman . . . we would wait in the lounge for the phone calls. Whoever was there answered and you could find yourself going down Watling Street to St Albans with despatches or to the Admiralty.'

There was no let-up in pace, or indeed in focus and concentration. In December 1944, Hugh Alexander set up Naval Section IIJ specifically to make further inroads into the main Japanese naval code. And there were still outbreaks of tension between the military and Bletchley Park. That same month the Park found itself being blamed for failing to give warning of a surprise attack in the Ardennes, when the British and Americans found themselves facing fourteen infantry and seven Panzer divisions along a 75-mile front. The assault was termed by some as 'the most notorious intelligence disaster of the war'. Those who worked in Hut 3 defended themselves with the explanation that they had picked up word of an imminent assault – and indeed a date – but there was nothing in the transmissions that could have indicated a location.

Part of the problem, it seemed, was that the Germans had used skilful deception – misdirection in the matter of troop deployments – as well as a tactic of radio silence. Moreover, the amount of decrypt material that Bletchley could harvest had decreased; rather than relying on radio transmissions, the Germans, back in their own territory, were using land-lines once more.

This ever-increasing intensity of work took its toll at the Park; by December 1944, it was estimated that the sick rate was running at four per cent, rather higher than normal. In the earlier years of the war, such intensity would have been tempered with the enthusiasm of youth. One can see all too easily, though, how the strict rota system, combined with the unremitting focus of the often repetitive and dull work, would have a corrosive effect. It is often said that for ordinary soldiers, any conflict is composed of moments of sheer terror and exhilaration, and the rest of the time of solid boredom. In the case of Bletchley, there was little in the way of exhilaration or terror.

Nevertheless, by January 1945, those in Hut 6 were cracking more German army signals than ever before, under the keys 'Puffin' and 'Falcon'. And even though the tide was flowing so strongly, the work did not let up. Against the backdrop of the Yalta conference of February 1945 – at which Stalin assured Churchill that there would be free elections in Poland after the war – there was another massive codebreaking setback when the Luftwaffe started to implement a new system of changing call-sign encryptions on a daily basis, and the frequencies every third day. Thankfully, some of the more experienced codebreakers and traffic analysts were still able to detect the individual traits of some individual enemy operators, which gave a way in to each code.

On the night of 29 April, those on duty at Bletchley Park found themselves witness to Hitler's increasing desperation. The Führer telegraphed Field Marshal Keitel from his bunker with three questions. 'Where are Wenck's spearheads? When will they advance? Where is Ninth Army?' Keitel's response was that all such forces were either stuck fast or completely encircled.

One might imagine a build-up of tremendous excitement in the huts at this time. But in fact, the events leading up to VE Day brought with them, surprisingly, an increase in security precautions. In late April, just days before German capitulation, the staff of Hut 3 were being told in memos that any decrypts involving mass German surrenders were to be extremely restricted in terms of circulation. On top of this, Director Edward Travis sent out a memo forbidding celebratory telegrams being sent out – unless they were in extremely special circumstances, in which case they first had to be presented for his approval.

Why the anxiety? First, the war with Japan was still going on. And also, even in the euphoria of victory, Travis and other senior staff at Bletchley Park would have been aware of the need to maintain security in the face of a new, chilly, geopolitical reality.

The collective image we now seem to carry of VE Day is of jubilant crowds in the streets of London, men and women with arms linked, people hanging on to lamp-posts, the night-time streets bathed in lights after the years of blackouts; people getting 'lit-up' themselves, as the singer Hutch put it, getting uproariously drunk, dancing and kissing that perfect night away.

And, despite the restrictions, nothing could stop the celebrations in Bletchley either. When the day came, one veteran recalls: 'We assembled on the grass outside the Mansion to hear that war with Germany was over. There was a huge cheer and great excitement – though our delight was muted as we still had the Japanese to finish before we could go home. So back to our decoding machines.'

There was another reason for going back to the machines. Even since the beginning of the war, it had not just been German traffic that was the target for the codebreakers; it was Russian traffic too. And in Bletchley – as well as in the wider Intelligence and military hierarchy – all thoughts were now starting to focus on 'the next war'; that was, the possibility of having to face a dominant Russia with plans of its own for European territorial gains.

Recall that as far back as the early 1920s, the British had been doing their best to monitor all Soviet secret traffic. Come 1939, there was no less reason to do so, especially in the face of the Molotov/Ribbentrop pact that foreswore any acts of aggression between Russia and Germany. So at the time of the Russian invasion of Finland in 1940, with the enormous amount of encrypted messages that were generated therewith, Bletchley managed to get a hook into the Russian codes. When the Germans invaded France, the Polish codebreakers who had been living in exile in Paris were forced to flee once more, to Britain. And from the outstation at Stanmore in Middlesex, these Poles were able to intercept and read Russian traffic emanating from the Ukraine.

When in 1941 Germany invaded Russia, the mighty bear appeared suddenly to be an ally of the British. It was officially put about that she was treated as such, and that Churchill especially ordered that any intelligence operations against Russia should desist. This was not entirely the case.

In September 1944, Sir Stewart Menzies, head of MI6, held discussions involving Sir Edward Travis, Gordon Welchman and Colonel Tiltman. These talks were about the urgent need to keep pace with (and, if possible, ahead of) Soviet encryption technology. Some personnel in Hut 3, including an American officer, were instructed to focus on the Red Army's most advanced equipment. And come VE Day, it was clear that even after the Japanese had been vanquished, a core of codebreakers would remain with the institution of Bletchley Park, even if they did not stay within the grounds of the Park itself.

Of course, like every other aspect of the war effort, the fact of VE Day in May 1945 didn't instantly mean that everyone could be released from their duties. As Jean Valentine recalls: 'When the war in Europe in stopped, my mother wrote to me in Ceylon and said, "Isn't it wonderful that war's over, when are you coming home?" My mother didn't see any reason why I couldn't come back immediately. I said, "Mum, excuse me, it's still going on here."'

But it was not just the fact that the war in the east was still rumbling on. Even in Europe, demobilisation was a complex business. Troops were not returned home instantly. And for the majority of the denizens of Bletchley Park, release from the work was slow. In the period between May and September of 1945, there were fresh tasks to address. Rather than decrypts, there was now the business of sweeping up after the destruction.

'Technical books came in in their dozens from Germany,' says Sheila Lawn of that time. 'And they had me and a few other girls just sitting and making details of the books so that they could be traced. The author and the way it was published and what the subject was.'

Her husband-to-be Oliver was engaged in similar mopping up. 'I was writing reports detailing what we had done. And we both left in September.'

'It was a sort of dribble down,' says Sheila. 'The numbers got less. Ten thousand, then eight thousand, however many it was, we didn't all leave at once.'

There is a curious poignancy about the annual report of the Bletchley Park Recreation Club at the end of 1945. In the previous year, the club had proudly boasted of 'play-readings', 'operatic performances', even a musical concert given by the Bletchley Park choir on the BBC, as well as 'fencing, chess, badminton and squash'. Now, though, the activities were fading as the young people began to move away. The floor of the hall no longer vibrated to the thump of couples ballroom dancing; there were fewer to take part in the specially organised cycling and hiking clubs. Even the 'swing music enthusiasts', as the Park's annual report referred to these daring souls, were dwindling in number. Bravely the club went on, meaning to carry on with all these impeccably middle-class activities until the very end.

In June 1945, there was a curious echo of Gordon Welchman's initial observation about codebreakers' aptitude for music. The BBC was already aware of the rich gathering of talented musicians at the Park, and had featured some of them in a previous broadcast. Now, startlingly, it was decided that there should be a broadcast from the Park itself. In one sense, it looked like surprisingly lax security – but then, of course, Bletchley's talented actors had been touring the local county, with their audiences aware of where they worked if not of what they did. So why not the BBC? Among the pieces performed were works by Ralph Vaughan Williams – a composer who, in his harking back to Tallis and to English folk melodies, reinforced a certain national sense of age-old coherence. The audience for the programme was not told what else the musicians had been achieving in recent years.

By that time, with Europe now silent, coming to terms with the devastation, grim news was still reaching Bletchley Park from across the world. In August 1945 intelligence was received that atom bombs had been dropped on the Japanese cities of Hiroshima and Nagasaki. Rosemary Calder told Michael Smith of what it was like when the messages started coming in. 'I was on a day-watch by myself,' she said. 'I didn't know the bomb had been dropped but you could tell from the disruption of all the messages that something terrible had happened. You could just feel the people standing there, screaming their heads off.'[3]

But it was finally over. A copy of a rather stiff memo on the subject of 'Re-Distribution of Surplus Staff' survives. Intended as a generic letter to all staff members, it begins:

Owing to the cessation of hostilities, there is no further work for you to do in this organisation. In these circumstances, there is no object in continuing to report here for duty, and with effect from . . . [blank space left for date], you are free to absent yourself. You must, however, present yourself, with this letter, to the Staff Officer, Hut 9, before your departure, to give certain particulars for his records . . .

In accordance with Treasury regulations, your name has been forwarded to the Treasury for consideration for employment in other Government Departments.[4]

This transition was by no means instant, and nor was it painless. With personnel leaving, those left behind were juggling new and awkward shift systems to keep up with the remaining work. The Bletchley Park directorate made some proposals concerning weekend leave, which one might imagine would have been welcomed after all those years of seven-day shifts. Curiously, these met with fierce resistance: what worked in peacetime for 'family and friends', as one Park staffer put it, was not right for this organisation. At Bletchley, the shifts worked best when the staff could 'choose' which days off they wanted. And what, this staffer added, would be the benefit of having every Sunday off?

'Shopping is impossible on Sundays anywhere,' said the staffer in a memo of protest. 'So no shopping would be possible one week in three (according to the BP shift system). In London, shopping is only possible in the forenoon of Saturdays. Those making appointments – hairdressing, dentistry, interviews for jobs – would be severely handicapped.'

Perhaps even more persuasively, added the staffer, 'Entertainment facilities are rare on Sundays and overcrowded on Saturdays. Difficulties would be greatly increased if all BP personnel were free at weekends.' And possibly the clincher? 'Billeted personnel are in many cases obliged to be "out" for the midday meal. They are doubly unwelcome on Sundays, when the billetor is himself at home, and on Sunday, it is more difficult than on weekdays to get a meal elsewhere.'[5]

John Herivel took a slightly more emollient line in the debate over compulsory weekends off, though he felt that in his own department, he and his colleague Macintosh should carry on as before. 'If we were to confine our leave to Saturdays and Sundays,' he wrote in another memo still held in the archives, 'there would be some days when neither of us were on. This could be very inconvenient.'[6]

Nevertheless, the slow, careful dismantling of the operation was under way. And the image of Bletchley Park in the later months of 1945 seems to be one of once-teeming blocks now lying empty; of sparse huts, and of many of the rooms in the house itself now starting to echo. 'It was so strange,' said one veteran. 'It was already nearly empty – a ghost town with just a few removal men shifting furniture. Thousands of people just walked out of the gate never to return.'

Actually the clear-up was a shade more complex than that; given the intense secrecy and security, every square inch of the house, and all the huts, and all the blocks, had to be combed and sifted for any hint of coding material or even machine components to ensure that absolutely nothing had been left behind.

The operation was largely packed up: some (though by no means all) bombes were dismantled. Some Wrens were gleeful about these acts of destruction, for they had come almost to hate the machines. Now, instead of having to treat them with the utmost care, they let parts drop and fall and roll on the floor, and they shouted with enthusiasm.

Meanwhile, bonfires of paperwork were made in the grounds of Bletchley Park. The huts, the house, all areas had to be combed for any bits of paper that might have got away. Some decrypts were found jammed into the gap of a window frame; the huts had been so draughty in winter that they were used to muffle the cold.

The Colossus and Heath Robinson machines were also taken to pieces. Anything that remained was kept either at Stanmore or Eastcote in Middlesex. The bombe machines that remained at Eastcote, however, did not stop, for they now had other sorts of traffic and signals intelligence to decode.

For most of those who had worked at the Park though, the conflict was over; and many of those young people now had a shattered country to rebuild. One is tempted to look back across the years and see idealism in that enthusiasm; but it might be more accurate to say that this was a time for unflinching realism, and even a certain sense of apprehension.

26 1945 and After: The Immediate Aftermath

All the thousands of young cryptographers and linguists and Wrens were at last able to turn their thoughts to the futures that they had planned for themselves, futures that had been held in limbo for the last six years. Yet there was also a destabilising sense of abstraction, like walking out into a white fog. According to a few of the veterans, there was, surprisingly, no intensive debriefing session. Apart from the instruction that silence was to be maintained at all costs, these young people went out into the world to begin their careers.

'There was nothing,' says Oliver Lawn of his final days at Bletchley Park. 'Nothing at all. You signed the Official Secrets Act.' His wife Sheila says: 'I don't remember any final lecture. We had just escaped from this dreadful war, and therefore anything that was secret then was secret now.'

For Roy Jenkins's fellow 'Tunny' codebreaker Captain Jerry Roberts, his military role was not to end for some time, an experience common to many. Immediately after Bletchley, he was seconded into War Crimes work.

'I regarded my time in War Crimes as a great nuisance,' he says. 'I wasn't demobilised until 1947. And looking back, I regard it as the only time in my life where I didn't make progress and didn't contribute an awful lot. But shortly after that, I met a middle-aged Belgian lady. Her husband had been a lawyer, and during the war, they had sheltered British airmen, or Allied airmen, shot down, and trying to make their way back to Britain to join the air force again.

'She had written a diary – they actually had an airman hidden in the house when the Gestapo came to call. The Gestapo searched up and down, but didn't find him, and went away disappointed. So the airman emerged and everybody congratulated themselves. And the Gestapo came back. Because that is what they did, that was their trick. This Belgian woman never saw her husband again. She got away by pretending to be doolally. The president of her tribunal was a civilised man and let her go.

'But she had this diary and she wanted someone to translate it. So I did that and it was published as a book.'

After that, though, Captain Roberts found that he had to find a career that was rather more diverting than the one that he had originally planned: 'When I studied German, at University College, London, it had been with the purpose of joining the Foreign Office. I am eternally grateful that I never joined the Foreign Office. I went into market research side of an international advertising agency.' The work took him all over the world at a time when not many British people travelled at all. 'And for the rest of that time,' he says, 'it was market research, which I thoroughly enjoyed. I had my own company in the 1970s. The travel was very welcome!' It was also sufficiently absorbing to counter the frustration of never being able to talk about Bletchley.

Similarly, for Gordon Welchman, who had brought so many invaluable innovations and systems to Bletchley Park, the end of the war marked a turning point; the prospect of returning to his old, academic life in Cambridge seemed utterly impossible. Towards the end of the war, and with his enthusiasm for the nature of organisations, he had began to help in drafting the future of Government Communication Headquarters – what was later to become GCHQ.

His belief – one that flew in the face of established civil service practice – was that talented cryptologists should be able to reach the highest salary rung without also having to undertake administrative work. This was based on his experience in Hut 6, when he saw at first hand the benefits of mutual co-operation, freeing up time for thinking.

However, he found himself up against more stubborn attitudes. On top of this, Welchman believed that the British computer industry was fatally held up by the government's reluctance to fund research – the attitude seemed to be that the government would wait until such technology was developed commercially, and then find a use for it.

He recalled that by then, he was a changed person who had been 'thoroughly shaken out of my old academic way of life by my challenging experiences at Bletchley Park and in the United States, and it seemed impossible to return to what I had been doing before the war'. With appropriately golden references from Hugh Alexander, Welchman took up his colleague's old post as Director of Research at the John Lewis Partnership. While being a very fine position, this does leave one wondering whether the years that immediately followed the war seemed a little anti-climactic. In 1948, Welchman discarded the department stores and set sail with his family to America, to work in the burgeoning field of computer technology. Later he joined the organisation MITRE, looking into such matters as battlefield communications systems.

For in one sense, the war hadn't ended at all. The conflict had simply become frozen. Britain, America, and western Europe were facing an opponent every bit as implacable as Nazism. Welchman had joined the strategic struggle against the forces of the Warsaw Pact, and of Soviet military might.

Indeed, Welchman's preference for the American way of doing things led him, eventually, to take on American citizenship. One now senses that his view of the British authorities was a little stronger than that of simple distaste. 'People have a tendency to filter out what they do not want to hear,' he wrote of the pre-Second

World War government. 'An appeasement-minded government in England filtered out the information on Hitler's Germany that they were receiving from their Secret Service.'

But for other key players from Bletchley Park, life in the immediate post-war years lost that lustre of intensity. John Herivel – whose flash of inspiration one night in 1940 had had an incalculable effect upon the war effort – first went into teaching. He returned to his native Belfast, joined a school there and pretty soon found the rowdy boys absolutely intolerable. So he returned to academia and found, despite his mathematical background, that history was his real passion. He was to go on to write a history of Newton's *Principia*, among many other subjects. 'And I found that I just didn't think about Bletchley Park,' he says.

Messenger and typist Mimi Gallilee, who of course was so very young when she started work at Bletchley, found the immediate aftermath to be rather unsatisfactory by comparison. She says: 'I think there were about 1,700 people left, and we went off to Eastcote, in Middlesex. We went into the quarters where the bombes were, and I think there was only one bombe left. I didn't know anything about the bombes. None of us knew. Those of us who had nothing to do with it wouldn't know. So we just moved in to where the Wrens had worked. I of course stayed within the directorate . . .

'Commander Loehnis was the head by then. That was in 1946. And a lot of Forces people were still at Bletchley Park. I don't think any Forces people went down to Eastcote.'

The move to London provided Mrs Gallilee with the first dusty taste of post-war austerity; even the matter of a daily Tube fare could put a serious dent in one's weekly living wage. Life was a constant effort to scrimp.

'I was living in Bayswater and I would have to pay the full fares all the way to Eastcote,' she says. 'On such a low salary. I don't think I stayed there for longer than six months. They tried to do something for me in the way of an increase in pay but you just didn't have that kind of system and I had so long to wait until I was twenty-one. The Civil Service was very rigid, and there were no such things as merit awards in those days. The government wouldn't have had the money to pay us anyway.'

So, after the relative comfort and even romanticism of Bletchley Park, this new prospect of dull work for low wages began to gnaw at her. 'I hadn't got enough money to live and stay in London,' she says. 'So I said I'd take the first job that I could get as long as it paid more money. And the first job I went after was as a copy typist for Burroughs Wellcome, the research chemist outfit. They took me on. I earned a pound a week more, straight away. That was a hell of a lot of money.

'But after maybe just a couple of days, I thought – I can't stand this. I felt as though I had been dropped from one world into another. It was nothing like anything. Perhaps I thought everywhere would be like Bletchley Park.

'I used to say, "I feel as though I'm in a different world altogether." I saw a job advertised in the *Telegraph*, for BOAC [the British Overseas Airways Corporation, a precursor of British Airways]. I applied there, and got that, and I stayed with them from 1947 until about 1953. I was married by then.'

For two of the codebreakers, there was a move, conscious or not, towards helping to rebuild both the nation and its remaining colonies. Keith Batey recalls: 'I left Bletchley Park in August 1945. I decided – wrongly, I think now, though it seemed right at the time – that I wasn't going to go on with mathematics, so I tried for the administrative Civil Service. I got in, so for some reason I opted for the Dominions Office.

'I had six months in the Foreign Office while I was waiting for the Civil Service exam, in the South American department. I was working with Victor Perone, who had finished a very successful career as Her Majesty's Representative in the Vatican. A typically Edwardian gentleman, very portly, with a great gold chain across his chest. The man I really did like – I being a junior dogsbody, of course – was the chairman of the Bank of London and South America. He was Samuel Hoare – and a more polite, considerate and charming chap I have never met.'

But there was an element of an upper-class world that already seemed to be vanishing fast. Hoare, it seems, was slightly bewildered by the provenance of this new Foreign Office recruit. In the years before the war, many of those who worked for the Foreign Office very often came from the grander, titled families; they tended to have substantial private incomes, upon which they were expected to live. This was not the case with Keith Batey.

'Samuel Hoare was puzzled,' Mr Batey continues. 'He couldn't understand how there could be anyone in the Foreign Office whose name he didn't recognise. He would call me Mr Beety.' But it was Batey who was emblematic of the future, not Sir Samuel Hoare. Mr Batey and his generation were helping to forge a new era of administration in which old school contacts were not the most important thing.

Similarly, for Oliver Lawn, the Civil Service seemed the logical career path. 'I had a very frantic one-term lecturing in mathematics at Reading University in September 1945,' he says. 'By that time, I had more or less forgotten all my mathematics, in five years of doing codebreaking.

'Then I took the Civil Service exams in the spring of 1946. I could have gone scientific or administrative civil service. I was successful in both but I decided, on the whole, to go for the administration, rather than the specialist science as a mathematician. I joined the civil service around July 1946.'

As he says, Mr Lawn was 'directed', as indeed was everyone else after the war. Despite the fact that almost any occupation would seem drab after the pressurised life he had been leading, this was also the correct thing for a young man of his upbringing and background. Britain was smashed to pieces, bankrupt, fading and peeling and shabby. It needed clever, expert administrators; not politicians, but men who really knew how things worked. It was Mr

Lawn's generation that was to exert the real influence in Britain in the coming years, in everything from the rebuilding of inner cities to the dismantling of Empire.

For the women who were to become their wives, this was still an era in which ladies were not expected to go out to work, despite the mass mobilisation of the female population throughout the war. When a wife became pregnant, it was understood that her career was over and that she would become a mother and a homemaker.

Having said all that, it would clearly have been a travesty if the women of Bletchley Park had led their intellects slide into abeyance. Happily, for both Sheila MacKenzie and Mavis Lever, this was emphatically not the case.

Sheila continued academically. However, her original plan to teach on the continent was still looking extremely uncertain. What shape would that continent now be taking? How much of it would be subsumed by the heavy mass of the Soviet Union? The war forced a geographical change of Sheila's plans. She had to confine herself to British opportunities.

'I did what you can do in Scotland, a general degree,' Mrs Lawn says. 'Based on the previous subjects I had done. That was quite hard work over the year. And then I did a year in Birmingham University, a post-graduate diploma in Sociology and then I went in for personnel management. A complete change. It still wasn't easy to get abroad.'

She and Mr Lawn felt the full icy blast of austerity Britain in their first two winters after the Park. It is one of those periods which now, with some distance, is almost as difficult to imagine as the war itself. As Sheila recalls: 'Oh, but it was cold. There was very little fuel and very little hot water. That was even worse than during the war. Everything was rationed, including potatoes and bread. And clothes were rationed until 1952, I think. When Oliver and I were married, we could only get dockets for basic furniture. But Oliver had a great-aunt who died and some of her beautiful furniture came to us. So we got a bedroom and a living room from that.'

The scrimping that went on for Sheila and Oliver's wedding day now seems almost unthinkable. 'My mother made do and mended. She was very good with her needle. For instance, out of two beautiful silk jumpers of the 1920s, which she had kept in a trunk, my mother was able to make three jumpers; I had two and she had one. And she remade some of her frocks for herself and for me. And my going-away – I was married in borrowed clothes, very successfully.

'I had a lovely veil which belonged to our minister's wife and had come through her family. I went away in army blankets, dyed a lovely maroon colour. They were made by a cousin of mine who was learning to be a tailoress. And with the tailoress she was working with, she made a suit for me – skirt, waistcoat and coat. I wore it for years. It was much admired. My undies were parachute silk. Gorgeous stuff to use. It was "make do and mend" with a vengeance!'

Mavis Batey also felt certain that her future was of an academic nature, though the duties of bringing up a young family with her new husband Keith came first. 'We were in Oxford, we went back to Christ Church, and I didn't really get back into any kind of intellectual activity until my three children were grown. After that, I could go to the Bodleian Library every day. So I eventually picked up.'

But what of the Park's most famous innovator and presiding genius? For Alan Turing, still only thirty-four at the end of the war, technology was drawing closer and closer to enable him to realise his concept of a 'Turing Machine'; equally, though, his homosexuality, and the British establishment's attitude towards it, were to contribute to his tragic – and wholly pointless – death.

The transition from war to peace seemed, initially, to make little difference to Alan Turing's working life. After his removal as head of Hut 8 and his return from the United States, he came back to intense research. But we might also see that the post-war world outside the hermetically sealed atmosphere of Bletchley – a country with a shifting, faintly neurotic moral climate – was one in which it would be extremely difficult for him to thrive.

Late in 1944, Turing still had further cryptological challenges to take on, and he did so both at Bletchley Park and the nearby communications base, Hanslope Park. Building on ideas he had seen in the United States, he was working on a new speech encipherment system, to be given the name 'Delilah' – that is, a deceiver of men.

It was extraordinarily complex stuff, involving sound frequencies and bandwidths. According to Andrew Hodges, Turing, together with two new young recruits, Robin Gandy and Donald Bayley, installed himself in a corner of a Hanslope laboratory. Though this establishment, in contrast to Bletchley, was assuredly military, Turing was still very much the archetypal wartime boffin, in shiny trousers and with his unkempt hair and the unselfconsciously strange noises that he would make while working.

Turing was remarkably good with electronics, given that he was entirely self-taught, but it was Bayley who provided a certain level of organisation. There was one bout of turbulence when Turing told Bayley of his homosexuality; Bayley had only heard of such things through smutty jokes and was horrified. What might have ended in embarrassed silence escalated into a shouting match. But somehow, the two men were able to find an understanding, for Bayley continued to work with Turing, whatever he might have felt about his orientation. Indeed, their collaboration was to prove quite remarkable – if anyone could ever have realised it.

Turing first of all chose to sleep in the old house of Hanslope itself, and then, rather like Bletchley, moved into a cottage near the Park's kitchen garden, accompanied by Robin Gandy and a ginger cat. The two men would go for walks, and the ginger cat, unusually, would go with them. If Turing was annoyed at work, or by the behaviour of those around him, he would, as ever, go off on long runs around the countryside.

Although still a top secret base, Hanslope Park wasn't Bletchley; but in one other curious respect, it was very similar. And that is that Turing found himself pulled into a social life, a sense of community. Although more military in flavour – mess jackets at smart dinners (a dinner jacket in Turing's case) and so forth – there were parties, dances with ATS girls, gossip and social intrigue. Turing was rather popular.

Holding as he did the unique position of eccentric boffin, he combined this with a surprisingly youthful outlook – to some he could seem even younger than thirty-four – which made him a draw for both men and women. It was an appeal that crossed ranks; he seemed to mingle as happily with the working-class Tommys as with anyone else. He even gave complicated mathematical lectures.

And as 1945 dawned, Turing and Bayley persisted with the labyrinth of wires and valves that comprised the Delilah system, conducting ever more complex work with equations and frequencies and kilohertz. By the spring, they had succeeded in enciphering a recording of a Churchill speech – the coded version sounded like the hiss of white noise. But the conflict was nearly over and there was no longer any sense of urgency. No matter how extraordinary the technical achievement, the military powers had other matters on their minds now. Encryption of this sort was low on the list of priorities.

The question now was: what parts of Turing's scientific work would find government or even private sponsorship in peacetime? His Fellowship at King's College was renewed for another three years, which would give him £300 per annum and academic freedom. He was also awarded the OBE; for reasons of security, such awards were rare, for fear of the citation giving away some element of the work that had been done.

However, with the lack of enthusiasm for the Delilah system – it seems the Post Office was working upon its own commercial sound encryption techniques – Turing wanted to return to the question that had been haunting him since the 1930s, that of constructing a thinking machine – an electronic brain. A Universal Turing Machine. A machine of such complexity that it could not only speedily handle any kind of mathematical calculation, but also store a memory of the process within itself.

In the 1930s, while the theory had been revolutionary, it was difficult to see how the current valve technology could keep pace with such a thing. Come 1943, and the successful operation of the Colossus machine, with its thousands of valves working in unison, and suddenly a whole new realm of possibilities opened up.

King's was to wait: for the mathematicians and physicists at the National Physical Laboratory in south-west London had – despite the security and secrecy of the last few years – come to hear of Turing's reputation, and wished to hire him. Turing saw this as a potential avenue for at last realising his vision. The goal was simple: the logical functionings of the mind could surely be replicated inside the electronic pulses of a machine.

In the months and years that were to follow, this work – the construction of a vast room-filling machine, all dials and wires and valves   would eventually take Turing to the University of Manchester. He bought a house in a suburb, made good friends with his next-door neighbours; and began to investigate those areas of the city in which like-minded men and opportunistic youths flashed understanding glances at one another.

Turing became involved with a young man called Arnold Murray, inviting him home for dinner. After several of these dinners, Murray was invited to stay the night. Their relationship, by Andrew Hodges' account, was at once awkward, odd, and in some curious way affecting, with the lad finding Turing's intellect and superior social class eye-opening.

But then money started to go missing; Turing instantly suspected Murray. Words were exchanged. After Turing's house was burgled, Murray, slipping up, admitted that he knew the burglar in question – a lad he called Harry – and had happened to meet him a short while back when Harry had been planning a crime. Turing went to the police with the information on 'Harry'.

But it all suddenly backfired on Turing. The police caught up with Harry, who in his statement gave an account of Arnold Murray's numerous visits to Turing's home. The police now decided to turn their attention to Turing.

Turing made no bones about the allegation of homosexual behaviour – indeed, while Detective Mills was round at his house, Turing gave him wine and entertained him with a few old melodies on his violin. To his closest friends, Turing had always been open about his orientation, even going so far as to make jokes about men that he found attractive. But in 1952, there was a sort of mini-hysteria in Britain surrounding the entire subject of homosexuality.

There was the celebrated case of Lord Montagu and the journalist Peter Wildeblood, not to mention an undercover officer entrapping the actor John Gielgud in a public lavatory. The subject made lurid headlines in the Sunday scandal sheets. Turing was charged with gross indecency. He did not seem to understand how anyone could possibly imagine that he had committed a crime.

At Turing's trial, Max Newman and Hugh Alexander, now at GCHQ in Cheltenham, appeared as character witnesses. Turing was found guilty, though spared prison. Hideously, though, as part of the condition of being bound over for a year, he was also required to submit, for a limited period of about a year, to 'Organo-Therapic Treatment' at Manchester Royal Infirmary. In short, this was an extremely primitive form of hormone treatment involving oestrogen. Turing was, for a time, rendered impotent, and grew breasts.

Nevertheless, although the trial had obviously caused a certain amount of disquiet within Manchester University – and even though GCHQ had removed his security clearance – he had been allowed to hold on to his academic post. And by this stage, he was widely admired within the British scientific community. At conferences, mathematicians would vie for his attention. Work on the Mark II Turing machine – an even larger computer than the first – was under way. He even managed a reunion with his old colleague Don Bayley, who now lived in Woburn Sands near Bletchley. And Turing remained defiantly unapologetic about his orientation, sharing the tale of a trip to Paris where he picked up a young man who insisted on putting his trousers under the mattress in order to keep the crease sharp.

Turing nevertheless started to go for sessions with a psychiatrist. It seemed clear to some that despite his energy and good humour, the events of the trial, and the sentence, weighed heavier upon him than he liked to suggest.

Turing's sentence expired in 1953. The University of Manchester appointed him to a Readership in the Theory of Computing, which would have made him financially secure for a great many years to come. Turing also enjoyed foreign holidays – a genuine rarity in the pre-jet age 1950s.

So there remains at least some ambiguity about the circumstances of his suicide in 1954, at the age of forty-two. He was found in bed by his housekeeper, with white foam around his mouth. There was a jar of potassium cyanide in the house, and of cyanide solution. On his bedside table was an apple, out of which several bites had been taken. The obvious conclusion: the apple had been dipped in cyanide. Indeed, author Andrew Hodges went so far as to recall how, some years back, Turing had become fascinated with the film *Snow White and the Seven Dwarfs* and the wicked queen's chilling incantation: 'Dip the apple in the brew/Let the Sleeping Death seep through'.

According to Hodges, Turing had prepared a new will several months earlier. But the fact that he left no note, and indeed no indication whatsoever that such a course might be on his mind, has led others to speculate that his death might have had an even more macabrely random element about it.

Keith Batey is one who cannot quite believe that Turing committed suicide. He recalls: 'When I was secretary at the Royal Aircraft Establishment, I overlapped with James Lighthill. He'd been Professor at Manchester with Turing. James said he didn't believe Turing committed suicide. He said that he [Turing] was a great man for experimenting and he was experimenting with acidification of cyanide on coke. James said he did this while he was eating an apple and that's how he got poisoned. He went on to say that [Turing] had bought himself two pairs of new socks three days previously. And he wouldn't have done that if he was going to commit suicide.'

In the acclaimed Turing play *Breaking the Code* (1988) by Hugh Whitemore, the dramatist delicately hints at another possibility. In the final scene, Turing is enjoying a Greek holiday. He has picked up a young man. The young man says nothing and Turing assumes that he cannot speak English. As they recline, Turing, now talking almost to himself, finally talks out loud about Bletchley – about the work he did, the breakthroughs he achieved, the intolerable burden of security and secrecy. And still the Greek boy says nothing.

But from this we suddenly, chillingly, infer: what if the Greek boy was a set-up? A Soviet spy? Such things were known. If that were the case – if the boy understood every word and reported it back – would it have become plain to British security services that Turing had leaked the vital information? And if so, could they not have arranged to have had him conveniently removed?

The play ends as our speculation begins. But that is simply theatre. These days, Turing is rightly remembered for his achievements, as opposed to his eccentricities and foibles. A bust of his head now stands in the Bletchley Park museum. And in September 2009, the Prime Minister Gordon Brown apologised – on behalf of the government and, we presume, the nation – for Turing's prosecution. 'He was a quite brilliant mathematician,' said Mr Brown, praising his contribution to 'Britain's fight against the darkness of dictatorship'.

'The debt of gratitude he is owed,' continued the Prime Minister, 'makes it all the more horrifying, therefore, that he was treated so inhumanely. In 1952, he was convicted of gross indecency – in effect, tried for being gay . . .

'Alan deserves recognition for his contribution to humankind . . . it is thanks to men and women who were totally committed to fighting fascism, people like Alan Turing, that the horrors of the Holocaust and of total war are part of Europe's history and not Europe's present.'

Quite so. In this day and age – one that Turing might possibly have felt more comfortable in – there is a greater general understanding of his philosophy concerning the nature of the mind, and in particular of the electronic mind. The work that he began has led to illimitable advances.

27 Bletchley's Intellectual Legacy

'There was a pub in the village of Stony Stratford that some of the chaps at Bletchley went to,' says Y Service veteran Geoffrey Pidgeon. 'And it was there you'd get the sight of, say, four chaps, all gathered together with their beers, and talking in Greek.'

In discussing the Park and its impact on the lives of those who worked there, a great many veterans acknowledge the other side of what they gained; it was a kind of university education by proxy, even if their own academic studies had become a little fuzzy round the edges. The full range of what the Park gave them only became clear to them in the years that followed the war.

In general terms, the Second World War brought with it not merely a will to win, but also a determination that what came afterwards would make life better for everyone. It was during the years of the war that the great social changes of the National Health Service and of the Welfare State were conceived, proposed through the Beveridge Report, debated and agreed.

But there was more than that; in cultural terms, there seemed a strong thirst for the wider dissemination of knowledge. The notion that great art, and literature, and music, and thought, should be shared among as many people as possible, as opposed to simply appealing to privileged elites. Rather than being a 'pause' in their young lives, Bletchley provided an unexpected and unusual further education, as many veterans of the Park have told me; an education which they would never have had in any other circumstances.

The question of money was very important; in the years before and during the war technological developments were already putting great works of art directly into more hands. Bryan Magee recalls in his memoirs that when he was a boy in the 1930s and 40s, gramophone records became slightly cheaper and more widely available; this in turn allowed him, as a boy, to listen to more and more great performances of classical music. And the effect of this was life-changing; the music alone awoke in him the sense of so many other possibilities, so much other art to be explored.[1]

Those years also saw the introduction of the paperback book, which instantly made literature affordable for many more people. Previously, most had to rely upon their public libraries; wonderful though these institutions once were, you could only borrow a book for two weeks at a time. If you could actually buy it, and own it, your time spent studying it was limitless.

We learn through the diaries of Mass Observation that the war years brought an even greater enthusiasm for cinema, and in particular the glossy, expensive escapism of Hollywood. We also learn, though, through some of these day-to-day diaries that most people seemed to have a highly tuned critical faculty, and that some films that we would regard today as classics were dismissed sharply at the time as nonsense by these diarists.

For the young people of Bletchley, this sense of intellectual openness and curiosity was strong. Even for those who were not drawn directly from university, there had been a sense of culture in the air. Mimi Gallilee recalls with especial fondness the library within the house itself. Others had brought their libraries with them.

'We were much into Freud,' recalls Mavis Batey. 'Pelican published sixpenny editions of *The Psychopathology of Everyday Life*. If you had been an undergraduate, as we were, then you were pretty much bound to have had one.' Bletchley Park codebreaker (Lord) Asa Briggs subsequently saw his *Social History of England* published by Pelican. In many ways, the imprint was a synecdoche for a younger generation eager to absorb as much as they could. From economics to psychology to linguistics, those blue spines were signifiers of educational aspiration, a generation before Jennie Lee brought the Open University into being.

Like a surprising number of young people of the time, Mavis Batey had, just before the war, spent a little time on the continent for the purposes of study. 'I was much better acquainted than anyone else with Freud because I went to Zurich University,' Mrs Batey says. If one was a linguist, one normally had to go for a term in a German university. But since this was 1938, and the Germans had already moved into Czechoslovakia, she instead had to go to one that was German-speaking. 'And I actually heard Freud's disciple Carl Jung.'

One always imagines that the work of Bletchley Park would be enough of an intellectual demand on the young people who were working there. Yet as we have seen, aside from the odd lightning flash of genius, the business of decoding communications was more a question of patience, trial and error. Also, this particular generation of young people had hinterlands. Just because they had particular abilities in their own fields – mathematics, linguistics, the classics – didn't mean that their interests were circumscribed in any way.

'This is another thing you hear: that we were more or less incarcerated in Bletchley,' continues Mavis Batey. 'That isn't true at all, we could do anything in the town, and I enrolled for the Cambridge extra-mural course on psychology and used to go there with the townsfolk.'

She also recalls: 'Lord Briggs always said to me, as he did to a few other people: "It was our university, Mavis." Those five years are tremendously important at that age . . . what it did for me, that I was very grateful for, we were all thrown in at the deep end.'

Mrs Batey credits Bletchley Park with giving her a certain measure of confidence. 'I always wanted to be a historian – so I am a historian now – and I got into a particular field of landscape history as pioneered by W.G. Hoskins,' she says. 'He was my great guru.

'As time went on, I found myself on heritage committees, landscape heritage, National Trust. And because it was a new subject, I didn't have to know what Professor X or Professor Y had said – I was quite happy to have a bash at it, and then read what the others said after I had got some ideas myself. And that was what I realised was a gift, a legacy of Bletchley. You either do it or you don't, but no one else is going to do it if you don't.'

Similarly, Sheila Lawn was summoned to Bletchley before she had the chance to finish her degree. But the atmosphere of the Park suited her extremely well, as she recalls: 'It was stimulating to meet people, and to talk to them. I had friends, about my age group. I think I was the only half-baked MA, they all seemed to have completed theirs. They came from different universities, different parts of the country, different experiences, different subjects. Yes, that was the collegiate feel, all the different disciplines.'

The Hon. Sarah Baring had been educated only by governesses. Nevertheless, Bletchley Park seemed to her at times to have a distinctly campus feel: 'Of course the cryptographers were all brilliant mathematicians. And they were a class apart. Quite mad, some of them, quite potty, but very very sweet.

'I never went to university but here, I was lucky to be right at the centre of things and the people I worked with were so wonderful. And to have met Turing and all those sorts of people was just great.'

Another veteran, Gwen Watkins, recalled wanting to immerse herself totally in this strange intellectual whirlpool. And afterwards, when Bletchley Park was packed up and she was facing, like everyone else, the austere grind of post-war Britain, she felt a certain measure of gratitude to have been working in such a place. For in a sense, Bletchley Park gave her a grounding: 'To be with people for whom books, music, art, history, everything like that, was a daily part of their lives, it was an absolute blossoming for me.'[2]

Meanwhile, Mimi Gallilee had been given the chance to see how some of a generation's greatest minds disported themselves in everyday circumstances. What she witnessed are scenes that – if there hadn't been a war – might have been commonplace in Oxford or Cambridge, and which otherwise she would never have seen.

'Like, for instance, Alan Turing,' recalls Mimi. 'All of my memories of him are of seeing him walking along the path and turning left at Hut 9, always with his head down. He was a very intense young man, and he always looked worried.

'That's how people were there. You would have been frightened by Josh Cooper if you met him. He was a big man, and he was cumbersome. When he walked along, he would exclaim things like: "Pincers!"'

Josh Cooper's eccentricity did not end there. One story that did the rounds of Bletchley concerned the evening when he walked out of the Park gates with his hat clasped in his hand and a briefcase somehow balanced upon his head. One might easily imagine such a thing happening in an Oxford quad. As Mimi Gallilee says, 'We accepted it as normal. You didn't laugh at him really. You got used to it. There were so many like that. Brilliant people, in their own sphere.'

Elsewhere among the huts, there had also been perceived sexual eccentricity – again, the preserve of the older universities – which Mimi Gallilee says was viewed from a radically different point of view. And this in itself was an education to the young woman, doing much to colour her post-war view of such matters: 'When we were young, we were very ignorant, because we didn't know about homosexuality. If somebody seemed a bit effeminate, we'd just have a little giggle, but we didn't think beyond that. Was it innocence or ignorance? And you didn't hear that kind of thing being talked about anywhere – you certainly wouldn't hear it at home – so you really didn't know very much about anything.'

Being in the grounds of Bletchley Park was then, for someone as young as Mimi Gallilee, an education in itself. She says that she would sometimes look at these sophisticated people and know that she would not be able to casually drop into their conversations. 'The kind of conversations you would overhear would all be on a higher scale. If you overheard things in the cafeteria, they would be talking, discussing – obviously nothing about their work, but wider subjects – and it was a rarefied atmosphere.

'The majority of them were from university,' she adds. 'And now I can say that they wouldn't have sniggered and laughed at things that the ignorant would – such as I. They wouldn't perhaps have pointed and laughed at certain people, for instance. The more I think back, the more rarefied I realise it was.'

In the later years of the war, when Bletchley Park's numbers had multiplied and the Colossus decrypting machines had turned code-breaking almost into an industrial process, some were nevertheless keen to see the collegiate atmosphere continue. Professor Max Newman encouraged his senior staff to take time off 'to think'. He opened up 'research books', available should any member of staff be hit by a bright idea and wish to record it there and then. This book was open not just to mathematicians and linguists but to Wrens as well. And if enough people expressed interest in an idea, they could all be gathered together to discuss it at what would be termed 'a tea-party'.

Finally, a quick overview of how many Bletchley Park veterans dispersed in the post-war years gives us a vivid flavour of its intellectual and artistic mettle.

Jane Fawcett, who had worked in Hut 6, managed after the war to pursue a similarly academically satisfying career in architectural history that took in running the enormously influential Victorian Society (of which John Betjeman was so prominent a member) and the Royal Institute of British Architects.

Actress Dorothy Hyson not only returned to the West End; in 1945, she joined John Gielgud's Haymarket Company, newly formed and immediately set to become highly prestigious. In 1947, she went on to marry her second husband and sometime Bletchley colleague Anthony Quayle (her first husband, Robert Douglas, had died not long before). Not long afterwards, she retired from the stage in order to concentrate on bringing up their two children, while he became one of the most recognised faces on the cinema screen, going on to be knighted.

Writer Angus Wilson, who had found Bletchley so psychologically stressful, had his first volume of short stories, *The Wrong Set*, published in 1949. These were chilly portraits of contemporary upper-middle-class life. He was to achieve real fame with his first novel *Hemlock and After*, published in 1952. Wilson's colleague and friend Bentley Bridgewater subsequently became Secretary of the British Museum.

Meanwhile, reluctant 'Tunny' codebreaker Roy Jenkins was, after an unsuccessful attempt in Solihull, to win his first seat in Parliament – Southwark Central, in 1948. The seat soon disappeared in boundary changes, but Jenkins won another, Birmingham Stechford, in 1950. He went on to become one of the most influential politicians of his generation, rising in the 1960s to become Home Secretary and in 1967 Chancellor of the Exchequer. Like a great many politicians of that era who fought in the war – Edward Heath was another – Jenkins was very much in favour of the then Common Market. For greater economic union between member European states would help to ensure that no conflict like it could ever happen again.

Keith Batey's fellow billetee Howard Smith was later to become Ambassador to Moscow and head of MI5. David Rees went on to become a tremendously eminent Professor of Mathematics at Exeter University.

Elsewhere, the extraordinary musical traditions of Bletchley Park were upheld proudly in codebreaker Douglas Craig's subsequent career as an opera baritone, a creative executive at Glyndebourne and later Director of Sadler's Wells theatre. Colin Thompson, one of the men who later helped to crack the Italians' alternative cipher machine, the C 38M, went on to become curator of the Scottish National Gallery. Meanwhile, naval Ultra veteran James Hogarth eventually became a high-ranking official in the Foreign Office, while his colleague J.H. Plumb became a professor of history.

This brief run-down demonstrates that even though the central work of the Park may not have been directly stimulating, those young men and women who had applied themselves to the most intractable and daunting of problems had finally emerged from the institution ready to take their rightful places in government, the civil service, the arts, as though they had just matriculated from Oxford or Cambridge. Compared to their military equivalents, the young people of the Park had scarcely paused at all in their pursuits.

Unlike their military equivalents, however, they were not permitted the luxury of relating what they had achieved in the war. Exactly the reverse: with family, with spouses, with offspring – no Bletchley Park operative was allowed to say a single word about those extraordinary years.

28 After Bletchley: The Silence Descends

'My father died in 1951,' says John Herivel. 'And of course, he never heard anything about my war career. Although he knew I had been at Bletchley Park, he had no idea about what I had been doing. And there was a point, shortly before he died, when he experienced this tremendous frustration.

'I was a son who had promised great things after his school career, and who then seemed, to him, to be doing nothing during the war. And this frustration spilled out. My father said: "You've never done anything!"'

The Official Secrets Act, says Herivel, was so deeply impressed upon everyone who signed it that even under this terrible weight of provocation, he could not imagine himself breaking it. 'I did think he was perhaps not long for this world,' Herivel says of his decision not to tell his father anything, 'but really, out of all those people who had signed that act, I wasn't going to be the one who broke it.'

It was not just parents. There were also children who had to be kept in the dark, as Mavis and Keith Batey were to find. As the 1940s gave way to the 1950s and 60s, their children could not be told the slightest detail of what their parents had done throughout the war. And yet those tiny details could escape in the most surprising ways.

Mavis Batey says, for instance, that even the numerical positioning of each letter within the alphabet became ingrained to an extent that might have raised suspicions. She gives an amusing example: 'Some years ago, my daughter was working in the Bodleian Library, right down in J Floor. Ten floors down, I said, that's a long way. And she said "How do you know J is ten floors down?" I changed the subject. Little things like that could give you away.'

There were some, of course, who never strictly left Bletchley, but instead stayed with GC&CS through to its move a few years later to Cheltenham when it became GCHQ. Among them were Hugh Alexander and the widely liked Eric Jones, who went on to become head of GCHQ. For others, the silence of Bletchley had set in so far that they did not think about it any more.

Mimi Gallilee got a job in the news research department of the BBC. Although she enjoyed it, the urge to move on was strong. In the 1960s, Mimi went to America. When she came back, she found an odd and rather disconcerting echo of her old life.

'When I went for my interview at Bush House – I used to put on my applications that I worked at Bletchley Park, adding in brackets "Foreign Office Evacuated". One of the people on the board whom I didn't know, said, "I see you worked at Bletchley Park. What were you doing there?" So I said, "I'm very sorry, I can't discuss that,"

'My response to that interview question was a reflex action,' she says. 'I hadn't had time to think what would I say if they asked this. I always put it down openly, but only stating that it was a wartime base for part of the Foreign Office. That man on the board was Hugh Lunghi.'

Lunghi is a very distinguished figure; he was Churchill's interpreter at the Yalta conference of 1945, and in this capacity met Roosevelt and Stalin. He was also one of the first men into Hitler's bunker in 1945. It is interesting that when he interviewed Mimi Gallilee, the word Bletchley held such significance. 'And that was why I got the job at Bush House,' says Mrs Gallilee. 'I didn't know

then that the department I was going into was also under the aus-
pices of the Official Secrets Act – that was the World Service.'

Some were even more dedicated to keeping the secret. Frederick
Winterbotham's book on Ultra was published in 1974; Walter Eytan
(formerly Ettinghausen; he changed his name a few years after the
war when he left England for the Middle East, eventually to become
an Israeli diplomat), who had worked in Hut 4, recalled: 'I was
shocked to the point of refusing to read the book when someone
showed me a copy, and to this day I feel inhibited if by chance the
subject comes up.'[1]

In later years, especially in the wake of the publication of
Winterbotham's account, Bletchley veterans found themselves frequently bumping into one another. Keith Batey and Oliver Lawn,
both senior civil servants by the 1960s, often sat on important government committees together. Meanwhile, Roy Jenkins quite often
found himself at functions with people who would say: 'Were you at
the Park?' Once he met the Hon. Sarah Baring at a glittering party,
and there was a moment of amused, complicit acknowledgement.
'I'd never met him before but he was a lovely man,' says Sarah
Baring. 'But I knew. I asked him if the initials BP meant anything to
him and he laughed and said yes.'

However, those years of enforced silence also created moments
of great family upset for some codebreakers. 'You had forcibly to
forget for thirty years,' says Mavis Batey. 'Now, I have people writing
to me saying "My husband has died and I never knew what he did
at Bletchley Park. Can you tell me?" Well no, I'm afraid I can't – not
unless they worked in my section.' With all the huts so rigidly
demarcated, how could anyone know?

And even after the Bletchley secret was blown open for all to see
in 1974, many of Bletchley's operatives experienced a curious psychological side-effect. Although Winterbotham's book set off a
chain of other publications, a number of ordinary Bletchley-ites
could not bring themselves to even mention the place, let alone discuss their roles there. The need for secrecy had become ingrained

to the profoundest degree. There were a significant number, like Walter Eytan, who felt that Winterbotham himself was a disgrace for having gone into print. Others, even into the 1980s, would steadfastly refuse to disclose a single thing even to their closest family.

One codebreaking veteran in Scotland, a church minister, continued to tell his children that his war had consisted of his religious ministry, although they knew well that he had been ordained *after* the war. He absolutely would not mention Bletchley. It was simply a case of duty; a promise had been made, and it had to be kept.

In the case of Walter Eytan, the silence remained even in the face of matrimonial pressure: 'Security was second nature to us; my wife said she found difficulty in marrying a man who would not tell her what he did in the war. I did tell her that I had spent most of the time at a place called Bletchley, which meant nothing to her.'[2] Others were more pragmatic. 'I never told a soul,' says Jean Valentine. 'It didn't come up because you didn't discuss it. I married a man and didn't ask him about the secret things on the plane that he flew, and he never asked me what I had been doing.' One story concerns a husband and wife who finally, in the late 1970s, told each other what they had done at the Park while the husband was washing the car on a Sunday afternoon.

Then there was Mimi Gallilee's extraordinary case: she, her mother and her sister all worked at Bletchley in different capacities Mother was a waitress, and so rather less secret. But Mimi and her older sister – who worked in one of the huts – never discussed it after the war. Sadly, Mimi's sister died in the late 1960s. To this day Mimi has no idea what her sister was doing in that Hut. There are no official records – so how on earth is she to know?

There are numerous other poignant stories too, chiefly concerning young people who – like John Herivel – yearned as the post-war years went on to tell their parents what they had done in the war, yet never could; and whose parents then died, never having known. Some found it unbearable that there was no official documentation, as though those years had simply never happened.

Sheila Lawn recalls: 'What I regretted was that my father died long before I could reveal anything. He died in 1961. My mother died a lot later but by that time she wasn't very well. I am so sorry my father couldn't have . . . he would have been so interested.'

'My parents were the same,' adds Oliver Lawn. 'They both died in the 1960s. They were never curious. Many people were in the same situation. Relatives who should have known, but who couldn't be told. And then died.'

These days, some wonder exactly why everything had to remain so hush-hush for so long afterwards. One very simple reason was that the encryption techniques that Bletchley had managed to break into, either via Enigma or 'Tunny', were still current in other parts of the world – far-flung corners of the fast-fading British Empire included. Indeed, in its first few years under Communist rule, East Germany was still using the same Enigma; a fact that was exploited not merely by the British, but also by the East Germans' Russian overlords.

The second reason was the Cold War: Churchill's chilling 1945 speech concerning the Iron Curtain falling across Europe; the understandable paranoia when, in the immediate aftermath of the conflict with Germany, Stalin's Soviet Union went back on all its promises and not only swallowed up Poland but a vast chunk of Germany too, bringing the oppressive forces of Communism jutting into western Europe. In terms of the scale of territory, it was a breathtaking seizure; Churchill noted how very close the Soviets were now to France and Britain. Indeed, in a moment of desperation back in 1945, he openly mused about the possibility of flattening Moscow with the newly perfected atomic bomb.

Against this backdrop it was decided that the secrets of Bletchley must remain inviolate. In one sense, the conflict was not yet at an end. Throughout the campaigns of the early 1940s, Churchill had sanctioned careful releases to Stalin of information gleaned from Bletchley, while at the same time endeavouring as far as possible to disguise the source. It was deemed best that the

Russians should have no idea what sort of decrypting advances had been made.

Speaking of the Soviets, for Mimi Gallilee, work at BBC World Service in the 1970s offered a few faint echoes of the time that she had spent at the Park. 'We were keeping a watch on world communism. We weren't spies but we had a lot to do with dissidents Solzhenitzyn came over. My boss was the first to have an interview and to befriend him here in the UK.

'By the 1970s,' she adds, speaking of her own attitude to the past, 'Bletchley Park was dead. Nobody would have known what I was talking about. It wouldn't have meant anything to anybody.'

Even the physical fact of the place itself seemed a little abstract to her, until one day in the 1970s, she decided upon a day trip. By this time, Bletchley was little more than a satellite to the gleaming new town of Milton Keynes. She went there with a friend whom she had known since after the war. That friend did not have any inkling.

'At this stage, I still didn't know about the Enigma. The only term I knew was Ultra. I knew what it meant, though not in connection with anything else . . .

'So we drove along Wilton Avenue, got to the gate, and I said to my friend: "I used to work here during the war." She said, "Would you like to go in and have a look?" I said, "I'd love to." But there was no one there – not that I could see, at any rate.

'Anyway,' she continues, 'one day, after the Winterbotham book was out, it was mentioned on the TV news, and my friend was watching. They talked about what was going on at the Park. My friend rang me and said, "I felt so proud, I heard this thing on Bletchley Park and you never said what you did there!" And I said, "Well, there was nothing to say really . . ."'

The physical fact of the town might have helped as a visual reminder, keeping certain memories strong, but even the smallest changes could suddenly make memory more distant. 'I did not think Vicarage Walk could have changed a great deal, but it had,' wrote Gwen Watkins of the little lane in which she had been billeted during her time as a Luftwaffe codebreaker. 'It was full of parked cars and expensive bicycles lying about in the lane.'

Gwen Watkins had remembered an utterly quiet little lane, where the windows of the house were never opened and the front door was only ever used for special visitors and occasions. Now she saw a house with windows wide open, chintz curtains, music playing loudly from within. 'I only wish that it had not changed,' she wrote. 'I turned away, and never went there again.'[3]

Curiously, as Oliver and Sheila Lawn recall, there was little in the way of official pressure to keep this silence after their time at Bletchley. It was just understood. 'It was subconscious,' says Sheila Lawn, 'I just never thought about talking. You'd just say that it was war work.'

When the house and grounds were saved in 1991, they found themselves not only overwhelmed with memories, but also able to talk further with one another about all that they had done – some fifty years after the war had ended. They decided in the early 1990s to make a trip to see the Park once more. Just the sight of it was a curiously emotional experience for both of them.

'They had altered a lot since then,' says Mr Lawn. 'Buildings had been taken down. But there was much there that we remembered. It was like double vision. And I couldn't believe having forgotten everything. It was like having a bit of your life shown to you again.' Having made themselves known to the recently set up Bletchley Park Trust, the Lawns found that their connections to the place were firmly – and amusingly – re-established.

The Lawns, and thousands of others, had had a unique experience. Poet Vernon Watkins, who had served at Bletchley, said of his time there that it was 'a situation, an era and an excitement which cannot be repeated'. And one anonymous codebreaker, a few years ago, summed his own feelings just as acutely: 'No work I have ever done in my life,' he said, 'has been more fascinating or given me greater satisfaction.'

29 The Rescue of the Park

And so Bletchley Park's life as the centre of Britain's cryptographic effort ended; the duties of GCHQ were transferred first to a leafy London suburb, and then to the West Country.

But the old property in Buckinghamshire was kept going as a government concern, mainly for the training of Post Office engineers. In that immediate post-war period, the General Post Office, as it was then known, was a state-run concern. The business of telephone lines was masterminded by Whitehall as opposed to private firms.

In the 1960s, there were some unlovely architectural additions made to Bletchley Park in the shape of a stumpy pebble-dashed block of offices facing the gate nearest the railway station. Come the 1980s and following the privatisation of telephones – the new company was called British Telecom (BT) – and the advances being made in fibre-optic technology, the need for a specific training centre began to dwindle.

For a time the estate was multi-tasking. As well as the engineers, it also, for a while, provided a training centre for employees of GCHQ. There was also a BT management school, a teacher training college, and a branch of the civil service called PACE (Property

Advisers to the Civil Estate). But as the 1980s gave way to the 1990s, the old house itself was beginning to crumble, as were the many huts still dotted around. Even though the estate was handy for Milton Keynes, just a few miles away, it was clear that in business terms, its potential uses were dwindling. British Telecom did not own the land or the house; the government assumed, quite understandably, that it did. And so came the first germ of an idea to sell the land off and put it to more profitable use.

But the house didn't belong to the government. According to some reports, it belonged to the late Admiral Hugh Sinclair, the head of the Secret Intelligence Service, who had paid his own £7,500 for the estate back in 1937 when Whitehall was dragging its feet over the matter. The government had no business attempting to dispose of it.

And in 1991, the newly formed Bletchley Park Trust stepped in, determined quite rightly that a site of such significance had to be preserved properly, and in such a way that members of the public would eventually be able to visit.

The house by that stage was in a sorry state. The ballroom, with its elaborate carved and fretted ceiling, was semi-derelict and the ceiling itself had begun to disintegrate. Outside, the huts – which had survived all weathers over the space of fifty-odd years – were also in terrible condition. Yet it was immediately obvious to many – Bletchley Park veterans and non-veterans alike – that it would be worthwhile to turn the site into a proper museum where younger generations could learn of the vital work and the leaps of genius that had, arguably, made their own world possible.

Bletchley Park was not alone when it came to the question of the sale of former war sites. Go to Eastcote now, or Dollis Hill, and you will find that these once sprawling secret institutions have been turned over to the property market. In the case of Dollis Hill, the rooms in which Tommy Flowers and his team worked so brilliantly on Colossus are now swanky apartments; Eastcote, meanwhile, was clearly a slab of real estate in an extremely affluent suburb that was simply too valuable to be let go to waste, although it was only quite recently that it was sold to developers. It scarcely has to be added that all around the country, former air-bases have been transformed from semi-derelict wildernesses to business parks, eco-villages and the like.

Not all change is bad. There is a limit to the amount that one can learn from a potholed runway surrounded with weeds and roofless mess huts. But in the case of Bletchley, the case for preserving the site as close as possible to its wartime state was a great deal more important.

Through extraordinary efforts of persuasion and fund-raising, the Bletchley Park Trust painstakingly began work on transforming it into a place that the general public could come to visit, and learn. And in ensuing years, Bletchley Park has found new, and rather wonderful, life as a museum. The main exhibitions, involving reconstructed huts and displays of Enigma, the Colossus and bombe machines, are utterly fascinating, especially for younger visitors. For children – with computers in their classrooms and their bedrooms – the sight of these huge early proto-computers, with their drums and switches, wires and valves, hooks the imagination very strongly.

And the museum is extremely popular, with an estimated 200,000 visitors per year. It is a splendid achievement. Though some of the huts, as I write, are still crumbling away – blue tarpaulins flapping in every breeze – the place has at last received a special Lottery grant for the purposes of restoration.

To visit the Bletchley estate now is to get a vivid taste of what it must have been like to come through those main gates during the war. There is a security guard's booth, past which are the first of the concrete blocks and huts. Then, just a couple of hundred yards or so up the driveway, you see the lake and the house itself. At weekends, the place is teeming with visitors and very often the lawn in front of the house plays host to special events, such as vintage car rallies, editions of *Antiques Roadshow* or military remembrance services. In some of the huts can now be found recreations of wartime conditions – plain desks, radio transmitter sets – that give the visitor an inkling of what it might have been like to work here.

But the restoration of the Park serves an even better purpose. For the last twenty years or so, it has provided a wonderful point of focus for the people who were actually there. Even now, among the eight thousand or so Bletchley Park veterans, there are still those who have yet to identify themselves or are yet to revisit the Park. With each anniversary event, Ruth Bourne notes affectionately, 'more come out of the woodwork'.

Because no official staffing records were kept – if Bletchley was the utmost secret, then so also was the fact that one had worked there – it has been impossible for the Bletchley Park Trust to track all veterans down. Very often it has been a case of word of mouth, or veterans happening to have spotted a Bletchley Park-related item in the newspaper.

But for many veterans, Bletchley Park now is in some way a cross between a social club and a shrine; just to walk through its rooms, to gaze at the dark panelling of the hallway, to be reminded of a small pothole in the driveway, is enough to trigger a flood of memories that, for many years, had to be utterly suppressed.

Architectural historian Jane Fawcett – whose first visit back to the Park was in the autumn of 2009, some sixty-four years after she had left – recalled that the place was shabbier than it appears now. Oliver and Sheila Lawn, who had so loved the countryside around, made an expedition to drive along the green lanes that they had once cycled through; instead of which, they found themselves caught up in the endless roundabouts of Milton Keynes. Nothing ever stays the same. Yet the Park itself – together with the opportunities to meet up with people whom one was not even allowed to acknowledge for so many years – is a source of deep satisfaction, as well as enjoyment.

Everyone else in the war had their reunions; from the RAF boys to the Land Girls, bonds were formed, friendships sealed, that carried on through the years after 1945 in the form of regular socialising and regular commemorations. The men and women of Bletchley Park were denied all this. Instead of an annual dinner dance, or even simple meet-ups for a few pints at a chosen local, they were instead left with their silent memories. Whereas for everyone else of their generation, the war was understood as the most fundamental of formative experiences, Bletchley veterans instead had a hole where acknowledged experience should have been.

And as the 1950s, '60s and '70s wore on, there must have been a few private memories that became a little frayed. For if one can never discuss with anyone what one has experienced, then how is that remembrance to be kept pristine? But thankfully, the sheer intensity and uniqueness of life at the Park helped enormously in this respect, giving most recollection a laser beam quality. And interestingly, both the Bateys and the Lawns maintain that it was a shade easier for them altogether; even though, as married couples, they found that they did not discuss the Park after the war, there was none the less that element of shared experience. Even a little element of complicity.

These days, Bletchley Park veterans are most frequently asked: 'But why? Why did you have to stay absolutely quiet for so long?' When any of the codebreakers goes to give a talk at a school, the pupils' most frequently asked question is: 'How on earth did you manage to keep it all secret?' In an age of Twitter, of instantaneous global mass communication, such an idea seems genuinely baffling to the young. 'On top of this,' says Mavis Batey, 'you've got programmes like *Newsnight* talking about things like Osama bin Laden and giving away serious intelligence. It's as if the idea of secrecy has gone.' Author Neal Ascherson, whose sister had been a Wren at Bletchley, found her discretion both admirable and astonishing. 'That silence was very British,' he wrote in the *Observer* a few years ago. 'Nobody else could have kept it and nobody was rewarded for keeping it. We wouldn't be able to keep such silence today.'

One answer, as previously noted, is a large measure of Cold War paranoia on behalf of the authorities, mixed with a sharp sense that a number of countries were still using encryption systems similar to the Germans. Aside from this, though, a slightly more philosophical explanation for the all-pervasive silence – as might be surmised from a wider study of the history of the intelligence services – is that secrecy has, until recently at least, been something of a British fetish.

For secrecy, in some senses, is power; to know something that someone else does not know. The staggering achievement of Bletchley – the inspired lightning flashes of genius combined with the most dedicated work – was perhaps something that Britain could hold on to with pride as the aftermath of the war stripped the nation of its empire and its wealth, and left it desperately scrambling to find a position in this new world of East/West blocs. We might no longer have the firepower but we still did retain a native ingenuity (witness the ferocious 1950s pride concerning such innovations as the Harrier jet – we could still lead the world when it came to inventive genius). And as we moved from wartime espionage to the gathering possibilities of industrial espionage, the idea of staying mum retained not merely its importance but also its dignity.

There is an element of old-fashioned patriotism involved too. To this day, there are a few veteran codebreakers who will not speak of what they did, and who are infuriated by anyone who does, despite the fact that the subject has been openly known about, and discussed, since the 1980s. There were, and are, those who feel that Frederick Winterbotham – the first man to go into print to reveal the Bletchley secret in 1974 – was in his own way a traitor. These were secrets that had to go to the grave.

But there is also the other side of Bletchley Park story: the struggle for official recognition. Old soldiers have their medals; but what do the men and women of Bletchley Park have? In October 2009, Foreign Secretary David Miliband presided over a ceremony at Bletchley to award commemorative badges to all known veterans. It was a gesture, certainly, and came fast on the news of the Park's lottery grant, and also of the government's posthumous apology to

Alan Turing. But a commemorative badge is not quite the same as a medal.

One Bletchley veteran, during the course of the research for this book, wrote to say that she was 'sick to the back teeth' of articles about the Park placing so much emphasis on the 'dancing on the lawn' and the social side of it. This, she said, was a time of war and the work was extraordinarily hard, and it is that aspect that ought to be remembered.

Certainly it should; remembered and commemorated properly. Yet it would also be wrong to forget these other aspects of Bletchley life. The wonder of what all these men and women did is illustrated, in some ways, just as well by the recreational pursuits as the labour; for in both cases, astonishing efforts were made. The very idea of coming off a night shift having done hours of tiring, focused, pressurised work, and then turning one's mind to the staging of a play, seems to me both extraordinarily admirable and brilliantly sane. 'Even though I've had wonderful friends since,' recalled Gwen Watkins, 'I've never again experienced that atmosphere of happiness, of enjoyment of culture, of enjoyment of everything that meant life to me.'[1]

Nevertheless, it is daunting to consider now not merely the sheer intellect required, but also the powers of concentration and absolute, unsnappable patience that the work involved. And, as ever with these things, one always finds oneself asking: could this generation rise to a similar challenge?

By coincidence, the other day, two newspaper headlines jumped out at me; one concerning the ingenuity of British creators of modern video games, and the other concerning Gary McKinnon, the computer hacker who broke into the Pentagon system and who (as I write) the Americans are trying to extradite for trial.

I am not about to draw a parallel between these people and the Bletchley codebreakers. I merely observe that British computer game experts are leading the field in what is basically an extraordinarily abstract job of feeding codes into computers; while Gary

McKinnon, who is said to suffer from Asperger's syndrome, had the ingenuity – from a perfectly ordinary home computer in north London – to hack into a mighty military system and get past all the Pentagon's passwords and encrypted complexities. No wonder the American authorities have seemed so profoundly rattled by the case.

The other point is that there may never again be a challenge like that presented by Enigma; for in times of future war, intelligence and code experts are extremely unlikely to be drawn from a pool of untrained amateurs. They will be sleek professionals, working in synchronisation. Which only serves to highlight further the real achievement of all those men and women at Bletchley. Equipped with little more than intelligence, enthusiasm and determination, they got stuck right into the job, persisting until they succeeded.

It might be true that their story lacks the pyrotechnic thrills of the bomber boys, or the icy suspense of the Atlantic convoys, and it might well be that this is one of the reasons that recognition has been so long in coming. Yet, as Eisenhower said, these were the men and women who shortened the war by two years.

And there are countless thousands of people across the continent who survived, who just might not have done without the brilliance of Bletchley Park.

Notes

1 Reporting for Duty

1 Memo in the National Archives. Most documents cited in this book are held within the HW 62 series, with the exception of a few in HW 25 and HW 67

2 S. Gorley Putt, quoted in Margaret Drabble, *Angus Wilson: The Biography* (Secker and Warburg, 1995)

2 1938–39: The School of Codes

1 Ruth Sebag-Montefiore, *A Family Patchwork: Five Generations of an Anglo-Jewish Family* (Weidenfeld and Nicolson, 1987)

2 Penelope Fitzgerald, *The Knox Brothers* (Macmillan, 1977)

3 Documents in the National Archives

4 John Herivel, *Herivelismus* (M & M Baldwin, 2008)

5 Peter Hilton, interviewed by the BBC

6 Letter now in the National Archives

3 1939: Rounding Up the Brightest and the Best

1 F.H. Hinsley and Alan Stripp, *Codebreakers: The Inside Story of Bletchley Park* (Oxford University Press, 1993)

2 Professor E.R.P. Vincent, quoted in Christopher Andrew, *Secret Service: The Making of British Intelligence* (Heinemann, 1985)

3 Irene Young, *Enigma Variations: A Memoir of Love and War* (Mainstream, 1990)

4 Gordon Welchman, *The Hut Six Story* (Allen Lane, 1982)

4 The House and the Surrounding Country

1 Malcolm Muggeridge, *Like It Was* (Methuen, 1982)

2   Landis Gores, quoted by Kathryn A. Morrison in her monograph 'The Mansion at Bletchley Park' (English Heritage)

3   Bletchley Park Trust Archive, quoted in Marion Hill, *Bletchley Park People* (The History Press, 2004)

5   1939: How Do You Break the Unbreakable?

1   Robin Denniston, *Thirty Secret Years* (Polperro Heritage Press, 2005)

2   Aileen Clayton, *The Enemy Is Listening* (Hutchinson, 1980)

3   Denniston, *Thirty Secret Years*

4   John Herivel, *Herivelismus* (M & M Baldwin, 2008)

5   Jack Copeland, *The Essential Turing: Seminal Writings in Computing, Logic, Philosophy* (Clarendon, 2004)

6   Penelope Fitzgerald, *The Knox Brothers* (Macmillan, 1977)

7   Herivel, *Herivelismus*

8   Peter Twinn, interviewed by the BBC

6   1939–40: The Enigma Initiation

1   F.H. Hinsley and Alan Stripp, *Codebreakers: The Inside Story of Bletchley Park* (Oxford University Press, 1993)

2   This memo and many other communications from Dilly Knox are in the National Archives

3   Gordon Welchman, *The Hut Six Story* (Allen Lane, 1982)

7   Freezing Billets and Outdoor Loos

1   Baroness Trumpington, interview conducted at Bletchley Park by the BBC

2   Stuart Milner-Barry, quoted in F.H. Hinsley and Alan Stripp, *Codebreakers: The Inside Story of Bletchley Park* (Oxford University Press, 1993)

3   Irene Young, *Enigma Variations: A Memoir of Love and War* (Mainstream, 1990)

4   Memos on billets, National Archives

5   John Herivel, *Herivelismus* (M & M Baldwin, 2008)

8   1940: The First Glimmers of Light

1   Ruth Sebag-Montefiore, *A Family Patchwork: Five Generations of an Anglo-Jewish Family* (Weidenfeld and Nicolson, 1987)

2   Sir Anthony Quayle, *A Time to Speak* (Barrie and Jenkins, 1990)

3   William Millward, address to an Enigma symposium, Bedford, 1992

4   F.H. Hinsley and Alan Stripp, *Codebreakers: The Inside Story of Bletchley Park* (Oxford University Press, 1993)

5   Peter Twinn, quoted in Michael Smith, *Station X* (Channel Four Books, 1998)
6   Peter Calvocoressi, *Top Secret Ultra* (Cassell, 1980)
7   Marian Rejewski, quoted in Hugh Skillen, *Enigma and Its Achilles Heel* (Pinner, 1992)
8   F.L. Lucas, quoted in *Enigma: The Battle for the Code* (Weidenfeld and Nicolson, 2000)
9   Memo from Dilly Knox to Alistair Denniston, National Archives

9 1940: Inspiration – and Intensity

1   John Herivel, *Herivelismus* (M & M Baldwin, 2008)
2   Gordon Welchman, *The Hut Six Story* (Allen Lane, 1982)
3   Memo from Alistair Denniston, National Archives
4   Jack Copeland (ed.), *The Essential Turing: Seminal Writings in Computing, Logic, Philosophy* (Clarendon Press, 2004)
5   Memo from Dilly Knox, National Archives
6   Memo from Dilly Knox, National Archives
7   Welchman, *The Hut Six Story*
8   Aileen Clayton, *The Enemy Is Listening* (Hutchinson, 1980)
9   Andrew Hodges, *Alan Turing – The Enigma* (Burnett Books, 1983)
10 Gwen Watkins, *Cracking the Luftwaffe Codes* (Greenhill, 2006)

10 1940: The Coming of the Bombes

1   Captain Frederick Winterbotham, *The Ultra Secret* (Purnell Books, 1974)
2   Andrew Hodges, *Alan Turing, The Enigma* (Burnett Books, 1983)
3   F.H. Hinsley and Alan Stripp, *Codebreakers: The Inside Story of Bletchley Park* (Oxford University Press, 1993)
4   Memo from Frank Birch to Edward Travis, National Archives
5   Correspondence between Dr Dunlop and Commander Bradshaw, National Archives
6   Quoted in Paul Gannon, *Colossus – Bletchley Park's Greatest Secret* (Atlantic, 2006)

11 1940: Enigma and the Blitz

1   Peter Calvocoressi, interviewed by the BBC
2   Aileen Clayton, *The Enemy Is Listening* (Hutchinson, 1980)
3   Clayton, *The Enemy Is Listening*
4   Captain Frederick Winterbotham, *The Ultra Secret* (Purnell Books, 1974)
5   R.A. Ratcliff, *Delusions of Intelligence: Enigma, Ultra and the End of Secure Ciphers* (Cambridge University Press, 2006)
6   Roy Jenkins, *Churchill* (Macmillan, 2001)

12 Bletchley and the Class Question

1   Josh Cooper's account, National Archives
2   Recruitment documents, National Archives
3   Lord Dacre, interviewed by Graham Turner, *Daily Telegraph*, 2000
4   Quoted by Marion Hill, *Bletchley Park People* (The History Press, 2004)
5   Hairdressing facility memos, National Archives

13 1941: The Battle of the Atlantic

1   Joan Murray, quoted in *Enigma: The Battle for the Code* (Weidenfeld and Nicolson, 2000)
2   Jack Copeland (ed.), *The Essential Turing: Seminal Writings in Computing, Logic, Philosophy* (Clarendon Press, 2004)
3   Hugh Alexander, quoted in *Enigma: The Battle for the Code*
4   Asa Briggs, foreword to Gwen Watkins, *Cracking the Luftwaffe Codes* (Greenhill Books, 2006)
5   Memos concerning staffing, National Archives
6   Superintendent Blagrove, quoted in Marion Hill, *Bletchley Park People* (The History Press, 2004)

14 Food, Booze and Too Much Tea

1   Irene Young, *Enigma Variations: A Memoir of Love and War* (Mainstream, 1990)
2   Memos concerning Bletchley food, National Archives
3   Memos concerning tea consumption, National Archives
4   Memo from Captain Ridley concerning tea, National Archives
5   Memo from Denniston concerning tea, National Archives

15 1941: The Wrens and their Larks

1   Memo concerning Wren recruitment, National Archives
2   Documents donated by Felicity Ashbee to the Imperial War Museum
3   Documents held by Imperial War Museum

16 1941: Bletchley and Churchill

1   Gordon Welchman, *The Hut Six Story* (Allen Lane, 1982)
2   Quoted in Marion Hill, *Bletchley Park People* (The History Press, 2004)
3   Lecture to Sidney Sussex College given by John Herivel, 2005
4   Lecture to Sidney Sussex College given by John Herivel, 2005
5   Welchman, *The Hut Six Story*

17 Military or Civilian?

1   Peter Calvocoressi, *Top Secret Ultra* (Cassell, 1980)
2   Edward Thomas, essay in F.H. Hinsley and Alan Stripp, *Codebreakers: The Inside Story of Bletchley Park* (Oxford University Press, 1993)

3 R.A. Ratcliff, *Delusions of Intelligence* (Cambridge University Press, 2006)

18 1942: Grave Setbacks and Internal Strife
1 Kim Philby, *My Silent War* (MacGibbon and Kee, 1968)
2 F.H. Hinsley and Alan Stripp, *Codebreakers: The Inside Story of Bletchley Park* (Oxford University Press, 1993)
3 P.W. Filby, addressing an Enigma symposium, 1992
4 Robin Denniston, *Thirty Secret Years* (Polperro Heritage Press, 2005)
5 Denniston, *Thirty Secret Years*
6 Philby, *My Silent War*
7 Gordon Welchman, *The Hut Six Story* (Allen Lane, 1982)
8 Ralph Bennett, essay in Hinsley and Stripp, *Codebreakers*
9 Hugh Skillen, *Enigma and its Achilles Heel* (Pinner, 1992)
10 Hugh Denham, quoted in Michael Smith, *The Emperor's Codes* (Bantam, 2000)
11 Michael Loewe, essay in Hinsley and Stripp, *Codebreakers*
12 Maurice Wiles, quoted in Smith, *The Emperor's Codes*
13 Michael Loewe, essay in Hinsley and Stripp, *Codebreakers*
14 Hugh Denham, quoted in Smith, *The Emperor's Codes*
15 John Winton, *Ultra at Sea* (Leo Cooper, 1985)
16 Edward Thomas, quoted in Hinsley and Stripp, *Codebreakers*
17 Aileen Clayton, *The Enemy Is Listening* (Hutchinson, 1980)
18 Ralph Bennett, essay in Hinsley and Stripp, *Codebreakers*
19 Memos about blocks, National Archives
20 Hugh Alexander, quoted in *Enigma: The Battle for the Code*

19 The Rules of Attraction
1 S. Gorley Putt, quoted in Margaret Drabble, *Angus Wilson: The Biography* (Secker and Warburg, 1995)
2 Jon Cohen, interviewed by the BBC
3 Wren interview, Bletchley Trust Archive, quoted in Marion Hill, *Bletchley Park People* (The History Press, 2004)

20 1943: A Very Special Relationship
1 Michael Howard, *Times Literary Supplement*, autumn 2009
2 Barbara Abernethy, talking to Michael Smith, *Station X* (Channel Four Books, 1998)
3 Andrew Hodges, *Alan Turing – The Enigma* (Burnett Books, 1983)
4 Peter Calvocoressi, *Top Secret Ultra* (Cassell, 1980)
5 Telford Taylor, essay in F.H. Hinsley and Alan Stripp, *Codebreakers: The Inside Story of Bletchley Park* (Oxford University Press, 1993)
6 Christine Brooke-Rose, quoted in Smith, *Station X*

7   Harry Fensom, addressing an Enigma symposium, 1992
8   American soldier, quoted in Marion Hill, *Bletchley Park People* (The History Press, 2004)
9   Asa Briggs, foreword to Gwen Watkins, *Cracking the Luftwaffe Codes* (Greenhill Books, 2006)
10 Gordon Welchman, *The Hut Six Story* (Allen Lane, 1982)
11 John Winton, *Ultra at Sea* (Leo Cooper, 1985)

21 1943: The Hazards of Careless Talk
1   Memo from H. Fletcher, National Archives
2   Gordon Welchman, *The Hut Six Story* (Allen Lane, 1982)
3   Memo to Nigel de Grey, National Archives
4   Memo from Nigel de Grey to Colonel Wallace, National Archives
5   Memo to Mr Fletcher, National Archives
6   Internal memos, National Archives
7   Letter from Nigel de Grey, National Archives
8   Letter to Nigel de Grey, National Archives
9   Peter Calvocoressi, *Top Secret Ultra* (Cassell, 1980)

22 Bletchley and the Russians
1   Kim Philby, *My Silent War* (MacGibbon and Kee, 1968)
2   Henry Dryden, essay in F.H. Hinsley and Alan Stripp, *Codebreakers: The Inside Story of Bletchley Park* (Oxford University Press, 1993)
3   John Cairncross, *The Enigma Spy: The Story of the Man who Changed World War Two* (Century, 1997)
4   Andrew Sinclair, *The Red and the Blue: Intelligence, Treason and the Universities* (Weidenfeld and Nicolson, 1986)
5   Quoted in the *Independent*, 1994
6   Mavis Batey, *From Bletchley with Love* (Bletchley Park Trust monograph)

23 The Cultural Life of Bletchley Park
1   Lucienne Edmonston-Stowe, addressing an Enigma symposium, 1992
2   John Cairncross, *The Enigma Spy: The Story of the Man who Changed World War Two* (Century, 1997)
3   Irene Young, *Enigma Variations: A Memoir of Love and War* (Mainstream, 1990)
4   Tennis court memos, National Archives
5   Memos concerning journalists, National Archives
6   *Bletchley Gazette*, 1945

24 1943–44: The Rise of the Colossus
1   Dilly Knox poem, quoted in Penelope Fitzgerald, *The Knox Brothers* (Macmillan, 1977)

2   Dilly Knox farewell letter, National Archives
3   George Vergine, quoted in Virtual Jewish Library
4   Roy Jenkins, *A Life at the Centre* (Macmillan, 1991)
5   Harry Fensom, addressing an Enigma symposium, 1992
6   Harry Fensom, addressing an Enigma symposium, 1992
7   Letter from Gordon Welchman, National Archives
8   Tommy Flowers, interview for an Imperial War Museum video presentation, London

25 1944–45: D-Day and the End of the War
1   Quoted in Marion Hill, *Bletchley Park People* (The History Press, 2004)
2   Quoted in Hill, *Bletchley Park People*
3   Rosemary Calder, quoted in Michael Smith, *The Emperor's Codes* (Bantam, 2000)
4   Demobilisation memo, National Archives
5   Memo from Bletchley Park staffer, National Archives
6   Memo from John Herivel, National Archives

27 Bletchley's Intellectual Legacy
1   Bryan Magee, *Clouds of Glory* (Pimlico, 2004)
2   Gwen Watkins, *Cracking The Luftwaffe Codes* (Greenhill Books, 2006)

28 After Bletchley: The Silence Descends
1   Walter Eytan, interviewed by the BBC
2   Walter Eytan, interviewed by the BBC
3   Gwen Watkins, *Cracking the Luftwaffe Codes* (Greenhill Books, 2006)

29 The Rescue of the Park
1   Gwen Watkins, *Cracking the Luftwaffe Codes* (Greenhill Books, 2006)

Acknowledgements

With a great many thanks, first of all, to Kelsey Griffin, Director of the Museum at Bletchley Park, for introducing me to such brilliant people. Among all those, and other, brilliant people, thanks are also due to the Honourable Sarah Baring, to Mavis and Keith Batey, Ruth Bourne, Mimi Gallilee, Simon Greenish, John Herivel, Oliver and Sheila Lawn, Trudie Marshall, Geoffrey Pidgeon, Veronica Plowman, Nicolas Ridley, Captain Jerry Roberts, Sarah and John Standing and especially to Jean Valentine. Thanks also to the Bletchley Park Trust – which has made the museum such an invaluable and fascinating draw for generations to come.

Index